PROVENCE & THE CÔTE D'AZUR

Chrissie McClatchie, Ashley Parsons, Nicola Williams

Feast on a sun-spun bounty of hues, scents and tastes at the market or *à table*. Embrace old-school glamour on the glittering Riviera. Motor from handsome hilltop village to village, lingering perhaps to lunch on a jasmine-shaded terrace or stargaze after dark. Shred alpine powder. E-bike through a Cézanne canvas. Explore ancient Roman ruins, contemporary art and an intoxicating new world of locavore spirits and botanicals. Sip rosé by the pool or at a château on the sand. Island-laze.

This is Provence and the Côte d'Azur.

**TURN THE PAGE AND START PLANNING
YOUR NEXT BEST TRIP →**

Serres

Grignan

Nyons

Pont-
St-Esprit

Curel

Bagnols-
sur-Cèze

Malaucène

Orange

Baron

Avignon & Around
184

Carpentras

Sault

Banon

Pont du
Gard

Digne-
les-Bains
2.15hrs

Forcalquier

Avignon

Coustellet

Cereste

St-Rémy
de Provence

Cavaillon

Apt

The Luberon
204

Manosque

Nîmes

Tarascon

Parc National
Régional des
Alpilles

Durance

Cadenet

Pertuis

St-Gilles

Arles

Salon-de-
Provence

Meyrargues

Aigues-
Mortes

Grand Rhône

Mas
Thibert

Aix to Arles
156

St-Cannat

Aix-en-
Provence

St-Maxi
la-Ste-Ba

Parc Naturel
Régional
de Camargue

Étang
de Berre

Vitrolles

Cabriès

Trets

Stes-Maries
de la Mer

Monaco
3.15hrs

Golfe de
Beauduc

Port St-Louis
du Rhône

L'Estaque

Marseille

Aubagne

Marseille 126

Cassis

Ollioule

N
0   50 km
0
25 miles

Seafront, Menton (p73)

4

Contents

Above Camargue horses, Parc Naturel Régional de Camargue (p179)

From the 5th century CE until the French Revolution, the kings of France were baptised with silken olive oil from St-Rémy de Provence.

BON
APPÉTIT!

Thinking, dreaming and living food is the norm in Provence, where most people's days revolve around satisfying their natural appetite for dining exceedingly well – for good reason. Provençal cuisine is reputed the world over for its exceptional sun-blessed produce, seafaring booty and brigade of innovative chefs. Any dish *à la Provençal* invariably involves garlic, tomatoes and olive oil, but travel a little and exciting regional differences quickly emerge.

→ FLORAL FEASTS

Provençal chefs use the aromatic lavender flowers to flavour herbal teas, tart up desserts and spice grilled meats. Its leaves float in soup.

▶ Discover how local chefs, distillers and perfumers are making magic with lavender on p228

Left Garlic, tomatoes & olive oil
Right Dried lavender **Below** *Herbes de Provence*

MMEEMIL/GETTY IMAGES ©

SPECIALIST FOOD MARKETS

- Garlic Market – daily, late June and July in Marseille
- Melon Market – mornings, May to September in Cavaillon
- Black Truffle Market – Saturdays, November to March in Richerenches

RIGHT: BRENT HOFACKER/SHUTTERSTOCK ©
LEFT: LA P'TITE CUISINE DE PAULINE/GETTY IMAGES ©

↑ HERBAL SCRUB

Provence's heavenly herbal array is a legacy of its scented *garrigue* (scrubland). *Herbes de Provence* mixes dried basil, thyme, oregano and rosemary (the secret to eternal youth in medieval Provence).

▶ Pick your own wild *herbes de Provence* on p215

Best Foodie Experiences

▶ Tuck into oven-warm *socca*, *pan bagnat* oozing olive oil and other traditional street food at Nice's Port Lympia (p46)

▶ Enjoy the sweet taste of winter mimosa with a Mandelieu-La Napoule pastry chef (p78)

▶ Feast on marsh-to-menu gastronomy fresh from the rice paddies and salt flats of the Camargue (p178)

▶ Splurge on the catch of Monaco's last fisherman (p95)

▶ Dine at sunset on a roof garden in Saignon (p220)

The Côte d'Azur ('Azure Coast') is named after the region's original guidebook, published in 1887 by Cannes lawyer Stéphane Liégeard.

Hitchcock's *To Catch a Thief* (1955) was partly filmed at Villa Leopolda, the world's most expensive private villa, in Villefranche-sur-Mer.

RIVIERA
HIGH LIFE

From bottle-top-covered nipples to cleavage-inspired architecture, billion-dollar penthouses and Champagne-fuelled hedonism aboard mega yachts, there's no disputing the intoxicating glitz of the Côte d'Azur. The coastline stretches west from lemon-scented Menton by the Italian border to palm-stitched Hyères, just short of Toulon, and is among Europe's most celebrated beach strips. Tread the boards here to rub shoulders with myth, legend and the occasional celebrity scandal.

→ FAIRY-TALE LAND

A Hollywood queen weds a Monégasque prince: visit Monaco's royal palace and risk a little in Monte Carlo's world-famous Belle Époque casino.

▶ Take a walk through Princess Grace's legacy on p100

Left Villefranche-su-Mer **Right** Palais Princier de Monaco **Below** Hôtel du Cap-Eden Roc, Cap d'Antibes

WALK OF FAME

Trail film stars along Cannes' fabled seafront, La Croisette: find your matching celebrity handprint and pose on the steps of Palais des Festivals.

↑ OLD-SCHOOL GLAMOUR

Epitome of Riviera romance, Cap d'Antibes' Hôtel du Cap-Eden Roc marries the original hotel (1889) with Eden Roc, the 1914 tearoom around which a swimming pool was dug from rock.

▶ Read about the surprising history of tourism on the Côte d'Azur on p74

Best Riviera Experiences

▶ Trail F Scott Fitzgerald and other Jazz Age hedonists in Antibes and Juan-les-Pins (p72)

▶ Dance with world-class DJs on the sand in Cannes at Les Plages Electroniques (p89)

▶ Play *pétanque* and beach-chill in St-Tropez (p110)

▶ Motor or e-bike in cinematic style along Nice's trio of mythical corniches (p80)

▶ Walk a lap of the Monaco Grand Prix street circuit (p98)

PROVENCE & THE CÔTE D'AZUR BEST EXPERIENCES

ALLAN BAXTER/GETTY IMAGES ©

RIGHT: ARCHIVE PHOTOS/GETTY IMAGES © LEFT: ARNDALE/SHUTTERSTOCK ©

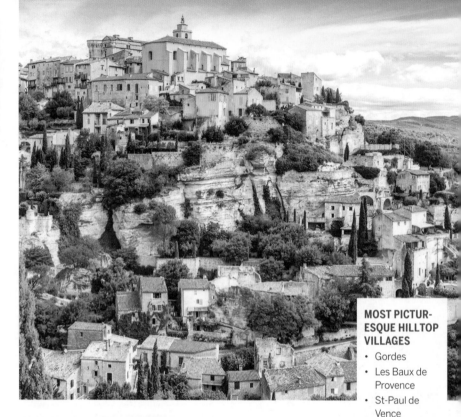

**MOST PICTUR-
ESQUE HILLTOP
VILLAGES**

- Gordes
- Les Baux de Provence
- St-Paul de Vence
- Èze
- Ménerbes

HILLTOP
SAFARI

There's no escaping *villages perchés* (hilltop villages) in Provence. Round a hairpin and another cluster of old stone houses teetering precariously atop a rocky crag peers down at you. A signature speciality of the Luberon and less-explored backcountry Var, these eagle-nest villages cropped up from the 10th century as villagers moved from plain to hilltop to better defend themselves against Saracen attacks.

→ CELEBRATE THE UNSUNG

Southeast of Carpentras spills the seldom-explored but beautiful Pays de Venasque – a scattering of teeny hilltop villages around the village of Venasque.

Left Gordes **Right** Venasque **Below** Ste-Agnès

À TABLE!

A highlight of every hilltop-village foray is a lazy *auberge* lunch, on the jasmine-shaded terrace of an old buttermilk house with peppermint-green shutters and a village-fountain view perhaps.

↑ EXPLORE ON FOOT

Don't miss the 2km footpath linking 12th-century château ruins in hilltop hamlet Ste-Agnès with Gorbio, a flower-filled hilltop village 10km northwest of Menton.

▶ Reach spectacular heights on the Côte d'Azur's three corniches on p81

Best Hilltop Experiences

▶ **Chase bougainvillea blooms in medieval Grimaud** (p119)

▶ **Drink mountain beer at a brewery in St-Martin-Vésubie, gateway to the remote Mercantour national park** (p89)

▶ **Pair hilltop-hopping by pedal-power with scenic hikes in the southern Luberon** (p218)

▶ **Swoon over stars with an astronomy guide in Joucas, Murs or Buoux** (p212)

▶ **Celebrate a *fête votive* with song, dance and a giant aïoli in a medieval village** (p200)

GREEN
ESCAPES

Eco-explorers seeking tranquillity won't struggle in this gloriously green region made for go-slow road-tripping. Back roads ribbon through a mesmerising kaleidoscope of landscapes: purple lavender fields, silver olive groves, maquis-cloaked hills, pink-hued salt pans and snow-crowned mountains. France's deepest canyon is here, not to mention a stash of spectacular *cols* (mountain passes) and the Mediterranean itself – a silken swathe of azure blue mirroring sky-high cliffs, golden beaches and endless china-blue skies.

Montagne Ste-Victoire
A post-impressionist muse
Lose yourself in the serene tableaux of post-impressionist painter Paul Cézanne – in the very mountains where he set up his easel. E-biking is the loveliest way to roam the familiar landscape of red sandstone, fresh green meadow and eagle-encircled crests.

🚴 15mins from Aix-en-Provence
▶ p164

Camargue
Untamed wildlife wetland
There is no other landscape like it in France. Where the Petit Rhône and Grand Rhône meet the Mediterranean, rises the hauntingly beautiful Camargue: 930 sq km of salt flats, *étangs* (small saltwater lakes) and marshland, interspersed with waterlogged rice paddies and paddocks of grazing black bulls. Cycling, bridle and hiking paths are abundant.

🚴 1hr from Arles
▶ p178

Massif des Calanques
Wild beaches by paddle or foot
From downtown Marseille, it's an easy flit to the dramatic Massif des Calanques, a sun-parched world of rocky creeks and prickly barbary figs. Begin your coastal trek, by sea kayak or on foot, in the end-of-the-world hamlet of Callelongue. Bring water – lots.

🚐 20mins from Marseille
▶ p155

Géoparc de Haute-Provence
Open-air geological 'museum'

With its HQ at the Musée Promenade and five driving itineraries across rural Haute-Provence, this gargantuan geological reserve assures adventure and green peace in spades. Each route includes breakaway walks, visits to nature museums and fossil and geological sites.

🚗 40mins from Sisteron

▶ p234

Gorges du Verdon
Europe's Grand Canyon

A great escape if you avoid the high-season crowds, this jaw-dropping canyon slices 25km across Haute-Provence's limestone plateau to the Alps. Some cliffs are twice the height of the Eiffel Tower and safeguard a colony of vultures. Hike the dramatic Sentier Blanc Martel.

🚗 30mins from Castellane

▶ p232

Grasse
A cheesy bike tour

Perfumery hub Grasse is the fragrant starting point for a six-day epicurean cycling tour north into Provence's remote alpine foothills. En route the Grand Tour des Préalpes d'Azur passes stark lime-stone plateaux, isolated hilltop villages, and goat farms selling home-crafted cheese and ice cream.

🚗 40mins from Cannes

▶ p86

CLOCKWISE FROM LEFT: JEF WODNIAK/SHUTTERSTOCK ©, CHRIS HELLIER/SHUTTERSTOCK ©, MARCO RUBINO/SHUTTERSTOCK ©,

0 — 20 km
0 — 10 miles

ROMAS_PHOTO/SHUTTERSTOCK ©

ROMAN
HOLIDAY

▬▬ Ancient Roman ruins transport visitors to a very different Provence. Gloriously intact, carefully preserved amphitheatres, triumphal arches, baths and other public buildings evoke the very period in its rich history that gave Provence – the first Roman *provincia* (province) – its name. Throw the region's gutsy and gregarious festive spirit into the ancient arena, and Roman Provence suddenly becomes bags of fun.

Best Roman Experiences

▶ Admire the awe-inspiring Pont du Gard from an alternative angle afloat a canoe or sprawled on a beach (p190)

▶ Go underground beneath Arles' Roman forum (p175)

▶ Shop for hand-made jewellery inspired by ancient Roman fashion (p174)

▶ Enjoy opera in Orange's Roman theatre during France's oldest festival (p18)

Just as many wine-producing châteaux and *domaines* (estates) in Provence offer *dégustation* (tasting) in situ, so do many craft breweries and distilleries.

Check if an advance reservation is required before visiting.

Some run hands-on *ateliers* (workshops).

Best Drinking Experiences

▶ Pair Niçois street food with tasty cocktails at Babel Babel (p59)

▶ Drink agave-distilled Josiane at Tuba (p141)

▶ Shop for citrus-fruit spirits and beers in 'lemon capital' Menton (p89)

▶ Taste local basil gin and olive-laced rum in a rooftop bar in Nice (p62)

▶ Sample a rosé winemaker's pink gin in a secret garden near St-Tropez (p115)

ON THE
ROCKS

▬▬ Nothing evokes Provençal *art de vivre* quite like an aperitif – traditionally a glass of Côtes de Provence rosé (pictured) or aniseed-flavoured pastis – on a shaded terrace. Yet drinking trends evolve, and while the beach crowd now sips bowl-sized cognac glasses of light and floral Rosé Piscine on the rocks, hipsters are tapping into sassy new spirits by artisan distillers. The source? Provence's beautiful abundance of natural botanicals.

OUTDOOR
ACTION

▬▬ With its varied landscapes – cavernous gorges and alpine mountains, flamingo-pink wetlands and glittering coastline – the region has an outdoor activity to match every mood and moment. Hiking, biking, sea kayaking, snorkelling: whatever your chosen action, exploring outdoors is a deep dive into the very best of backwater Provence.

Best Outdoor Experiences

▶ Dive into marine gardens, underwater museums and film sets in Golfe-Juan, the Var and Marseille (p84, p120, p136)

▶ Enjoy a walk in the Massif des Maures and watch cork being harvested (p119)

▶ Fly down winter slopes with Med views in Côte d'Azur ski resorts (p78)

▶ Razz up Nice's legendary corniches by e-bike (p80)

▶ Horse trek across wetlands and beaches with Camargue cowboys (p181)

★ TRAIL TIP

Save glittering clifftop and coastal trails in Les Calanques for spring or autumn. Risk of forest fire can shut trails July to mid-September.

→ HIGH-SUMMER HIGH

Don't miss St-Martin-Vésubie in Haute-Provence's Vallée de la Vésubie, with guided hikes into the remote Vallée des Merveilles, littered with Bronze Age rock carvings.

Above Gorges du Verdon (p232)
Left St-Martin-Vésubie

LEFT: BOIVIN NICOLAS/SHUTTERSTOCK © BOTTOM: MICHEL PERES/SHUTTERSTOCK ©

SUR LA
PLAGE

Cats on leads, dogs in handbags and prima donnas dusting sand from their toes with shaving brushes are madcap sights to lap up on the glorious beach-laced Côte d'Azur. Anything goes, but it pays to know your *plage:* ceramic-smooth pebbles in Nice, soft and golden in St-Tropez (pictured), strictly *naturiste* (nude) on Île du Levant, as wild as the wind in the untamed Camargue...

Best Beach Experiences

▶ Sail the length of Plage de Pampelonne in a Polynesian pirogue (p112)

▶ Feast on fresh seafood with locals in a clandestine beach shack (p125)

▶ Trade sardine-packed summer sands for river beach on the Gardon (p191)

▶ Forage for your own private beach on an island idyll – by bicycle or on foot (p121)

▶ Enjoy a guided wine tasting in a seaside château on the sand (p114)

High season peaks in August – avoid autoroutes and major roads on Saturdays when half of France it seems clogs up roads.

Beautiful Beaches

Few French beaches rival the Côte d'Azur for celebrity glitz. Porquerolles' golden sands are among the region's most untouched.

♥ Île de Porquerolles, p124

Lavender Fields

Purple lavender colours Plateau de Valensole and the gardens around Abbaye Notre-Dame de Sénanque from late June. Smell the harvest mid-July to mid-August.

♥ Plateau de Valensole, p228

▶ Abbaye Notre-Dame de Sénanque, p220

↖ Les Chorégies d'Orange

France's oldest festival stages operas at Orange's incredible Roman theatre in July, an unforgettable night if you bag tickets.

▶ choregies.fr

JUNE

Average daytime max: 24°C
Days of rainfall: 4

JULY

Provence & the Côte d'Azur in
SUMMER

↘ Festival d'Aix-en-Provence

A month of world-class opera, classical music and ballet lures culture buffs to the elegant city of Aix.

📍 Aix-en-Provence, p162

▶ festival-aix.com

↓ Fireworks

Spectacular fireworks illuminate night skies in Cannes and Monaco during hotshot pyrotechnic festivals in July and August.

Festival d'Avignon

Theatre in every guise at this renowned three-week theatre fest, equally brilliant off stage as on.

📍 Avignon, p188

▶ festival-avignon.com

AUGUST

Average daytime max: 27°C
Days of rainfall: 2

Average daytime max: 28°C
Days of rainfall: 3

PROVENCE & THE CÔTE D'AZUR PLAN BY SEASON

Demand for accommodation peaks in July and August. Book tours and overnight adventures in advance.

Packing Notes

Sunglasses, hat, sunscreen and insect repellent are essential. Some festival spirit is handy too.

Alfresco Dining

September is your chance to enjoy the region's signature summertime terraces, urban rooftop bars and star-topped garden restaurants. Remember to bring a sweater.

↓ Hit the Trail

September is an ideal month for hiking and cycling in the region. Tackling Mont Ventoux and Nice's three corniches are off-season, two-wheel classics.

● Mont Ventoux, p194

▶ Nice's three corniches, p80

Grape Harvest

The harvest is already in full swing in August in Provence's most southern, sun-drenched vineyards; September sees pickers in Châteauneuf-du-Pape harvest grapes by hand.

↑ Dramatic Drives

Quieter roads make September a perfect time to road-trip around hilltop villages or along the Routes des Vins (Wine Roads).

▶ routedesvinsde provence.com

SEPTEMBER

Average daytime max: 24°C
Days of rainfall: 6

OCTOBER

Provence & the Côte d'Azur in
AUTUMN

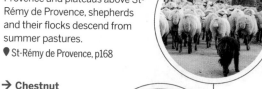

→ La Transhumance

In the hilly Alpes-de-Haute-Provence and plateaus above St-Rémy de Provence, shepherds and their flocks descend from summer pastures.

 St-Rémy de Provence, p168

→ Chestnut Festivals

Harvest, feast on, learn about and celebrate the region's sweet chestnuts in every guise at village-fuelled *fêtes des châtaignes.*

 Massif des Maures, p122

↓ Artist Palette

Mellow autumn days spun from bewitching colour and light lure art lovers to St-Tropez, Cassis, Montagne St-Victoire and other summer-packed art destinations.

PROVENCE & THE CÔTE D'AZUR PLAN BY SEASON

NOVEMBER

Average daytime max: 21°C
Days of rainfall: 8

Average daytime max: 17°C
Days of rainfall: 8

→ Epicurean Feasts

Fresh syrupy figs, the tail end of summer's fresh almonds, forest-foraged *cèpes* (porcini mushrooms) and game appear in markets and on locavore restaurant menus.

Packing Notes

Sunscreen, light sweater or waterproof jacket and swimmers for warm-day dipping.

Bitterly cold mistral wind aside, winter charms with chilly but bluebird-sky days and a serenity impossible to find other times of year. Olives are harvested.

← Mimosa Magic

Europe's largest mimosa forest bursts into golden bloom late December to early March. This is the time to road-trip along Route du Mimosa.
● Bormes-les-Mimosas, p78

A Provençal Christmas

Families celebrate Noël with midnight Mass, Provençal chants, 13 desserts and nativity scenes starring traditional santons (terracotta figurines) made in Marseille.

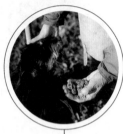

↙ Truffle Season

November to March gourmets feast on black truffles, sniffed out by dogs in wintery woods around Carpentras, Vaison-la-Romaine and Richerenches in the Vaucluse.

DECEMBER

Average daytime max: 14°C
Days of rainfall: 7

JANUARY

Provence & the Côte d'Azur in
WINTER

→ Fête du Citron

'Exotic and eccentric' best sums up the monumental sculptures and floats crafted from zillions of lemons at Menton's two-week Lemon Festival.

📍 Menton, p79
▶ feteducitron.com

Say it with Violets

Adopt the old-school tradition of offering a bouquet of wild or locally cultivated violets to your Valentine on 14 February. The fragrant purple flower blooms November to April.

📍 Tourrettes-sur-Loup, p88

↗ Hit the Slopes

The ski season in small, family-friendly resorts north of Nice runs from December to mid-April. February holidays get packed.

📍 Isola 2000, p78

PROVENCE & THE CÔTE D'AZUR PLAN BY SEASON

Average daytime max: 13°C
Days of rainfall: 6

FEBRUARY

Average daytime max: 13°C
Days of rainfall: 5

↘ Carnaval de Nice

Decorated floats, flower battles and the crowds are equally gigantic at this flamboyant Mardi Gras street parade, celebrated since 1293.

📍 Carnaval de Nice, p77
nicecarnaval.com

Packing Notes

Hat, gloves and a warm coat. Bring binoculars for watching wintering birds in the Camargue.

May is 'bank-holiday month', with four *jours fériés* (public holidays) and extra days slotted in to make long weekends. Plan ahead for reservations – it gets busy.

→ To Market

Shop local. Stalls at open-air food markets are piled high with local produce: Cavaillon melons, Apt cherries, strawberries, asparagus, apricots the size of tennis balls...

Deep Dive

Easter weekend traditionally raises the curtain on the diving season (until October) on the Côte d'Azur.

↗ Gardens of Eden

There is no lovelier time to visit the region's honeypot gardens, a ravishing rainbow of Mediterranean flowers in bloom.

📍 Villa Ephrussi de Rothschild, p75

▶ villa-ephrussi.com

MARCH

Average daytime max: 15°C
Days of rainfall: 5

APRIL

Provence & the Côte d'Azur in
SPRING

↘ Festivals Galore

From the world-famous Cannes Film Festival to a smorgasbord of staunchly local, teeny village *foires* (fairs) and *fêtes* (festivals), spring is the start of festival season.

↓ Monaco Grand Prix

Formula One's most anticipated race, May's Monaco Grand Prix tears around the municipality in a haze of Champagne, VIPs and after-parties.

◉ Monaco, p98

▶ acm.mc

Fête des Gardians

As flamingos nest in nearby *étangs,* Camargue cowboys celebrate their bull-herding and equestrian skills on 1 May.

▶ thegoodarles.com

MAY

Average daytime max: 17°C
Days of rainfall: 8

Average daytime max: 20°C
Days of rainfall: 7

← Bravade de St-Tropez

Join the crowds in traditional costume and 140 musket-firing *bravadeurs* celebrating St-Tropez' namesake and patron saint.

◉ St-Tropez, p125

🧳 Packing Notes

A light sweater, comfy shoes and insect repellent to repel March mosquitoes.

VAUCLUSE
Trip Builder

TAKE YOUR PICK OF MUST-SEES AND HIDDEN GEMS

▬▬▬ Named after France's most powerful natural spring, Vaucluse in western Provence is all about cinematic vineyards, abbeys, fruit orchards and fragrant lavender fields. Rampart-ringed Avignon is the art-fuelled urban hub. In the south, the rural Luberon seduces with go-slow green scapes sprinkled with traditional hilltop villages and squirrelled-away, epicurean *auberges*.

🗺 Trip Notes

Hub towns Avignon, Orange, Carpentras, Apt

How long Allow 1 week

Getting around Pick up a hire car or e-bike to get off the beaten track and hop at your own pace between hilltop villages. Buses link towns. Cycling tours are popular.

Tips A car in Avignon is a headache. In July and August traffic jams clog up bend-laced access roads to key villages and car parks on village outskirts fill fast.

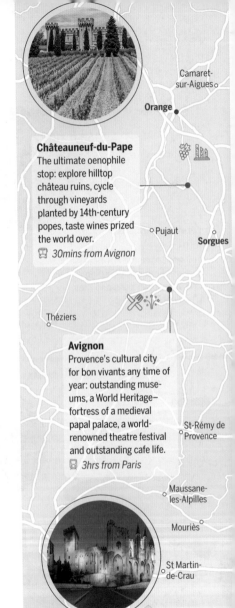

Camaret-sur-Aigues

Orange

Châteauneuf-du-Pape
The ultimate oenophile stop: explore hilltop château ruins, cycle through vineyards planted by 14th-century popes, taste wines prized the world over.
🚆 30mins from Avignon

Pujaut

Sorgues

Théziers

Avignon
Provence's cultural city for bon vivants any time of year: outstanding museums, a World Heritage–fortress of a medieval papal palace, a world-renowned theatre festival and outstanding cafe life.
🚆 3hrs from Paris

St-Rémy de Provence

Maussane-les-Alpilles

Mouriès

St Martin-de-Crau

Beaumes-de-Venise

Sample sweet Muscat wines, buy olive oil at the mill and admire exquisite Romanesque chapel Chapelle Notre-Dame d'Aubune in this eponymous viticultural village. Gorgeous *chambres d'hôte* too.

🚗 *30mins from Avignon*

Rustrel

Walk along ochre trails punctuated with dramatic, fire-red rock formations at Colorado Provençal, an ochre quarry until 1956. The less-crowded option to famously red Roussillon.

🚲 *40mins from Apt*

Apt

Info point for the hiking-trail-stitched Parc Naturel Régional du Luberon, this vibrant market town is worth a pit stop. Taste and buy *fruits confits* (candied fruits).

🚆 *1¼hrs from Avignon*

Buoux

Rock climbing, mountain biking and crumbling village ruins to uncover on foot: this teeny village in Le Grand Luberon, within easy striking distance of lavender-strewn Plateau des Claparèdes, is for outdoor explorers.

🚲 *50mins from Apt*

La Roque-d'Anthéron

Lavender-lovers flock to 12th-century Abbaye Notre-Dame de Sénanque near Gordes to admire its gardens, but for an alternative dose of medieval elegance, consider Abbaye de Silvacane in La Roque.

🚗 *1hr from Avignon*

Ansouis

Ramparts, watchtowers and gateways ring medieval Ansouis. Village highlights: lavender- and apricot-laced cakes at Pâtisserie Volpert and a long, lazy lunch alfresco at La Closerie.

🚗 *30mins from Aix-en-Provence*

N

0   10 km
0   5 miles

Violes
Malaucène
Gigondas
Le Barroux
Sarrians
Carpentras
Mazan
Villes-sur-Auzon
Monieux
Sault
Monteux
Pernes-les-Fontaines
Murs
St-Saturnin-lès-Apt
Villars
Oppedette
L'Isle-sur-la-Sorgue
Viens
Caumont-sur-Durance
Goult
St-Martin de Castillon
Cereste
Cavaillon
Le Colombier
Orgon
Parc Naturel Régional du Luberon
Vitrolles-en-Luberon
Parc Naturel Régional des Alpilles
Vaugines
Lauris
La Motte-d'Aigues
Cadenet
Eyguières
La Tour d'Aigues
Salon-de-Provence

BOUCHES-DU-RHÔNE
Trip Builder

TAKE YOUR PICK OF MUST-SEES AND HIDDEN GEMS

███ For a whirlwind trip through regional history, dig into this wildly contrasting part of Provence where the mighty Rhône splits before spilling into the Med. From the pulsating Provençal capital Marseille, springboard into an outdoor playground of pine-scented coastal uplands, turquoise creeks and cowboy-specked wetlands.

🗺 Trip Notes

Hub towns Marseille, Aix-en-Provence, Arles, St-Rémy de Provence

How long Allow 1 week

Getting around Trains and buses link towns, and seasonal boats yoyo along the coast. Postcard coves in Les Calanques are only accessible on foot. Cycling is the way to go in Montagne Ste-Victoire, Les Alpilles and the Camargue.

Tips Ditch the car in Marseille and Aix. The coast gets packed in July and August – expect traffic jams and tricky parking.

Avignon ●

Tarascon
●

St-Rémy de Provence
○

Stes-Maries-de-la-Mer
Hit the beach and devour fish *à la plancha* in this whitewashed seaside town. Roma pilgrimages fuel chaotic crowds of carnivalesque guitarists, dancers and cowboys on horseback.
🚗 *40mins from Arles*

Fontvieille
○

Maussane-les-Alpilles
○

● Arles

St Martin-de-Crau
○

○ Mas Thibert

Étang de Vaccarès

Parc National de Camargue

Les Salins de Giraud
○

Domaine de la Palissade
Trek on horseback or foot, birdwatch and forage for sea lavender and marsh samphire around flamingo-specked lagoons in the hauntingly beautiful Camargue wetlands.
🚲 *2½hrs from Arles*

Parc Naturel Régional des Alpilles

Spot Egyptian vultures along hiking trails in this silvery chain of craggy limestone peaks. Tour hill villages and olive groves by bike from St-Rémy de Provence.

🚗 *30mins from Avignon*

Senas

Eyguières

Miramas

St-Chamas

Fos-sur-Mer

Port de Bouc

La Couronne

MEDITERRANEAN SEA

Salon de Provence

St-Cannat

Étang de Berre

Châteauneuf-les-Martigues

Carry-le-Rouet

Apt

St-Martin de Castillon

Sivergues

Cucuron

Lourmarin

Cadenet

Pertuis

Durance

Rognes

St-Canadet

Couteron

Marignane

Cabriès

L'Estaque

Ventabren

The real reason to visit this pretty hilltop village is to dine at Dan B, a gourmet address with panoramic terrace and creative locavore cuisine.

🚗 *30mins from Aix-en-Provence*

Aix-en-Provence

Revel in elegant architecture and fine arts in this former Roman spa town, handsomely at home in Cézanne's beloved Pays d'Aix (Aix Country).

🚊 *40mins from Marseille*

Châteauneuf-le-Rouge

Cassis

Gateway to the iconic Massif des Calanques, picture-book Cassis enchants with its fishing-village vibe, vineyards and boat trips into cove-laced Parc National des Calanques.

🚊 *40mins from Marseille*

Côte Bleue

Explore the unsung Blue Coast, beaded with limestone coves, walking trails, unpretentious fishing villages-cum-holiday towns and – in winter – bucketfuls of sea urchins to devour.

🚊 *20–50mins from Marseille*

Marseille

Urbanites can't resist this ancient Greek colony with its gritty port and markets, pulsating nightlife, edgy art scene and beach-strewn suburbs.

🚆 *3¾hrs from Paris*

La Ciotat

Port d'Alon

0 —— 10 km
0 —— 5 miles

THE CÔTE D'AZUR
Trip Builder

TAKE YOUR PICK OF MUST-SEES AND HIDDEN GEMS

▬▬▬ Magical and mythical, this captivating string of dazzling beaches and pebble coves extends from St-Tropez to the Italian border. Framed by offshore islands one side and lively cities, medieval hilltop villages, historic gardens and hiking paths on the other, this coastal strip panders to every mood, moment and hedonistic desire.

🗺 Trip Notes

Hub towns Nice, Cannes, Antibes, St-Tropez, Monaco

How long Allow at least a week

Getting around Trains and buses run east–west along the coast. The Grande Corniche, Gorges du Loup and villages around Menton are the only places you'll really need a car. Public-shared bikes and e-bikes are handy everywhere.

Tips In summer hit the road early when riding bus 100 along the coast – or risk standing the entire way.

Île de Porquerolles
Paradise on earth (outside high season): cycling, swimming in gin-clear water from powder-soft sand beaches, wine tasting and playing *pétanque* on the village square sums up island life.
⛴ *50mins from Le Lavandou*

Aups ○

○ Draguignan

Le Muy ○

○ Le Thoronet

○ Le Cannet des Maures

○ Brignoles

Ste-Maxime ●

○ Gonfaron

Grimaud ○

Collobrières ○

Ramatuelle

Cuers ○

La Rayol-Canadel ○

Le Lavandou

Hyères ○

La Tour Fondue ○

Îles d'Hyères

Île du Levant

Île de Port Cros

ITALY

Ste-Agnès
The road trip here – across Col de la Madone de Gorbio – is as spectacular as the coastal village, Europe's highest. Embrace culinary highs on the rooftop of hotel-restaurant Le Saint-Yves.

🚗 *50mins from Nice*

Monaco
Homegrown oysters, the world's first 100% organic Michelin-starred restaurant, luxuriant rose gardens, open-air movies, Formula 1: the world's second-smallest country is a once-in-a-lifetime experience.

🚆 *25mins from Nice*

Grasse
Swap the tourist razzmatazz of downtown Grasse for the heady scents of rose, jasmine and tuberose grown exclusively for Dior at flower farm Domaine de Manon.

🚗 *30mins from Cannes*

Plan-du-Var

Var

● Menton

Vence

Côte d'Azur

Nice
Riviera queen Nice blends old-world opulence with modern-day grit: old town with bustling markets, dimly lit churches, artist studios, sun-fuelled dining and brilliant nightlife.

🚆 *6–7hrs from Paris*

Tourettes

Lac de St-Cassien

Antibes

Cannes

Théoule-sur-Mer

Cap d'Antibes
Cicada song reaches fever pitch on this exclusive cape where centurion parasol pines shade sumptuous villas and billionaire mansions. Snorkel, swim, stroll the scenic coastal path, gawp at Villa Eilenroc.

🚶 *1hr from Antibes*

Fréjus

Île Ste-Marguerite
Offshore from Cannes, sail to this eucalyptus-perfumed island to stroll scenic trails and snorkel in an underwater eco-museum showcasing works by British sculptor Jason deCaires Taylor.

⛴ *20mins from Cannes*

St-Tropez

Ramatuelle
Ensnaring the famously glam beaches of Pampelonne, a flowery hilltop village and Côtes de Provence vineyards, this bewitching chameleon rivals neighbouring St-Tropez in celebrity-seduction stakes.

🚲 *40mins from St-Tropez*

MEDITERRANEAN SEA

🧭 N
0   20 km
0   10 miles

THE ALPINE VALLEYS
Trip Builder

TAKE YOUR PICK OF MUST-SEES AND HIDDEN GEMS

▬▬▬ North of Nice, rising like a tooth-lined jawbone along the French–Italian border, lie the majestic Alps – haven for mountaineers, hikers and wildlife spotters, and home to some of Provence's most unforgettable scenery. Six main valleys linked by steep, hairpin-laced *cols* (mountain passes) slice through the Alpes-de-Haute-Provence, making this untamed backcountry a road-tripper must.

🗺 Trip Notes

Hub towns Digne-les-Bains, Sisteron, Castellane, Manosque

How long Allow at least a week

Getting around Your own wheels – two or four – are essential. Phone connection is patchy so download road maps before departure to access on the road offline.

Tips Heavy snowfall can shut the highest *cols* above 2000m; many are only accessible May to September and those that remain open require a minimum of snow tyres.

FROM LEFT: SAMUEL BORGES PHOTOGRAPHY/SHUTTERSTOCK ©, PATRICK ROUZET/SHUTTERSTOCK ©, JEAN-PIERRE PIEUCHOT/GETTY IMAGES ©

Aiglun
Cruise by vintage car along mapped driving routes in the Unesco-listed Géoparc de Haute-Provence. Overnight in Aiglun, an isolated 15th-century hilltop village with *gîtes ruraux* (holiday cottages).
🚗 *15mins from Digne-les-Bains*

Serres

Pays de Forcalquier
Give your taste buds a tour in this fertile, off-track wedge between alpine foothills and the Luberon: saffron, absinthe, lavender, Banon goat's cheese and decadent black truffles (mid-March to mid-November).
🚗 *1¼hrs from Marseille*

St-Geniez

Sisteron

Château-Arnoux St-Auban

Les Mées

Mane

Oraison

Reillanne

Volx

Manosque

Valensole

Riez

Durance

St-Paul-lès-Durance

Plateau de Valensole
Summer is prime season for mountain biking across this vast plateau of lavender fields and farms. Visit distilleries, scoff farm-made lavender ice cream, smell the August harvest.
🚗 *1¼hrs from Apt*

Vallée de l'Ubaye
Learn how wild hyssop flowers are foraged and distilled to make artisanal liqueur at Distillery Lachanenche in Méolans-Revel, a hamlet in this end-of-the-world, little-visited valley.
🚗 *1¼ hrs from Sisteron*

St-Dalmas-le-Selvage
Join snow-sports enthusiasts in winter to ice climb, ski tour, snowshoe and cross-country ski from this quaint mountain hamlet in the Vallée de la Tinée.
🚗 *2hrs from Nice*

Seyne-les-Alpes

Barcelonnette

Le Sauze

ITALY

Demonte

Barles

Thoard

La Javie

Colmars-les-Alpes

St-Martin d'Entraunes

Isola

Isola 2000

Le Boréon

St-Martin-Vésubie

Guillaumes

Valberg

La Colmiane

Lac Allos
Away from the coast the air is fresher, the pace of life 'slower' – frolic with whistling marmots on a family walk to Europe's highest natural lake at a cooling 2200m.
🚗 *2¾hrs from Nice*

St-André-les-Alpes

Barrême

Daluis

Puget-Théniers

Parc National du Mercantour
Home to rare wildlife, isolated villages and pristine natural habitats, this national park begs slow, thoughtful exploration. Keep the camera handy: there's an Instagram story around every corner.
🚗 *1hr from Nice*

Parc Natural du Verdon

Moustiers Ste-Marie

Castellane

Greolières

Lac de e-Croix

Baudeun

La Palud-sur-Verdon

Trigance

Gorges du Verdon
Nothing beats Europe's 'Grand Canyon' for high-octane drama and outdoor action: hiking, canoeing, climbing, vulture-spotting, bungee jumping, sunset walks with a night sleeping under the stars.
🚗 *2½hrs from Nice*

Èze

Nice

Grasse

Aups

Mediterranean Sea

Antibes

Cannes

7 Things to Know About
PROVENCE &
THE CÔTE D'AZUR

INSIDER TIPS TO HIT THE GROUND RUNNING

1 Un Ricard, S'il Vous Plaît

A summer classic, this anise-flavoured drink should be enjoyed *à l'ancienne*, by pouring one part pastis followed by five or six parts water into a glass and then adding ice cubes. If you add ice cubes before the water, it cuts the pastis' ability to release aromas; don't be surprised if locals refer to you as *un parisien* afterward.

▶ Try creative twists on the classic spirit on p140

2 Dream of the Côte d'Azur

Each evening a night train leaves Paris. Direction: the Côte d'Azur. Reserve a space in a four- or six-person couchette, or a private 1st- or 2nd-class compartment. A special service bunks solo female travellers with other women. Go to sleep in Gare d'Austerlitz and awake in Marseille, Toulon, Les Arcs Draguigan, St-Raphaël Valescure, Cannes, Antibes or Nice!

▶ Find more transport tips on p244

3 An Accent that Sings

The Provençal accent differs from the French you learned on Duolingo. Adding an 'ng' sound to words ending in 'ain', like *pain*, might help locals understand you better.

▶ Brush up on your French on p254

4 The Best Bouillabaisse

Once a poor fisherman's staple, the Marseillais dish of bouillabaisse stews for hours and requires fresh ingredients. To taste an authentic version, you'll need to reserve in advance. Expect to pay between €40 and €50 per person.

▶ Track down the best bouillabaisse on p134

5 Know Your Lavender from Your Lavandin

The lavender season lasts from early June to mid-July, after which the flowers are cut. Visiting in late July? Try the fields in higher altitudes like Sault, Thoard or Argens, which are cut later.

The bright purple flowers often seen in photos are *lavandin*, grown for industrial purposes. Real *lavande*, used for perfume, is greyer and grows at higher altitudes.

▶ Visit picture-perfect lavender fields on p228

6 Where the Mistral Blows

Notice a lot of references to something called *le mistral*? Cafes, songs and books often reference this northern wind. There is a long-standing Provençal belief that when the mistral says *bonjour*, or begins to blow in the morning, it will continue for three, six or nine days. If it says *bonsoir*, and begins blowing in the evening, it will only last through the next day.

The wind whips down through the Rhône Valley, accelerating as it races to the sea. Its gusts have reached up to 320km/h, tormenting farmers, locals and tourists wherever it blows, from Orange, Avignon or the Luberon, all the way to Marseille. Farmhouses traditionally faced south to protect their entryways from this 'naughty son' of the 2nd-century god Vintur. Chilling the area and sweeping away moisture, the mistral is nothing to joke about: make sure you have a windbreaker or jacket in your bag!

7 Keep It Human

Are you tempted to visit Cassis, Aix-en-Provence, the Luberon and Avignon in two days? And what about Nice, Cannes and the Côte d'Azur? What you'll really see is a lot of road. Rather than rush from site to site, choose a region or theme and build your trip from there.

▶ Tailor your trip on p26

Read, Listen, Watch & Follow

 READ

Voyeur (Francesca Reece; 2021) A beach read with a strong female protagonist.

The Man Who Planted Trees (Jean Giono; 1953) Simply written parable for the modern world.

A Year in Provence (Peter Mayle; 1989) Discovering Provençal living from a newcomer's view.

Tender Is the Night (F Scott Fitzgerald; 1934) Classic novel set on the French Riviera in the Jazz Age.

 LISTEN

13 Organisé (Various artists; 2020) Collaborative rap album with 50 rappers mainly from Marseille.

Une Partie de Pétanque (Various artists; 2010) Provençal songs compiled in one place, including 'Un Pastis Bien Frais' and 'La Bouillabaisse'.

Fais Comme L'Oiseau (Michel Fugain & Le Big Bazar; 1972) Seventies' vibes beach album to have a summer fling to.

Aller-Retour (Bon Entendeur; 2019) Electro collective mixing classic sounds into new dance hits. Perfect for blasting on the radio as you drive the coast.

MÉLANIE LEMAHIEU/SHUTTERSTOCK ©

Bichon (Julien Doré; 2011) Pop that feels drenched in Riviera romance.

▷ **WATCH**

Jean de Florette, Manon des Sources
(1963) Heart-wrenching two-part series about Provençal farmers and family.

Taxi (1998; pictured bottom right) Police comedy filmed in Marseille.

Pierrot le Fou (1965) Directed by Jean-Luc Godard, it's French Riviera meets midlife crisis.

La Baie des Anges (1963) A gambling romantic drama set in Nice, full of intrigue and seduction.

La Gloire de Mon Père, Le Château de Ma Mère (1990; pictured top right) Another two-part classic, a Provençal coming-of-age tale.

PHOTO 12/ALAMY STOCK PHOTO ©

MOVIESTORE COLLECTION LTD/ ALAMY STOCK PHOTO ©

 FOLLOW

@Foodlovers_provence
Cuisine and restaurant features across the region.

LUBERON
SUD TOURISME
@luberon.sud. tourisme
Events and travel in the Luberon.

@CuriousProvence
Daily updates from a Provence-based photographer and local guide.

FR
FRENCH RIVIERA
@FrenchRivieraGuide
Inspirational travel and Riviera lifestyle.

Belle Provence Travels
(belleprovence travels.com) Travel tips and Provence lifestyle blog.

NICE

BEACH | FOOD | OUTDOORS

Experience
Nice online

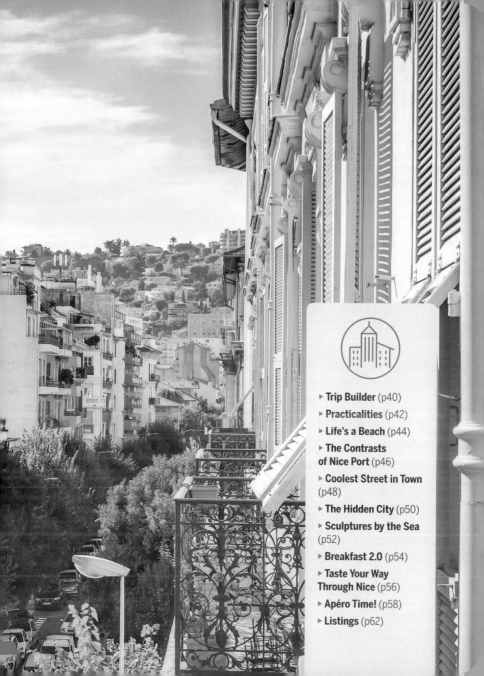

NICE
Trip Builder

A breezy palm-fringed beachfront framed by matching Mediterranean sea and sky blues, heritage architecture the colours of sunshine, shady terraces for alfresco living and an increasingly inventive food and drink scene. If you could bottle that holiday feeling, Nice would be a bestseller.

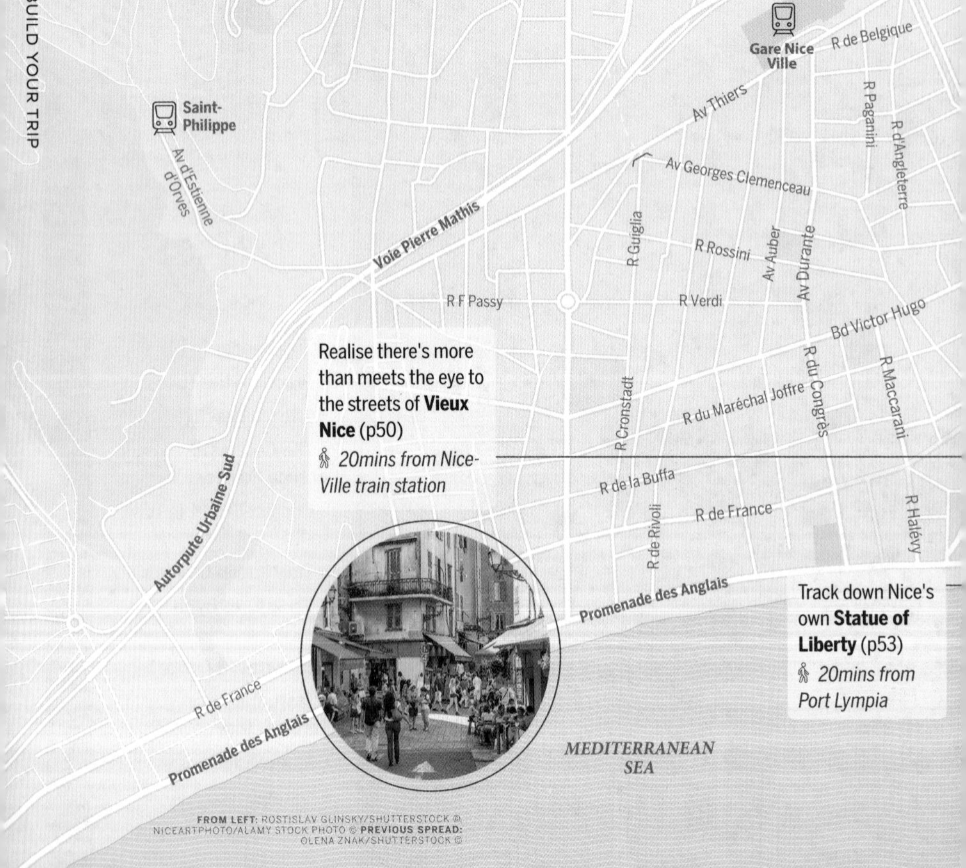

Sip on a Spritz at sundown at a real local favourite, **Altra Casa** (p59)
🚶 *20mins from place Masséna*

Saint-Philippe

Gare Nice Ville

Realise there's more than meets the eye to the streets of **Vieux Nice** (p50)
🚶 *20mins from Nice-Ville train station*

Track down Nice's own **Statue of Liberty** (p53)
🚶 *20mins from Port Lympia*

Av Borrigilione
Av Villermont
Av Raymond Camboul
Bd Joseph Garnier
Av Mirabeau
R Marceau
Voie Pierre Mathis
R de Belgique
R Paganini
R d'Angleterre
Av Thiers
Av Georges Clemenceau
R Guiglia
R Rossini
Av Auber
Av Durante
R Verdi
Bd Victor Hugo
R du Congrès
R Maccarani
Voie Pierre Mathis
R F Passy
R Cronstadt
R du Maréchal Joffre
R de la Buffa
R de Rivoli
R de France
R Halévy
Av d'Estienne d'Orves
Autoroute Urbaine Sud
R de France
Promenade des Anglais
Promenade des Anglais
MEDITERRANEAN SEA

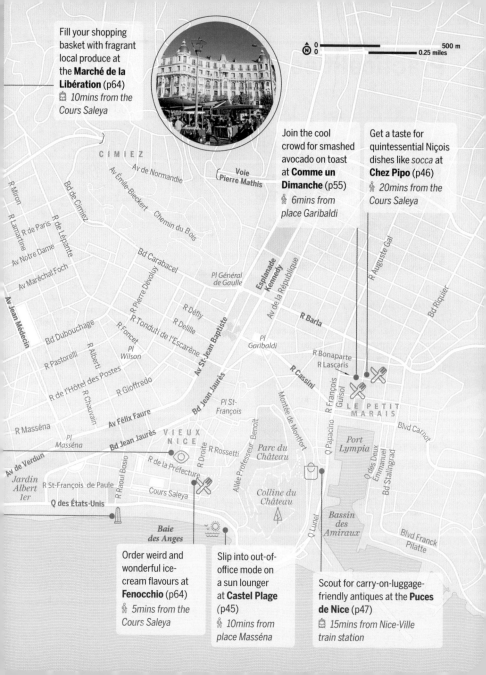

Fill your shopping basket with fragrant local produce at the **Marché de la Libération** (p64)
🚋 *10mins from the Cours Saleya*

Join the cool crowd for smashed avocado on toast at **Comme un Dimanche** (p55)
🚶 *6mins from place Garibaldi*

Get a taste for quintessential Niçois dishes like *socca* at **Chez Pipo** (p46)
🚶 *20mins from the Cours Saleya*

Order weird and wonderful ice-cream flavours at **Fenocchio** (p64)
🚶 *5mins from the Cours Saleya*

Slip into out-of-office mode on a sun lounger at **Castel Plage** (p45)
🚶 *10mins from place Masséna*

Scout for carry-on-luggage-friendly antiques at the **Puces de Nice** (p47)
🚋 *15mins from Nice-Ville train station*

Practicalities

EQROY/SHUTTERSTOCK ©

ARRIVING

Aéroport Nice-Côte d'Azur Nice's airport (pictured) is France's second busiest after Paris. A 15-minute taxi ride will get you to the centre of town for €32, but the newish tramline is a much cheaper (€1.50) and only marginally slower option. It leaves from Terminals 1 and 2.

Nice-Ville station If your destination isn't within walking distance of the main train station, the tramline passes just outside (tickets €1.50).

HOW MUCH FOR A

Glass of rosé
€5

Pan bagnat
€5.50

Parasailing on the Prom
€70

WHEN TO GO

DEC–FEB
Mild days and cooler nights punctuated by colourful seasonal festivals.

MAR–JUN
Return of the private beaches, warm days, fewer crowds.

JUL–AUG
Peak season: busy streets, overcrowded public transport and opportunistic pickpockets.

SEP–NOV
Often still T-shirt weather into October, with cool evenings and cosy heated outdoor terraces.

GETTING AROUND

Walking With mostly flat terrain, Nice's central neighbourhoods are easy to navigate by foot.

Bus & Tram Lignes d'Azur, the city's comprehensive bus and tram network, is frequent and cheap. One-way tickets for both start at €1.50 and allow unlimited onward connections for 74 minutes. Purchase on board buses or at tram-stop kiosks. Day passes cost €5 while 10-trip multi-tickets cost €10. The bus service slows down after 8pm with just a handful of irregular night buses. The tram runs until midnight.

Bicycle With 125km of bike lanes, Nice is a city for cyclists. Sign up for the VéloBleu *(velobleu. org)* city bike and e-bike share scheme, with over 120 docking stations.

EATING & DRINKING

A blend of French, Italian, alpine and maritime influences, Niçois cuisine brims with the products of its warm-climate soils (courgettes and peppers especially), small fish found close to its rocky shores and lashings of olive oil. *Socca* (pictured top right), made from chick-pea flour, is the signature snack, although that's a position closely contested by the *pan bagnat* sandwich (pictured bottom right). Local flavours are no longer the domain of casual street eateries – you'll find regional dishes now elevated to a fine-dining setting.

Best cocktail list
Babel Babel (p59)

Must-try breakfast pastry
Lavender croissant at
Boulangerie Roy Le Capitole (p55)

CONNECT & FIND YOUR WAY

Wi-fi Sign into the city's Spot Wifi Nice network in main public places including the Cours Saleya, place Garibaldi et Promenade du Paillon, place Masséna and the quai des Etats-Unis. Network access can be hit-and-miss in the backstreets of Vieux Nice.

Navigation Apart from the maze-like alleys of Vieux Nice, Nice is a simple city to navigate with a grid of streets fanning out from the south-facing waterfront.

FRENCH RIVIERA PASS

For an initial outlay of €26/38/56 for 24/48/72 hours, the French Riviera Pass unlocks reduced rates and free access to a large selection of sites and activities.

WHERE TO STAY

The choice of accommodation has ballooned with the arrival of platforms like Airbnb. For the pick of the crop, book well in advance.

Neighbourhood	Pro/Con
Vieux Nice	Private lets in old buildings along narrow alleyways. Always something going on. Noisy late into the night.
Carré d'Or	Grand residences set back from wide, leafy streets close to the beach. Cool boutique hotels.
Thiers	Budget-friendly choices blend in with fast-food joints around the train station.
Port	Ultra-hip waterfront district with great dining and drinking scene. More Airbnbs than hotels.
Jean Médecin	Convenient if a bit characterless. Nice's main shopping street.

MONEY

Nice is one of the more expensive cities in France, especially in terms of food and drink, but good deals such as the lunchtime *plat du jour* (dish of the day) exist. While most shops accept card payments, carry some small change for bus and tram fares, as well as public toilets.

01

Life's a
BEACH

BEACH | ACTIVITIES | SUN LOUNGING

There's no escaping the beach in Nice, but then again, you probably don't want to. What seems like one long 6km stretch – almost the entire breadth of the city – is actually made up of over a dozen beaches. Above it, with its wide pedestrian pavement and cycle lanes, sits the city's heartbeat: the sweeping Promenade des Anglais.

CHRISPICTURES/SHUTTERSTOCK ©

How to

Cost It's free to access any of the public beaches. Private beaches have their prices on display at the entrance.

Stone's throw If you find the smooth pebbles that cover the beach, called *galets*, painful to walk on, beachfront tourist shops sell swim shoes.

Blue chairs First installed in the 1950s, the blue chairs that line the Promenade are a beloved symbol of Nice.

Local spot Tucked away to the east of the port, Coco Beach is a low-key, local favourite.

SABINO PARENTE/SHUTTERSTOCK ©

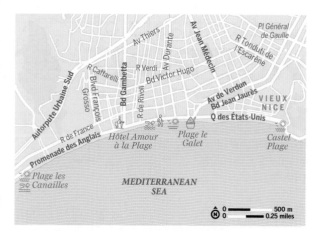

Top left Castel Plage. **Bottom left** Promenade des Anglais

Active morning Swimmers, joggers, dog walkers, strollers – the Prom, as it is affectionately known, stirs to life at first light. While a few hardy souls brave the water all year round for a brisk early-morning swim, the warmer months see organised classes such as **aquabiking** (aquabike06.com) at Ruhl Plage return to the water, as well as activities such as beach volleyball. The dedicated cycle lanes flow freely and go all the way to the airport. If you don't feel like turning back, the path continues another 14km to Antibes. **Roller Station** (roller-station. net) across from Castel Plage rents out bikes, rollerblades, electric scooters and skateboards by the hour or the day.

Relaxing afternoon Just below the #ILoveNICE selfie spot, LGBTIQ+ friendly **Castel Plage** is the oldest of Nice's private beaches. Snotty service is the price you'll pay for excellent food and the last of the day's sunshine. The owners of **Plage le Galet** bring the generous portions and oversized desserts that have made their Vieux Nice restaurants La Voglia and La Favola so popular to the beach. **Hôtel Amour à la Plage** is the waterfront address of the trendy boutique hotel a few streets behind it, while **Plage les Canailles** has a plunge pool that lights up during party nights.

As the sun sets Do as the locals do and pick up a takeaway pizza and bottle of rosé for a sunset picnic on the beach.

Top Tips for Prom Shots

Visit the Prom at different times of the day and week to experience the various moods and light conditions.

Use the blue chairs: they are a wonderful graphic element in photos and complement the different blues of the water and sky.

Avoid the light-swallowing grey pebbly beach in your frame by taking your photos from a low angle – this magnifies the space given to the sky. Align the handrail with the horizon for a graphic effect.

Try different points of view. An interesting perspective appears when you look up to the Prom from the beach, for instance.

■ Recommended by **Annette Lang**, street photographer in Nice @luxtasia

The Contrasts of
NICE PORT

EATING | SHOPPING | CULTURE

Trendy clothing boutiques, organic food shops, Michelin-star dining and LGBTIQ+ bars now call Nice's port home but as this increasingly hip neighbourhood comes of age, it hasn't come at the expense of local heritage, history and roots. Take your time wandering the streets that fan back from the harbourfront and see if you can spot the old from the new.

🗺 How to

Getting around The port area is easily explored on foot with plenty of outdoor cafes for rest breaks.

When to go Mid to late morning for fresh fish and the early-bird antique finds. Lunch and dinner for foodie feasts or street snacks. The *Lou Passagin pointu* is in the water from May to August, 10am till 7pm.

Napoleon's house As the name of the street suggests, Napoleon Bonaparte lived at 6 rue Bonaparte for nine months in 1794.

Stars and shacks South African chef Jan Hendrik van der Westhuizen put rue Lascaris on the Michelin map with his modern South African meets South of France cuisine at **Restaurant JAN**. Newly starred **Les Agitateurs** on rue Bonaparte brings *bistronomie* (bistro-style gastronomy) to

a pretty, jasmine- and wisteria-covered venue. If you're craving more casual fare, **Chez Pipo** has been the name of reference for a hundred years for fresh-from-the-oven *socca* that is crispy at the edges and slightly gooier on the inside. Get in early to nab a seat on the terrace. It might

not look like much but experts in such things swear by the *pan bagnat* at **La Gratta** snack shack near the Corsica Ferry Terminal.

Antiques and street art The **Quartier des Antiquaires** is a collection of art galleries and antique dealers clustered in the narrow triangle of streets

NICE EXPERIENCES

⛴ Boat Trip

Set against shiny super-yachts, *pointus*, as the brightly painted wooden fishing boats that line Port Lympia's eastern edge are called, bring a delightful splash of character to the harbourfront. While many are now privately owned pleasurecraft, the handful of fishermen who still cast a net in local waters sell their catch every day between 10.30am and 12.30pm on the quay opposite the Puces de Nice. It's only a short crossing from one side of the port to another, but hop aboard the city-operated *Lou Passagin* to get a feel for these traditional vessels for free. It leaves from quai Entrecasteaux and quai Lunel.

between place Garibaldi, Port Lympia and the Colline du Château. Bypass the stand-alone shops to hunt down a one-of-a-kind souvenir inside the **Village Ségurane** with its bric-a-brac stalls selling every-thing from palm-sized curios to heavy, ornate furniture. Just like the nearby **Puces de Nice** flea markets installed inside old fisherman's huts on Quai Lunel, the walls are covered in bright street art tagged by local artists such as Patrick Moya and François Nasica and are worth a visit for that reason alone.

Above Port Lympia

Coolest Street in Town

TRADITIONAL MAKES WAY FOR TRENDY ON RUE BONAPARTE

Once the heart of an industrial neighbourhood built on the old road to Villefranche-sur-Mer, a public gentrification program has transformed rue Bonaparte into the city's hub of all things trendy and cool. Conveniently located between place Garibaldi and Port Lympia, you'll find a crowd for morning coffee, evening cocktails and everything in between.

Left Place du Pin **Middle** Aerial view, Petit Marais Niçois **Right** Rue Bonaparte street sign

VV SHOTS/GETTY IMAGES ©

At 10 rue Bonaparte, the name is all that remains of Nice's first electrical store, Comptoir Central d'Electricité. Founded in 1905, for over a century it was the go-to name for generations of the city's electricians. They'd pull up on the kerb out front and disappear inside the bazaar-like store, emerging with lampshades, lightbulbs and other tools of their trade, thanking the staff who had become firm friends on their way out.

Neighbours included craft stores and *socca* stands. 'There was a real familial vibe, it was like a small village. We even had a local cinema,' says Brandon Esposito, the shop's owner. The friendly quarter has also long been a welcoming hub for the LGBTIQ+ community; **Malabar Station** next door is the city's most popular gay-only address (although the terrace is open to everyone).

A New Look

In 2011, municipal works to pedestrianise place du Pin, the small square across from the store, saw a drop in trade. The city was becoming prettier, but these long-standing businesses were feeling the squeeze. 'Our customers couldn't park up outside anymore,' Brandon continues.

The electrical store was out, and in its place a cool, boho bar with mismatched chairs and exposed concrete walls emerged. The new tenants kept (almost) the name, and suddenly Comptoir Central Electrique was the name on everyone's – not just the city's electricians – lips.

Le Petit Marais Niçois

More than a decade on, CCE is still one of Nice's trendiest bars. Around it, hipster cafes, upscale restaurants,

independent shopping boutiques and, of course, ubiquitous real estate agents, have opened their doors. Rue Bonaparte is officially Nice's coolest street. Millennials, families, retirees, members of the LGBTIQ+ community; people from all walks of life come for a long brunch at **Clay** (No 3), a Mediterranean street-food lunch at **Kalōs** (No 11), or tapas on the terrace at **Magnolia Cafe** for dinner (No 7). Nicknamed *le petit Marais Niçois*, a nod to Paris' famous bohemian gay quarter, the street is the undisputed LGBTIQ+ heart of the city. In 2020, inspired by San Francisco's Castro District, the road was painted blue.

> Nicknamed *le petit Marais Niçois*, rue Bonaparte is the undisputed LGBTIQ+ heart of the city.

As happens with gentrification, many of the original stores have left, pushed out by high rents and a changing clientele. Among the new arrivals, you can easily spot those who have remained: **Bonap**, a corner store, at No 13; **Pharmacie du Pin** at No 10; the **Bricolage** DIY store at No 5. Rising property prices have also changed the demographic of those who call the area home.

As for the original Comptoir Central d'Electricité? It has moved just around the corner, to a location where the street is wide enough for vans to double park outside. 'The new owners kept the name for the bar as it was such a point of reference in the city,' says Brandon. Does he mind? 'Not at all,' he smiles. 'But I'm never able to help the people who call up wanting to make a dinner reservation.'

✸ Hello, Dolly!

While there are LGBTIQ+ friendly venues across the city, the annual Dolly street party has really cemented rue Bonaparte's place as the city's gay-friendly area, explains Jameson Farn, blogger at Gay French Riviera *(gay frenchriviera.com)*. 'The street is blocked off, DJs are playing and the restaurants and cafes serve drinks on the terrace,' he says. 'The underlying theme for everyone attending is to wear white, and there is a sea of white as far as you can see. Heading into the streets filled with thousands of people of every age, weight, gender and sexual orientation, the Dolly party is a truly amazing experience!'

03 The Hidden CITY

HISTORY | CULTURE | WALKING

▬▬▬ Behind closed doors, below street level – even sometimes right in front of you – there's a whole different side of the city to uncover. Keep your eyes peeled for underground entrances, blink-and-you'll-miss symbols and remnants of the earliest architecture, or book on a tour that delves far beyond the ordinary. Nice's hidden side is out in the open, if you know where to look.

🗺️ How to

Getting around On foot, although prepare to be jostled along in summer by a crowd with little patience for *flâneurs*, or those walking at a leisurely pace.

When to go Wednesdays, Saturdays and Sundays for La Crypte Archéologique. Palais Lascaris is closed on Tuesdays.

Walking tour A private, three-hour Cathedral or Jewish Heritage Tour with Via Nissa will cost €500, but at that price you can bring up to eight people.

Map labels: R Tonduti de l'Escarène, R A Mortier, Pl Garibaldi, La Crypte Archeologique, R Miralhéti, Av Félix Faure, Promenade du Paillon, R de Pairolière, R Sincaire, Loge Communal, Bd Jean Jaurès, R du Collet, R Ste Claire, R de la Boucherie, R du Pont Vieux, R de la Loge, R de la Croix, Pl Rossetti, Palais Lascaris, Montée du Château, Allée Professeur Benoît, R Rossetti, R Droite, R St-Joseph, Cathédrale Ste-Réparate, R de la Condamine, R Pl Vieille, Église du Gesù, R de la Préfecture, VIEUX NICE, 100 m, 0.05 miles

In plain view Deep inside Vieux Nice, **Palais Lascaris** is a wonderfully preserved example of a 17th-century Baroque noble house, now a museum. Admire the richly detailed frescoes as you ascend the grand staircase to ornate reception rooms. Look out for the nearby **Loge Communale** (rue de la Poissonnerie), an easily missed outdoor gallery where a small but curious assortment of early architectural remnants like columns, lintels and even a pair of sphinxes are displayed behind a metal grill.

VIP access On a private cathedral tour, specialist tour guide Via Nissa (*vianissa. com*) unlocks closed doors and religious symbols of the ornate 17th-century **Cathédrale Ste-Réparate**. The walking tour is led by the Diocese of Nice in French but simultaneously translated into English and other languages. Step beyond the Baroque-style nave into the sacristy, where the cathe-

Three Streets ◎ Worth a Second Look

Rue Droite et rue de la Loge Look up and you'll spy a cannonball attached to the corner wall. This relic from the past was fired in 1543 by Turkish forces during the Siege of Nice.

Place Vieille This small square was once the site of a mushroom market but if the words *Interna Meliora* written above an unnumbered door next to No 5 are to be believed, what was 'better inside' were the delights of the neighbourhood brothel.

Rue de la Condamine Date-stamped lintels (horizontal beams) dot the door frames of Vieux Nice but the oldest dated architectural element still visible in Vieux Nice is from 1485. Next to No 15.

■ Recommended by Robert Levitt, *historian, Via Nissa*
@vianissa_nice

dral's collection of precious items is kept, and the bishop's private residence. From there, it's a short walk across place Rossetti towards the **Eglise du Gesù** for a similar behind-the-scenes experience. Via Nissa's other on-demand tours include a Jewish Heritage Tour, where you'll search for hidden messages carved out by families concealed in cellars below the city's Jewish ghetto during WWII.

Underground Delve into the depths of Nice's medieval era on a guided visit of **La Crypte Archéologique**, the ruined defensive walls below the modern city. Note that tours are in French only.

Above Palais Lascaris

04 Sculptures by
THE SEA

ART | OUTDOORS | WALKING TOUR

From Renaissance-style forms to more head-scratching works of modern art, you'll find a collection of public art along some of Nice's most scenic corridors. On this seafront walking tour, pause to contemplate both classic and modern masters.

OLGA355/GETTY IMAGES ©

🗺 Trip Notes

When to go Year-round, but try to avoid the midday sun in warmer months.

What to pack Hat, sunscreen and a water bottle; top up using the free municipal refill stations on the Promenade du Paillon.

Along the way Other art installations to look out for include the *Statue de Charles-Félix de Savoie* in the port, the #ILoveNICE selfie spot on quai Rauba Capeu and *La Chaise Bleue de SAB* on the Prom.

🚊 The Art Line

The west–east tramline also doubles as an open-air gallery. Along with *Lou Che* at Port Lympia, other tram stop art to keep your eyes peeled for include *Pépin, la Déesse et la Mer* at Garibaldi Le Château, *Soave* at Durandy, and *Fruitée* at Ferber.

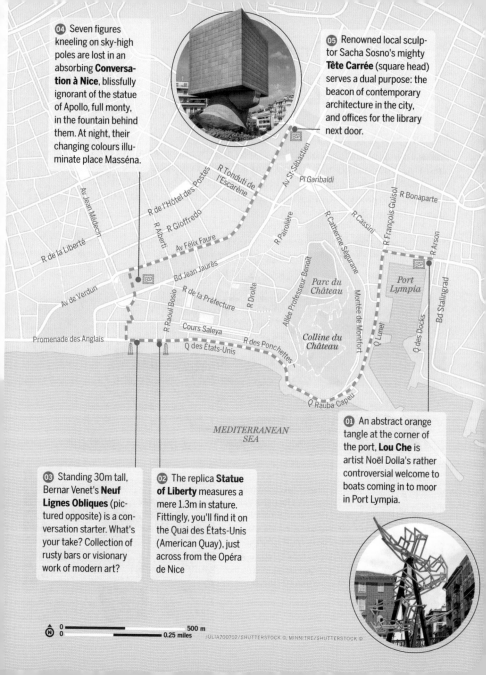

04 Seven figures kneeling on sky-high poles are lost in an absorbing **Conversation à Nice**, blissfully ignorant of the statue of Apollo, full monty, in the fountain behind them. At night, their changing colours illuminate place Masséna.

05 Renowned local sculptor Sacha Sosno's mighty **Tête Carrée** (square head) serves a dual purpose: the beacon of contemporary architecture in the city, and offices for the library next door.

03 Standing 30m tall, Bernar Venet's **Neuf Lignes Obliques** (pictured opposite) is a conversation starter. What's your take? Collection of rusty bars or visionary work of modern art?

02 The replica **Statue of Liberty** measures a mere 1.3m in stature. Fittingly, you'll find it on the Quai des États-Unis (American Quay), just across from the Opéra de Nice

01 An abstract orange tangle at the corner of the port, **Lou Che** is artist Noël Dolla's rather controversial welcome to boats coming in to moor in Port Lympia.

MEDITERRANEAN SEA

Av Jean Médecin
R de l'Hôtel des Postes
R Tonduti de l'Escarène
Av St-Sébastien
Pl Garibaldi
R François Guisol
R Bonaparte
R Gioffredo
R Alberti
R de la Liberté
Av Félix Faure
R Pairolière
R Catherine Ségurane
R Cassini
R Arson
Av de Verdun
Bd Jean Jaurès
R de la Préfecture
R Droite
Parc du Château
Port Lympia
Bd Stalingrad
Promenade des Anglais
R Raoul Bosio
Cours Saleya
Q des États-Unis
R des Ponchettes
Allée Professeur Benoît
Colline du Château
Montée de Montfort
Q Lympia
Q des Docks
Q Rauba Capeu

0 — 500 m
0 — 0.25 miles

05 Breakfast 2.0

EATING | CAFES | BRUNCH

▬▬▬ In neighbourhood bakeries across the city, a new wave of artisan bakers are using high-quality ingredients and a large serving of passion to take the classic baguette and croissant to a whole new level. The brunch scene is similarly brimming with fresh flavours and creative flair. It pays to wake up with an appetite in Nice.

AHANOV MICHAEL/SHUTTERSTOCK ©

🗺 How to

When to go Early morning for still-warm pastries, until mid-afternoon for brunch.

Cost Most baguettes, croissants and other breakfast pastries fall in the small change price range. Expect to pay a premium for those that use artisanal ingredients.

Waste not, want not You'll find a selection of the city's bakeries selling end of day food bundles on the Too Good To Go app.

REUTERS/ERIC GAILLARD/ALAMY STOCK PHOTO ©

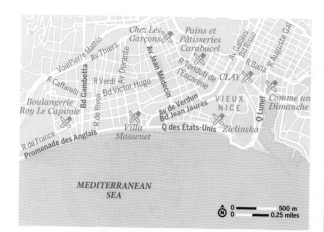

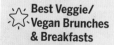

Top left French toast **Bottom left** All-butter croissants, Boulangerie Roy Le Capitole

☆ Best Veggie/ Vegan Brunches & Breakfasts

Amour Pâtisserie Végétale – Vegan Don't miss out on the raw patisseries or speciality chickpea omelette. Gluten-free and organic!

Paper Plane – Vegetarian You'll find avocado toast, açaí bowls and porridge for breakfast, or take the brunch deal for juice, a hot drink, something salty and something sweet!

SAJ – Vegetarian Authentic Lebanese bread with both savoury and sweet vegan toppings to choose from. Enjoy the artwork too.

The Healer – Vegan Make way for superfoods! Smoothies, juices, shakes and bowls of fruit/veggies to take away and enjoy in the park across the road.

The real deal At **Boulangerie Roy Le Capitole**, artisan baker Frédéric Roy's all-butter croissants are a labour of love that take three days to prepare. If you're lucky, you may also happen upon a batch of lavender croissants fresh from the oven – look closely and you can make out a faint violet hue. Another address to bookmark is the newly opened neighbourhood *boulangerie* **Pains et Pâtisseries Carabacel**, where Marc Payeur showcases skills sharpened in the kitchen of star chef Joël Robuchon and a preference for local ingredients. At **Zielinska** organic bakehouse and cafe in Vieux Nice, you'll find Warsaw-born, historian turned baker Dominika Zielinska using rare and long-forgotten flours. Her *pain nissart*, made from chickpea flour, is a homage to her adopted city.

Not breakfast, not lunch For smashed avocado with a continental twist, head to **Comme un Dimanche**, where owners Marie and Stéphane serve up a menu inspired by their three years spent living in Australia. The terrace fills up fast on warm mornings at **CLAY** on the ultra-cool rue Bonaparte. You'll find plates piled high with toasted sweet potato, avocado and pecan nuts that look too pretty to eat. **Villa Massenet** gets top marks for its friendly staff, relaxed atmosphere and Instagrammable decor. The cosy vibe and indulgent salted caramel brioche French toast at **Chez Les Garçons** are drawing the brunch crowd to the gentrified streets at the top of Jean Médecin.

■ Recommended by Morgan Crawford, *vegan blogger @morgancrawf*

Taste Your Way
THROUGH NICE

01 Socca

The quintessential Niçois street-food snack, this flat, wood-fired chickpea-flour pancake is best enjoyed hot and with lashings of ground pepper.

02 Pissaladière

Caramelised onions, garlic, olives, and – depending on who you ask – anchovies layered on a pizza base, served by the slice.

03 Salade Niçoise

The city's most famous culinary export is a summery mix of tomatoes, green peppers, spring onions, artichokes, tuna, anchovies, boiled egg, radish, olives and beans.

04 Pan Bagnat

Meaning 'wet bread' in local dialect, a *pan bagnat* is essentially a *salade Niçoise* in a round bread roll and the city's favourite sandwich.

05 Les Petits Farcis
A plate of locally grown vegetables – courgettes, peppers, onions – stuffed with meat and herb mix and oven-baked.

06 Fougasse
This flat Provençal bread is a twisty take on the baguette with ingredients like bacon, olives or chorizo often baked in.

07 Beignets de Fleurs de Courgettes
When these lightly battered courgette flowers start to appear on menus, it's a sure sign of summer's impending arrival.

08 Daube
Warm up a winter's day over a hearty *daube*, a Provençal beef stew usually accompanied by polenta or *raviolis Niçois* (pasta).

06 Apéro TIME!

DRINKING | SEA VIEWS | WINE

Come early evening, under the golden glow of the fading sun, Nice's outdoor terraces fill up with groups of friends catching up on the day's news over an *apéro*, as the pre-dinner aperitif is colloquially known. It's an easy custom to embrace.

Above Babel Babel **Bottom right** La Civette du Cours **Far right** Cave Bianchi (p61)

📖 How to

When to go Everyone's timekeeping varies but in general *apéro* starts anytime after 5pm.

Happy hour Many, but not all, bars and cafes do happy hour with discounted beers, wines and cocktails.

Mix and match Tapenade, an olive spread usually served with small toasts, is a traditional snack often served as an *apéro* accompaniment.

Sober curious For non-alcoholic drinks beyond the norm, try Miamici, Babel Babel, Casa Becchio and Cocoon Beach.

Name That Place

On sunny place Garibaldi, **Café de la Place** is a local favourite thanks to its good-value happy hour and cosy covered seating for the cooler months – even if the waitstaff seems a bit brisk at times. Across the road, **Le Garibaldi** has a family-friendly position next to the vintage carousel. At the start of rue Bonaparte, **Café de Chineurs'** eclectic, vintage vibe is popular with an after-work crowd. The trendy bars and restaurants along Les Ponchettes are blessed with beach-facing balconies – of them, **Babel Babel** is the top pick for inventive cocktails made with a Mediterranean twist. On the Cours Saleya, **Civette du Cours** is a prime spot for people-watching that can always be counted on for service with a smile. On the menu at **Altra Casa** on place du Général de

🍸 What's Hot to Drink Right Now?

Zaatar Negroni Gin fat-washed with olive oil, sweet vermouth infused with zaatar and Campari.

Momojito Rum, mint tea, vanilla syrup, lemon juice and soda water.

Spicy Margarita Prickly pear tree smoked with olive tree wood, white vermouth, lemon juice and chilli tincture.

■ **Recommended by Olivier Daniel,** *co-owner, Babel Babel* @olivier_brutevents

Gaulle in the Libération district is a friendly, neighbourhood feel and a refreshing Apérol Spritz.

Local Drops

It's always the rosé season in Nice, unsurprising considering the region's mild winter climate and proximity to the pink-hued vineyards of the Var. As the weather gets warmer, you'll notice people sipping from large glasses of rosé poured over a generous scoop of ice cubes – if you're intrigued, ask for a *rosé piscine* (it's also a thing for white wine). As well as the wines from Bellet, Nice's local wine appellation (see below), Made in Nice drinks to have on your radar include craft-beer labels **La Brasserie Artisanale de Nice**, a specialist shop turned urban brewer in Libération, and **Socca Bierra**, who brew a distinctly Niçois chickpea beer. **Blue Coast Brewery** has made an industrial zone at the edge of the city a destination for laid-back weekend sessions that all the family can

---

🍇 Nice Wine!

The existence of the Bellet AOC (Appellation d'Origine Contrôlée), or a group of nine boutique vineyards nestled among the sprawling villas and swimming pools of Nice's western flank, still flies under most travellers' radars. **Château de Crémat**, whose interlocking C logo was, according to local legend, 'borrowed' by Coco Chanel, and **Château de Bellet**, with its intimate tasting room inside a deconsecrated private family chapel, are the largest; **Domaine de la Source** is a sibling-run backyard operation. **Clos Saint Vincent** is regarded by many as the best expression of Bellet's pebbly terroir. The vineyards are open for tours and tastings – reserving in advance is strongly advised.

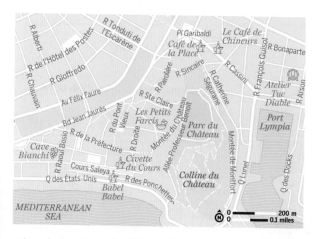

R. Alberti
R Tonduti de l'Escarène
Pl Garibaldi
Café de la Place
Le Café de Chineurs
R Bonaparte
R de l'Hôtel des Postes
R Giuffredo
R Sincaire
R Pairolère
R François Guisol
Atelier Tue Diable
R Arson
R Chauvain
Av Félix Faure
R Cassini
R Catherine Ségurane
R Ste Claire
Bd Jean Jaurès
R du Pont Vieux
Les Petits Farcis
Montée du Château
Montée Professeur Benoît
Parc du Château
Port Lympia
R Raoul Bosio
R de la Préfecture
R Droite
Cave Bianchi
Civette du Cours
Cours Saleya
Colline du Château
Montée de Montfort
Q du 11
Q des Docks
Q des États-Unis
R des Ponchettes
Babel Babel
MEDITERRANEAN SEA
0 — 200 m
0 — 0.1 miles

Left Château de Crémat **Below** Pastis de Nice

enjoy – but you'll also find this local label stocked in bars and shops across the city.

Craft Trends

The craft spirits wave hasn't bypassed Nice. Pick up a bottle of **Pastis de Nice**, made from a secret blend of 26 plants and spices from 21 Paysans (*21paysans.com*). **Atelier Tue Diable** (*tuediable. com*) distills a refreshing basil-flavoured gin, Le Galet, and olive-infused rum, Tue Diable Olive.

Tasting Times

For a more formal introduction to the wine of the region, mark out **Cave Bianchi** (*cave-bianchi.fr*) on your map: every afternoon, as the clock strikes 5pm, the cork is pulled on the first of four bottles to be sampled during a small group tasting session held in an atmospheric room behind the shop counter. Every Friday, also at 5pm, sommelier and cookbook author Viktorija Todorovska leads a relaxed class dedicated entirely to Provence rosé at **Les Petits Farcis** (*petitsfarcis.com*) cooking school. She serves up a selection of typical Niçois street-food snacks in accompaniment. Reservations recommended for both.

Listings

BEST OF THE REST

Not Michelin-Starred, but Still Very Cool

Lavomatique €€

So popular is this hip venue serving up modern tapas sharing plates, including finger-licking-good falafel and *panisse* (chickpea fries), that it doesn't need to open on weekends.

Epiro €€

One of the new addresses making bd Stalingrad in the port an up-and-coming foodie destination. Chic, cosy setting where perfectly portioned pastas matched with natural Italian wines are the main event.

La Merenda €

In a small, rustic Vieux Nice dining room, settle in to savour former two-star Negresco chef Dominique Le Stanc's perfectly executed local favourites. You'll see *pistou* (pesto) pasta in a new gastronomic light.

Babel Babel €€

Great for a drink but the exciting menu of fresh Mediterranean flavours is also a real treat. Add in the front-row sea views and a nightly DJ set, and you've got the city's best all-rounder.

Le Canon €€

Fresh fish delivered daily by a local fisherman and meat, where possible, from the Alpes-Maritimes region. Hyperlocal produce comes to the fore in this unpretentious but highly rated neighbourhood favourite.

Mallard €€

In the heart of increasingly hip Riquier, chef Guillaume Tran-tu's cosy neighbourhood bistro wouldn't be out of place in Paris. Think classics, but done to perfection.

Shout from the Rooftop Bars

Farago on the Roof €

Poolside tapas and cocktails atop the AC Marriott hotel; a superb vantage point for watching planes land. Vibe is casual, prices are not.

BOCCA Nissa €

This leafy restaurant and rooftop terrace is the perfect antidote to teeming summer crowds in Vieux Nice – but everyone else in the city thinks so as well, so reservations are a must.

Moon Bar at the Hôtel Aston €

Classy four-star hotel with an equally sophisticated top-floor space overlooking the terracotta rooftops of Vieux Nice and the sea beyond. Popular with a suited crowd who come for after-work drinks and stay for live music.

Rooftop Monsigny at the Hôtel Monsigny €

This hip hotel bar north of Nice-Ville station may lack ocean views but the twinkling hillside lights and jacuzzi give it an A+ for atmosphere.

Skylounge Nice Bar & Rooftop €

Split-level layout with free wi-fi overlooking the Basilique Notre-Dame inside the Mercure

Promenade du Paillon

Nice Centre Notre-Dame. Handy location for an *apéro* after an afternoon of high-street shopping on av Jean Médecin.

EssenCiel Restaurant €

To fully appreciate Nice's mountains-meets-sea location, there's no better spot than with a drink in hand on the 9th- and 10th-floor terraces of the Hotel Splendid.

 ## Foodie-Friendly Excursions

Secret Vineyards of Nice eBike Tour

Make easy work of the inclines along Nice's western flank on this e-bike wine tour from the city centre. You'll visit a boutique winery at the heart of the Bellet vineyards.

Les Petits Farcis

Follow Canadian writer Rosa Jackson through the flavours of the morning markets, before heading back to her cosy Provençal Vieux Nice kitchen to cook up a four-course Niçois feast.

Moments in Nice

Elena's dreamy Instagram feed (@elenasmoments) has made her – and her trusty 2CV – the go-to name for gourmet picnics laid out in some of Nice's most photogenic locations.

Nice Greeters

Volunteer residents who are glad to share their love for their city with you. Nice's Greeter program is a unique way to experience the local food and wine scene, among other themes.

The French Way

Come hungry on this morning walking through Vieux Nice where the best addresses for *socca*, olive oil, chocolate and wine are revealed. Expect a delightful side serving of local history.

 ## Green Spaces

Promenade du Paillon

More commonly called the Coulee Verte, this green artery transects the city and is broken up

Arènes de Cimiez

into zones with swim fountains, art installations and kids playgrounds as well as plenty of shady spots and park benches for easy lunch picnics.

Parc Vigier

A small, enclosed neighbourhood park across from Coco Beach popular with fitness groups and parents with prams. Conveniently located near La Gratta and its famous *pan bagnats*.

Colline du Château

The grass at the top of the Colline du Château is great for kicking a ball or throwing a Frisbee around. But don't forget to look up and out for some of the best water views in the city.

Jardin des Arènes de Cimiez

Sharing the same shady land as the Musée Matisse and the ruins of a Roman amphitheatre, this vast olive grove is one of the oldest – and most atmospheric – gardens in Nice.

Parc Forestier de Mont Boron

A 57-hectare forest park with plenty of hiking and running trails through scented pines. Best viewpoint is at the foot of the 16th-century Fort du Mont Alban for show-stopping views across the bay of Villefranche-sur-Mer.

Cascade de Gairaut

The waterfall may be artificial, but this quiet site north of the city is a good spot to escape the crowds and still savour sweeping sea views.

Inventive Ice Cream

Fenocchio €

The go-to name for can-you-believe-it ice cream and sorbet flavours such as tomato-basil, rosemary, olive and even *tourte de blettes,* with three addresses in Vieux Nice.

Oui, jelato €

Home-made, traditional Italian gelato and sorbets bursting with fresh flavours. Ice-cream biscuits are a particular treat.

Neron Glacier €

An ex-pastry chef brings his secrets – and ingredients – from fine-dining kitchens to this ice creamery in Vieux Nice. Tasty cakes, too.

Gelateria Garibaldi €

This busy roadside ice-cream parlour is a local favourite, executing the classics to perfection.

Arlequin Gelati €

Another must-do if unusual flavours are your thing. The lemon and ginger sorbet is particularly refreshing on a summer's day.

Wondrous Wine Caves

Cave de la Tour

An Aladdin's (wine) cave overflowing with character. The point of reference for local wines from Bellet and the Alpes-Maritimes region.

La Part des Anges

Voted France's best wine *cave* by esteemed magazine *La revue du vin de France* in 2020, this shop, bar and bistro is a treasure trove of natural and organic wine. Choose a bottle to open over lunch or take away to savour later.

Cave Caprioglio

Family-run wine shop in the heart of Vieux Nice. Check out the vaulted ceilings at the back, exemplifying Nice's earliest known architecture.

Cave Rembrandt

Find friendly service and a small but carefully curated collection of natural and biodynamic wines in this shop close to Riquier train station. Private tastings can be arranged in advance.

Le Glouphile

This new wine bar in the port has quickly become a must-visit address for its welcoming, knowledgable staff, exceptional produce and a cavernous collection of small-producer wines. Dine-in only.

Cave du Cours

One of local restaurant tsar Armand Crespo's many Vieux Nice spots, this cosy wine shop turns into a hugely popular bistro on weekend nights with crowds spilling onto the terrace.

Morning Markets

Marché de la Libération

Open-air neighbourhood markets just north of the train station with a big reputation for fragrant farm-fresh produce sold direct from local producers. Closed on Mondays.

Cours Saleya

Whether it's antiques on Monday or fruit and veg and cut flowers the rest of the week, these colourful markets are a feast for all the senses. One of the quintessential Nice experiences.

Cours Saleya food market

Marché Artisanal Nice Garibaldi

Over 60 stalls cram every corner of place Garibaldi one Sunday a month. Pick up handmade, one-off creations from local artisans to take home as a precious souvenir of the city.

Marché Brocante Palais de Justice

Hunt rare books, first editions, vintage posters and comic books at this small outdoor market held on the first and third Saturday of the month on the Palais de Justice in Vieux Nice.

Brocante du quai de la Douane

You never know what treasures you'll find among the trash at this flea market that spreads the length of the western edge of the port. Held one Sunday a month.

 **Must-Visit Museums**

Musée d'Art Moderne et d'Art Contemporain

Nice's premier modern art space celebrates influential contemporary artists such as Niki de Saint Phalle and Yves Klein. Big renovations are planned, so check for closures in advance.

Musée Matisse

The colours of the Côte d'Azur played muse to Henri Matisse for nearly 40 years and much of his artistic legacy, including almost all his sculptures, is on display inside a sunny terracotta red villa with the best trompe l'oeil facade for miles.

Musée International d'Art Naïf Anatole Jakovsky

Small but fascinating gallery of naïve art in a quiet neighbourhood. Still off the beaten track, even if now easier to reach on the tramline. The sculpture garden is an added treat.

Musée Massena

NICE REVIEWS

Musée Massena

The interior of this sumptuous beach-facing building is as much the star as the collection of art and artefacts that offer a snapshot of the city during the Belle Époque era.

Musée de la Photographie Charles Nègre

An old electric substation just off the Cours Saleya in Vieux Nice has been transformed into this bright, airy gallery dedicated to local and international photography. Keep an eye on the schedule of cool temporary exhibitions.

Musée National Marc Chagall

For fans of Marc Chagall's dreamy, whimsical brushstrokes, this bright museum at the foot of Cimiez is well worth an afternoon. The works of his *Biblical Message* are on permanent display.

Musée National du Sport

France's only national sports museum migrated south from Paris in 2013. In Nice, this celebration of a proud sporting nation has found a permanent home inside the nest-like Allianz Riviera Stadium.

 Scan to find more things to do in Nice online

THE CÔTE D'AZUR

COAST | VIEWS | NATURE

Experience
the Côte
d'Azur
online

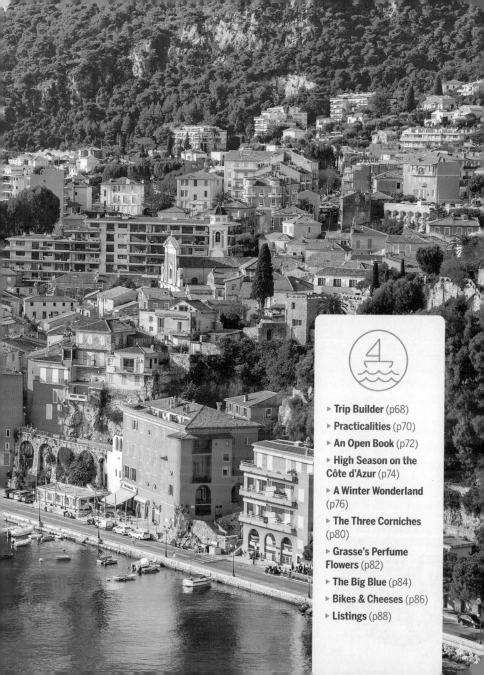

THE CÔTE D'AZUR
Trip Builder

Wake up with a swim in the Mediterranean, then be surrounded by a kaleidoscope of nature's greens just an hour later. Lunch in a bougainvillea-swaddled hilltop village before sipping chilled rosé in a hip beach bar before dinner. Be it your first time or 100th visit, the Côte d'Azur is ever the enchanting feast of landscapes, colours, flavours and scents.

Beuil

Guillaumes

Valberg

Gorges du Cians

Daluis

Entrevaux   Puget-
Théniers

Moustiers
Ste-Marie

*Parc Natural
Régional du
Verdon*

Castellane

La Palud-
sur-Verdon

Trigance

Breathe in the heady scents of perfume flowers at the **Jardins du Musée International de la Parfumerie** (p88)
🚌 + 🚶 *30 mins from Cannes*

Gourdon

Opio

Taste local cheeses direct at their mountain source at the **Chèvrerie du Bois d'Amon** (p87)
🚲 *1hr from Grasse*

Ste-Cézaire-
sur-Siagne

Grasse

Bargemon

Fayence

Mougins

Hike into Europe's largest **mimosa forest** in winter (p78)
🚌 *40mins from Cannes*

Cannes

La Napoule

St- Raphaël

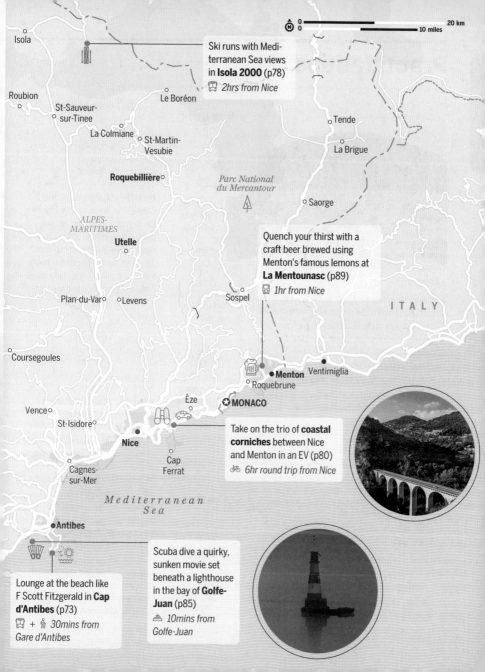

Ski runs with Mediterranean Sea views in **Isola 2000** (p78)

🚟 *2hrs from Nice*

Quench your thirst with a craft beer brewed using Menton's famous lemons at **La Mentounasc** (p89)

🚋 *1hr from Nice*

Take on the trio of **coastal corniches** between Nice and Menton in an EV (p80)

🚲 *6hr round trip from Nice*

Scuba dive a quirky, sunken movie set beneath a lighthouse in the bay of **Golfe-Juan** (p85)

🤿 *10mins from Golfe-Juan*

Lounge at the beach like F Scott Fitzgerald in **Cap d'Antibes** (p73)

🚟 + 🚶 *30mins from Gare d'Antibes*

Isola

Roubion

St-Sauveur-sur-Tinee

Le Boréon

La Colmiane

St-Martin-Vesubie

Tende

La Brigue

Roquebillière

Parc National du Mercantour

Saorge

ALPES-MARITIMES

Utelle

Plan-du-Var

Levens

Sospel

ITALY

Coursegoules

Menton

Ventimiglia

Roquebrune

Èze

✪ **MONACO**

Vence

St-Isidore

Nice

Cap Ferrat

Cagnes-sur-Mer

Mediterranean Sea

Antibes

Practicalities

ARRIVING

Aéroport Nice-Côte d'Azur Nice's coastal airport (pictured) is the air gateway to the Côte d'Azur. Nice Airport Xpress buses leave from Terminal 2 (Antibes €11, Cannes and Menton €22 one way; slight discount for a return ticket). Fixed taxi fares for Cap d'Antibes (€72) and Cannes (€85); rates vary for other destinations.

Train Continue onwards from the Gare de Cannes or Gare d'Antibes by foot, bus, taxi or Uber.

HOW MUCH FOR A

Sun lounger on a private beach
€40

Pint of beer
€7

Pizza in a water-front restaurant
€20

GETTING AROUND

Train The major towns of the Côte d'Azur are connected by the regional TER train network. Unfortunately flash strikes and other delays are all too common. Journeys during commuter hours are also standing room only, especially between Nice and Monaco.

Bus The Zou! intercity bus network is a slower, but often more scenic, alternative to the train. Fares are capped at €1.50 per ticket. The 100 bus is an attraction in itself, following the shimmering coastal road between Nice and Menton. It can be standing room only in summer.

Car You'll need your own transport the further inland from the coast you venture. Nice's airport is the main car hire hub.

WHEN TO GO

JAN–MAR
Sunny winter days and a golden mimosa bloom.

APR–JUN
April can be busy. Swimming weather from May.

JUL–SEP
Steamy summer days and nights. Packed beaches. Great music festivals.

OCT–DEC
Autumn is ideal for hiking and cycling the backcountry. First snow falls early December.

EATING & DRINKING

This coastal cuisine is increasingly bringing hyperlocal ingredients to the fore: rare lemons grown only in Menton, oils made from olive groves near Nice, sweet honeys from Grasse and goat's cheese from mountain herds in the Mercantour. You'll find what's considered Niçois cuisine — think *socca* and *pissaladière* (pictured top right) — is in fact the fare of the entire Côte d'Azur, although expect some tiny, but important, variations. Foodies shouldn't miss these morning markets: Marché Forville (Cannes), Marché Provençal (Antibes; pictured bottom left) and Marché des Halles (Menton's covered markets).

Best bakery
Ma Première Boulangerie (p88)

Must-try craft beer
Brasserie du Comté (p89)

MONEY

Expect medium-high prices to eat out in the main resort towns and coastal hinterland villages. There are still enough cash-only restaurants to warrant a reserve of euro notes. Public transport, however, is cheap and comprehensive.

CONNECT & FIND YOUR WAY

Wi-fi Most cafes, bars and hotels – even some towns – offer a wi-fi network you can log into.

Navigation The A8 is the highway connecting Cannes to Menton; traffic can be stop-start during peak hour and on Friday nights. Take the slower coastal roads for water's-edge views. Waze is a popular app with real-time updates from fellow drivers.

WHERE TO STAY

Beyond the high season, accommodation books up fast in February for winter carnivals; at Easter; and in May for the Monaco Grand Prix.

Place	Pro/Con
Cannes	Red-carpet town; full to the brim in May for the Cannes Film Festival.
Menton	Emerging foodie destination a stone's throw from Italy.
Villefranche-sur-Mer	Pastel pretty fishing village. Offers the pace of village life with Nice at your doorstep.
St-Paul de Vence	Art galleries, *pétanque* courts and medieval alleyways inland from the coast.
Parc National du Mercantour	Away from the coast, the air is fresh and the pace of life slower.
Èze village	Eagle's-nest village perched high above the Mediterranean. Touristy by day, tranquil by night.

TRAIN JOURNEYS

Two regional commuter train services connecting Nice with hinterland communities Chemins de Fer de Provence and Train des Merveilles also serve as charming day-trip options.

07

An Open
BOOK

LITERATURE | OUTDOORS | HISTORY

To visit the Côte d'Azur is to experience the light, colours and landscapes that have motivated countless great writers to pen new beginnings or compose fitting endings for some of the all-time classics. Along pine-scented walking tracks, inside Belle Époque villas and on sun-drenched beaches, to retrace their footsteps today is to realise that the Côte d'Azur is still one of the world's greatest muses.

JOSEPHWGALLAGHER/SHUTTERSTOCK ©

🗺 How to

Getting here The Sentier Nietzsche starts across from the Gare Èze train station. From Gare d'Antibes, take the Envibus line 2 to Cap d'Antibes (stop Fontaine).

Cost Mostly free, unless you upgrade to a sun lounger at the chic Plage Keller private beach on Plage de la Garoupe. Budget €24 for a gin cocktail at the Belle Rives.

Read For further reading, *The French Riviera: A Literary Guide for Travellers* by Ted Jones is an excellent introduction to the topic.

VALERY HACHE/GETTY IMAGES ©

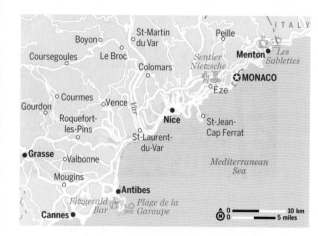

Top left Plage de la Garoupe, Antibes
Bottom left Sunbathers, Hôtel Belles Rives, Juan-les-Pins

🗺 X Marks the Spot

Play a game of plaque spotting on the Côte d'Azur:

- On the Hôtel Suisse in Nice where James Joyce wrote the first lines of *Finnegans Wake* overlooking the Baie des Anges.

- Outside the Hôtel Oasis at 23 rue Gounod where Anton Tchekov stayed during his stay in Nice.

- Attached to 26 av Pasteur in Antibes where Graham Greene lived and wrote seven books from 1966 to 1990.

- At 152 bd John Fitzgerald Kennedy, a 19th-century villa on the exclusive Cap d'Antibes where Jules Verne wrote part of *Around the World in 80 Days*.

- Where William Butler Yeats died in 1939 at 188 av Virginie Hériot, Roquebrune-Cap-Martin.

Around Nice Scale the **Sentier Nietzsche** in Èze, a steep hour-long trek from the seafront Èze-Bord-de-Mer to the perched medieval Èze village. As he cut through dense Mediterranean shrub, the German philosopher Friedrich Nietzsche found inspiration to complete the third part of *Thus Spoke Zarathustra*. Today, this well-trodden path is clearly defined, although even locals miss an unmarked turn-off around two-thirds of the way up that leads to a narrow waterfall.

The Antibes gang Laze on the beach like F Scott Fitzgerald, one of the Jazz Age pack of American novelists (including Ernest Hemingway) who had a scene at **Plage de la Garoupe** on leafy Cap d'Antibes. He called the waterfront Villa Saint-Louis in Juan-les-Pins, at the other edge of the peninsula, home; the wild party nights spurred him to complete *The Great Gatsby* and start *Tender is the Night* during his time here. Not long after he'd gone, the villa became the **Hôtel Belles Rives**. Splurge on a pretty cocktail in the hotel's elegant **Fitzgerald Bar** and you'll still sense the Roaring '20s vibe.

At the Italian border Splash around in the shallow waters of **Les Sablettes** in Menton where Vladimir Nabokov is said to have dipped his toes after days spent penning his last book written in Russian, *The Gift*. The cafe-lined beachfront, with a wide bike- and pram-friendly paved strip, remains the lively hub of local life.

High Season on the Côte d'Azur

WHEN WINTER WAS THE TRAVEL FASHION

Everyone from aristocrats to artists were initially drawn to the mild winters of the Côte d'Azur on doctor's orders, the sunshine thought to cure tuberculosis in particular. They returned every year for the colours, the light and the mild climate, making its wide waterfront boulevards and belle-époque gambling dens the place to see and be seen.

MARGARITA HINTUKAINEN/SHUTTERSTOCK ©

Left Russian Orthodox Cathedral, Nice **Middle** Queen Victoria in Hyères, 1892 **Right** Hôtel Regina, Nice

In 1859, gripped by consumption, physician James Henry Bennet bid farewell to his beloved London and set off on the long journey to Menton. 'I wrapped my robes around me, and departed southwards…to die in a quiet corner, as me and my friends thought.' It was not, as he continues in his 1866 treatise *Winter and Spring on the Shores of the Mediterranean*, to be. 'Under its genial sky…to my very great surprise I started to rally.'

Before antibiotics, the best medicine for tuberculosis and other turn-of-the-century afflictions was believed to be the mild climate of the French coastal towns between Hyères and Menton. Royalty, politicians, aristocrats, writers and artists; many came from England on Bennet's glowing recommendation, taking the newly forged railway line that made short work of what had been a two-week slog, or from frozen northern European countries and Russia.

Royal Seal

Queen Victoria led the way, her first voyage to Bennet's beloved Menton in 1882 marking the start of an almost 20-year winter love affair with the region. The British monarch had many favourite pockets along the coast, including the fit-for-a-queen Grand-Hôtel du Cap-Ferrat, but it was the newly built Hôtel Regina residence, high up in the Cimiez neighbourhood of Nice, where she felt most at home. So much did she grow to rely on her annual jaunt south that, on her deathbed in 1901, she is reported to have said, 'If only I was in Nice, I would get better.'

Not everyone came brandishing a doctor's prescription for a restorative winter in the Mediterranean sun, however. As news of the growing Côte d'Azur scene spread, British

aristocrats would pack their finest for afternoon strolls along Nice's Promenade des Anglais and try their luck in Monaco's Charles Garnier–designed Belle Époque casino.

These *hivernants* (the French word for winter tourists) left their mark in the period architecture that remains, such as the gilded-onion-domed Russian Orthodox Cathedral in Nice and the extravagant Villa Ephrussi de Rothschild in St-Jean-Cap Ferrat, as well as the golden mimosas they brought as cuttings in their luggage that, fittingly, burst into bloom between late December and March.

> On her deathbed in 1901, Queen Victoria is reported to have said, 'If only I was in Nice, I would get better.'

Changing Fashions

So what caused the seasonal switch? Many lay responsibility squarely at the feet of expat American socialite couple Gerald and Sarah Murphy, the wealthy benefactors of the Roaring '20s Cap d'Antibes cohort that included Pablo Picasso and F Scott Fitzgerald (in Fitzgerald's *Tender is the Night,* Dick and Nicole Diver are modelled on them). Their convincing pleas to the manager of the Hôtel du Cap (today the fabulously exclusive Hôtel du Cap Eden-Roc) to keep some rooms open for their friends over the summer spelled the end of one chapter – and the start of another.

Almost a century on, this storied stretch of coast continues to draw crowds in summer, leaving locals to reclaim their quiet village streets come October. But there's a crisp, fragile beauty during the shorter winter days, when the snow-covered Alpes-Maritimes form a protective ring around the region against the worst of the weather. Visit for yourself and you'll understand: they were onto something, these early tourists.

📖 What's in a Name?

In 1887, not long after Queen Victoria first wintered in Menton, a French writer by the name of Stéphen Liégeard set off on a journey along this stretch of coast, his experiences spilling out in a book he titled *La Côte d'Azur.* Maybe it was the sheer luck of timing, but the name quickly stuck. Liégeard's Côte d'Azur spanned from Genoa, in Italy, to Marseille, a definition geographically outdated today. But the exact start and finish point of the Côte d'Azur continues to generate debate. Does it extend from Menton to Hyères? Or is St-Tropez the western extreme? For many, however, the true 'blue coast' is just the length of the Alpes-Maritimes.

08

A Winter
WONDERLAND

FESTIVALS | SNOW | WINTER

▬▬▬▬ Nice's recent Unesco World Heritage listing as a winter resort town is a reminder that today's low season was the preference in the 19th and early 20th centuries. Come today for sunny ski slopes, colourful festivals and February blooms. With mild days and fewer crowds, the Côte d'Azur still packs a punch in the cooler months.

📱 **How to**

When to go February for festivals. The ski season typically runs from early December to mid-April.

Getting around The Bus 100% Neige connects Nice with Auron and Isola 2000 and is great value at €12 return. Make sure to book in advance.

Sweet treat Restaurant L'Oasis in Mandelieu-La Napoule celebrates mimosa season with a limited-edition gourmet creation: mimosa tarte or macaroon, exactly what depends on the year and the pastry chef's imagination!

Festival Fun

February's **Carnaval de Nice** program of lively street parades and perfumed flower battles is heavily ticketed, meaning locals stay away most days. Join in on the last night when many do venture out to witness the traditional burning of the king. If you walk past the **Maison de Carnaval** (rue du Dr Pierre Richelmi), a cavernous warehouse where the towering floats and *grosses têtes* (big heads) are stored during the two-week event, you may also chance upon a sneak preview for free. In Contes, a village 20 minutes from Nice, a young couple have channelled their passion for the tradition into a vibrant permanent exhibition space. Their **Musée de Carnaval** (*museeducarnaval.com*) may be small, but surrounded by vintage posters, elaborate costumes and even life-

Top & bottom left Parade, Carnaval de Nice

sized floats, you'll still be swept away to an imaginative, exuberant place.

Road Trip

Europe's largest mimosa (*Acacia dealbata*) forest bursts into golden bloom between late December and early March in the **Massif de Tanneron** mountain range to the west of the region. Starting in Bormes-les-Mimosas (in the Var), and ending in Grasse, set off on the **Route du Mimosa** to follow a 130km floral road trip recommended during the winter flowering

season. Stay for a while in **Mandelieu-La Napoule**, considered the mimosa capital. Each February the coastal town hosts the annual **Fête du Mimosa**. At the heart of its oldest neighbourhood, Le Capitou, over 100 varieties of the plant from around the world are scattered between picnic tables and a children's playground at the **Parc Emmanuelle de Marande**. To really dive deep into the bloom, the local tourist office is a departure point for daily hikes along mimosa trails with qualified

Four Essential Winter Villages

St-Dalmas-le-Selvage Ice climbing, ski touring, snowshoeing, cross-country skiing, Nordic skiing – this cute village has everything and is just 90km from Nice.

Le Boréon A great spot for ice climbing with artificial ice folds. Also an excellent starting point for Nordic skiing, but more limited for snowshoeing.

Isola 2000 Mainly known as a ski resort but at this altitude you're guaranteed snow, whatever the season is like. Great for snowshoeing and Nordic skiing.

Beuil The Plateau de St-Jean has beginner-friendly snowshoeing and cross-country skiing trails with lots of sun.

■ Recommended by Onil Wood, *mountain guide, Vallée de la Tinée*
@guidestinee

☀ Citrus Celebrations

From the larger-than-life floats made solely out of citrus fruit at February's Fête du Citron to the renaissance of the local Citron de Menton variety in the terraced groves behind the border town, Menton's lemons are another shade of yellow you'll notice lights up winter on the Côte d'Azur.

nature guides such as Maddy Polémi (*maddy polomeni.com*). *Mimosistes,* as the growers are known, such as **Colline des Mimosas** (*lacolline desmimosas.fr*) in neighbouring Pégomas, sell big bunches of freshly cut flowers directly.

Seaside Slopes

There aren't many places where you can swim in the sea in the morning and ski before lunch but that's all in a winter's day – if you dare – on the Côte d'Azur. The nearest slopes are just an hour's drive away from the main resort towns. **Gréolières-les-Neiges**, a small resort high on a plateau behind Grasse, is the closest to the coast and is particularly busy on Wednesdays when the area's schools are closed. Further north into the Alpes-Maritimes, **Auron** has a pretty alpine feel and a decent après-ski scene. **Isola 2000** rivals it for slopes, but the soulless '70s architecture makes it a place for a day rather than a long stay. Nestled among three valleys, **Valberg** was the first ski resort in the region and remains its most family- (and pet-) friendly. **Turini Camp d'Argent** is recommended for beginner skiers.

Left Isola 2000 **Top right** Fête du Citron, Menton **Above** Auron

09

The Three
CORNICHES

VIEWS | SLOW TRAVEL | ROAD TRIP

▬▬▬ Basse, Moyenne, Grande: take the three coastal corniches between Nice and Monaco at a slower pace to appreciate show-stopping views and new perspectives on eagle's-nest villages. Local small-electric-car vlogger Tim Fountain recommends his top itinerary to drive all three.

OLGA VORONTSOVA/SHUTTERSTOCK ©

🗺️ Trip Notes

When to go The Grande Corniche flows all day long, but the Moyenne and Basse Corniches can clog up during Monaco's morning and afternoon commuter rush.

Rent a car MobilizeShare *(share.mobilize.fr)* is Nice's electric car share scheme with a flexible rent by the hour or day pricing structure (from €7 an hour).

Bike-friendly Experienced cyclists will find the Col de la Madone de Gorbio a thrill to conquer – or you can hire an e-bike in Nice.

■ **Itinerary by Tim Fountain,** *writer and EV vlogger, Villefranche-sur-Mer.* YouTube: *@meandmonami*

ⓘ Power Up

Register with Prise de Nice *(prisedenice.fr)* to access over 300 charging stations in the Nice metropolitan region. The first two hours are free. If you don't want to sign up, you can pay by credit card or use Charge-pass, our go-to card for access to multiple systems.

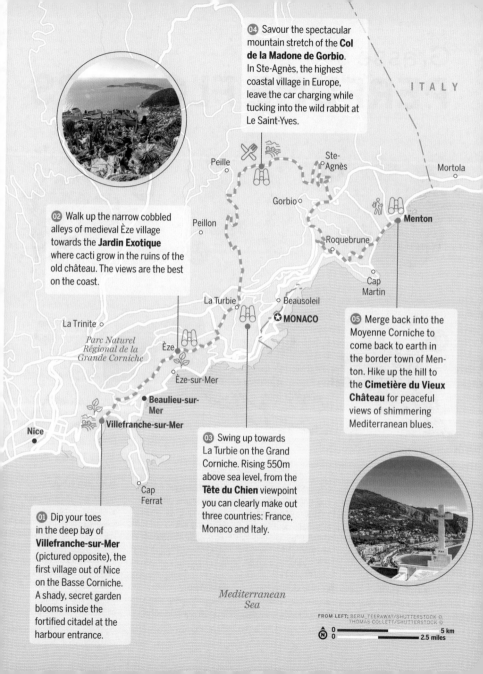

04 Savour the spectacular mountain stretch of the **Col de la Madone de Gorbio**. In Ste-Agnès, the highest coastal village in Europe, leave the car charging while tucking into the wild rabbit at Le Saint-Yves.

ITALY

Peille

Ste-Agnès

Mortola

Gorbio

Menton

02 Walk up the narrow cobbled alleys of medieval Èze village towards the **Jardin Exotique** where cacti grow in the ruins of the old château. The views are the best on the coast.

Peillon

Roquebrune

La Turbie

Beausoleil

Cap Martin

La Trinité

★ MONACO

Parc Naturel Régional de la Grande Corniche

Èze

Èze-sur-Mer

05 Merge back into the Moyenne Corniche to come back to earth in the border town of Menton. Hike up the hill to the **Cimetière du Vieux Château** for peaceful views of shimmering Mediterranean blues.

Beaulieu-sur-Mer

Villefranche-sur-Mer

Nice

03 Swing up towards La Turbie on the Grand Corniche. Rising 550m above sea level, from the **Tête du Chien** viewpoint you can clearly make out three countries: France, Monaco and Italy.

Cap Ferrat

01 Dip your toes in the deep bay of **Villefranche-sur-Mer** (pictured opposite), the first village out of Nice on the Basse Corniche. A shady, secret garden blooms inside the fortified citadel at the harbour entrance.

Mediterranean Sea

FROM LEFT: BERM_TEERAWAT/SHUTTERSTOCK ©;
THOMAS COLLETT/SHUTTERSTOCK ©

0 — 5 km
Ⓝ 0 — 2.5 miles

Grasse's
PERFUME FLOWERS

01 Rose de Mai
Also called the Rose de Grasse, the smallest but more aromatic of all rose varieties is the base of the iconic Chanel N°5.

02 Jasmine Grandiflorum
The other emblematic flower of Grasse's perfume industry is hand-harvested at dawn to capture its powerful yet sweet fragrance.

03 Mimosa
Europe's largest mimosa forest abuts the southern slopes of Grasse. This winter bloom adds rich, honeyed notes to scents.

04 Lavender
Grown higher up in the plateaus and mountains behind Grasse. Lavender's herby hints are a highly prized addition to many scents.

05 Broom
Yellow flowering shrub that goes wild in warm climates but starts to lose its fragrance as soon as its flowers are cut. Smell it in Dior's Dune.

06 Tuberose
Intensely fragrant, sensual white bell-shaped flower with a long stem. Said to have been a particular favourite in

the court of the Sun King, Louis XIV.

07 Iris
A six-year commitment is required to cultivate this tall plant for perfume: three years for growing and another three for drying. Only the rhizomes are used.

08 Violet
Violet's delicate petals give off no scent, so the leaves are used instead. Traditionally grown around the hillside village of Tourrettes-sur-Loup.

09 Bitter Orange
Called the 'perfumer's tree', every part of this

sunny Mediterranean bloom can be used to create raw material. Thrives around Vallauris-Golfe-Juan and Le Bar sur Loup.

10 Geranium
When the budget doesn't extend to roses, perfumers turn to geranium,

whose leaves have the same minty scent.

11 Narcissus Poeticus
Close relation to daffodil, valued since ancient times. Rare and expensive ingredient, used to add green floral tones to luxury perfumes.

10 The Big
BLUE

DIVING | DAY TRIP | OUTDOORS

▬▬▬ There's a whole other world below the azure Mediterranean Sea, where soft meadows of Posidonia seagrass cover the ocean floor and dusky groupers dart in and out of canyons, caves, wrecks and even a quirky sunken movie set. With sheltered sites that are ideal for beginners, why not dive in for a new perspective of the Côte d'Azur?

YANN COATSALIOU/GETTY IMAGES ©

🗺 **How to**

When to go The Easter weekend is considered the traditional curtain-raiser of a season that runs through until October.

Cost Budget around €70 for a beginner's dive.

Hold your breath Freedivers will meet kindred spirits in the bay of Villefranche-sur-Mer, the home of the sport in the region.

Underwater museum The six towering statues submerged on the ocean floor of the **Ecomusée Sous-Marin** underwater museum off the Île Ste-Marguerite are strictly visit by snorkel only.

FREDERIC.LOEWER/SHUTTERSTOCK ©

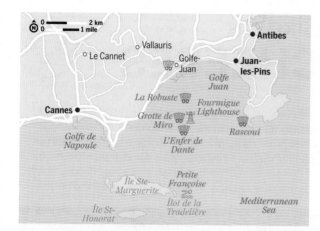

Top left Freedivers, Villefranche-sur-Mer **Bottom left** Beach, Cap d'Antibes

Try dive The sheltered dive sites off Golfe-Juan, Cap d'Antibes and the Îles de Lérins offer beginner divers protection from the elements. In easterly winds, dive boats head towards **Rascoui**, a rich shallow plateau and drop-off towards the leafy Cap d'Antibes peninsula. When the wind is coming from the opposite direction, the **Petite Françoise** off the Îlot de la Tradelière allows first-timers to swim alongside big grouper.

With Open Water Certification Inside the **Grotte de Miro** underwater cave, a bust of Commandant Yves Le Prieur, the Frenchman who invented the earliest scuba equipment, is surrounded by a colourful display of corals and soft sponges. Close by, **l'Enfer de Dante** (Dante's Inferno) is a smart name for a plunging vertical drop of over 50m. Also in the vicinity, **La Robuste** is an old wooden tugboat that sank after WWII. Resting at depths of 25m, it is considered one of the best wreck dive training sites in the region.

Mini Atlantis Local legend has it that a miniature underwater village below the Fourmigue Lighthouse in the bay of Golfe-Juan was built in the 1960s for a movie that never made it to the big screen. The tiny houses and other buildings such as a hotel, a hairdresser, and even a Roman amphitheatre still remain and, over the years, have been painstakingly restored by local divers. A site for more confident divers to visit accompanied by an instructor.

⚲ Dive On In

Vis can reach up to 30m along the Côte d'Azur and these optimal conditions are perfect for spotting some of the region's most common marine life, from octopus, cuttlefish, barracuda and dentex to grouper, the emblematic fish of the Mediterranean. There's also Posidonia, or seagrass, in abundance. In summer the water temperature goes as high as 27°C but my favourite months to dive are September and October when the conditions are still great yet the dive centres aren't as busy and instructors have had a chance to recover from the exhaustion of the high season.

■ Recommended by **Alex Diamond,** *dive instructor, Golfe-Juan, Diamond Diving @diamonddiving*

11

Bikes &
CHEESES

CYCLING | FOOD | DAY TRIPS

■■■■ Grab your bike for a tasty adventure in the backcountry of the Côte d'Azur. The five Vélo et Fromages itineraries range from short, family-friendly circuits to multi-day itineraries through the dizzying mountain passes and dramatic ochre-red gorges of the Parc National du Mercantour. No matter which one you choose, you'll meet small, artisanal cheese producers hungry to share their produce and passion.

RUDIERNST/SHUTTERSTOCK ©

📷 **How to**

When to go From March to November – that's when you'll see animal herds in the countryside.

Getting there By car for greatest flexibility, although Zou! bus 790 from Nice stops at both Guillaumes and Touët-sur-Var. Vence and Grasse are well served by bus lines; the Train de Merveilles connects Nice with La Brigue.

Bike rentals Options are limited in the back-country; best to hire all equipment on the coast beforehand.

LUC BIANCO/SHUTTERSTOCK ©

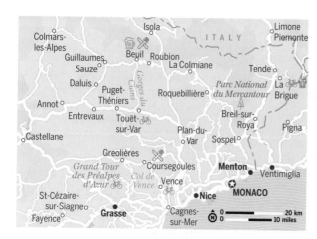

Top left Gorges du Cian **Bottom left** Rocky plateau, Col de Vence

Mountain circuits The 8km **La Brigasque** ride follows a family-friendly bike path in La Brigue. Flocks of the celebrated local sheep breed, Brigasca, graze on the grassy mountain pastures. Stop at Auberge St-Martin and Fleurs des Alpes, hotel-restaurants with a stock of local cheeses for sale.

There are 22 switchbacks on the 9km road ascent from **Guillaumes to Sauze**, one of four sub-routes of the **Variations Autour de Guillaumes** itinerary. Book ahead to visit La Ferme de Sauze Vieux where a small mountain cow herd is the prized source of a yummy Tomme de Vache.

Starting and finishing in Touët-sur-Var, **À la Découverte des Gorges Rouges** is a scenic but challenging 83km route through the sheer canyons and ochre red landscapes of the Gorges du Cian and Daluis. Don't miss La Petite Ferme de Péone for its organic products and dramatic mountain setting.

Sea views Closer to the coast, both the 55km or 86km itineraries on the **Autour du Col de Vence** take in the testing Col de Vence mountain pass. On the rocky plateau at Coursegoules, Gaec du Cheiron is a family-run farm rearing a medley of farm animals, including goats for yogurts and cheese.

Six days is recommended for the **Grand Tour des Préalpes d'Azur**, setting off from Grasse on a twisty 265km route through perched villages and across stark limestone plateaus. The circuit counts over 20 sites of cheesy interest; specialities at **Chèvrerie du Bois d'Amon** in St-Cézaire-sur-Siagne include goat's cheese ice cream and soap.

Top Bistros en Route

Along À la Découverte des Gorges Rouges, take a break at the **Relais du Mercantour** in Beuil where mountain beer chills in the fridge and the *plat du jour* changes every day.

Both Autour du Col de Vence and Le Grand Tour des Préalpes d'Azur pass the **Bistrot de Sophie** on the square in Coursegoules. Admire views from the terrace and refuel on a menu of regional recipes.

L'Auberge de Sauze's reputation for hearty homemade dishes using local ingredients is tempting more and more people to tackle the ascent towards Sauze on the Variations Autour de Guillaumes.

Listings

BEST OF THE REST

 Perfume-Scented Gardens

Domaine de Manon
Immerse yourself in the heady scents of rose, jasmine and tuberose grown exclusively for Dior. Opens just once a week for garden visits according to the flowering season.

Parfum Isnard
Enchanting perfumer's garden brimming with perfume flowers, fruit trees and aromatic herbs. Daily tours (except weekends) in July and August. On request for other months. Book online (isnardgrasse.com).

Mas d'Olivine – Au Pays d'Audrey
Family estate in Peymeinade which crafts a selection of candies, syrups, rose water and other delicacies from perfume plants grown on-site.

Jardins du Musée International de la Parfumerie
This multi-sensory museum garden encourages tactile discovery of the world's greatest perfume flowers. Particularly pretty in spring when the bushes of Rose de Mai burst into bloom.

La Bastide aux Violettes
Tourrettes-sur-Loup's Victoria violets are the other great flower of the Côte d'Azur. Learn more about their cultivation and uses at this Provençal villa turned museum and garden. Entrance is free.

Cool Bakeries

Mitron Bakery   €
Three-Michelin-starred chef Mauro Colagreco's Menton empire expands with this artisanal bakery where ancient flours play the starring role. Also inside Monaco's La Marché de La Condamine.

Ma Première Boulangerie   €
It's worth making a trip to La Turbie just to bite into one of Pierre Briand's buttery croissants or crusty baguette judged the best in the region. Don't be put off by the queue outside.

Boulangerie Veziano   €
Jean-Paul Veziano is quite the local celebrity (he baked the bread for a Monégasque royal wedding in 2011), but his breads and *pissaladière* live up to the hype.

Lou Bara de Pais   €
Baguettes and breads, cakes, pastries and pizza wood-fired in the old communal oven of Coursegoules, a small village on the plateau behind Grasse. Go to taste tradition.

Mama Baker   €
This central Nice neighbourhood bakery-cafe has been baking organic bread fresh daily since 2015. Considered a regional pioneer.

 Coastal Hikes

Sentier du Littoral
You'll need both swimmers and sneakers to tackle this coastal trail between Nice and Villefranche-sur-Mer. The path can be quite narrow and bushy in parts and is popular with runners.

Île St-Honorat
Just a 15-minute ferry ride from Cannes, you'll feel like you've escaped to another world on this serene monastic island. A 3km pine-scented path hugs the coast.

Tour du Cap Ferrat
Classic 6km path that traces the craggy coastline of the billionaire's Cap Ferrat headland. Not recommended in windy weather, when large waves break over the coastal path.

Promenade Maurice Rouvier

This easy 20-minute walk along the flat, pram-friendly path from Beaulieu-sur-Mer's Baie des Fourmis to the pleasure port in St-Jean is an ideal pre- or post-lunch stroll.

Cap d'Antibes

You'll find shallow spots to swim or snorkel on this scenic trail. Combine with a visit to Villa Eilenroc, a sumptuous private residence open to the public on Wednesday and Saturday.

 ## Crafty Beers & Liqueurs

Brasserie du Comté

Newly rebuilt in St-Martin-Vésubie after Storm Alex devastated the valley in 2020; you decide if the spring water from the Mercantour is what makes this mountain beer so thirst-quenching.

La Mentounasc

Menton's emblematic lemon is the inspiration for this sunny craft beer. Call ahead to confirm your visit; this small operation is less half an hour from the beach by foot. Mondays are brew days.

Bacho Brewery

Relaxed taphouse in Tourettes-sur-Loup where comfy outdoor seating, a *pétanque* court, sharing plates and the soothing sound of a nearby waterfall encourage you to stay for a while.

Au Pays du Citron

Rare lemons and other citrus fruit grown on the slopes around Menton, infused into a vodka, liqueur, even a pastis. Head to the shopfront in Menton to pick up your new favourite drink.

 ## Hot Summer Festivals

Festival Nuits du Sud

For over a quarter of a century, Vence's restaurant-lined place du Grand Jardin has

Les Plages Electroniques

grooved to an eclectic mix of world beats come eight nights in July.

Les Nuits Guitares

Summer nights don't get more atmospheric than this intimate stage set inside a fairy-light-lit olive grove across from the port in Beaulieu-sur-Mer. Chilled vibe so pack a picnic rug.

La Crème Festival

This hip boutique festival inside Villefranche-sur-Mer's citadel has fast become a must-do in June. Hot indie acts on stage; yoga, *pétanque*, natural wine tasting and vintage markets off.

Jazz à Juan

Rivals the Nice Jazz Festival for the title of the premier music event on the Côte d'Azur but takes the crown because of the pine-tree-fringed, waterfront setting.

Les Plages Electroniques

This epic three-day dance festival on the sandy beach in Cannes has welcomed headline French acts like David Guetta and DJ Snake. A party boat is a hot new addition to the line-up.

THE CÔTE D'AZUR REVIEWS

 Scan to find more things to do on the Côte d'Azur online

MONACO

GLAMOUR | ROYALTY | FOOD

Experience
Monaco
online

MONACO
Trip Builder

Turn your back to a superyacht and you'll probably spot a supercar whizz past: yes, Monaco is still the playground of the ultra rich. But, increasingly, another side is coming to the fore. Meet modern Monaco, a small principality with big, bold green ambitions.

Eat like a local in friendly neighbourhood eatery **Sexy Tacos** (p102)
🚶 30mins from Port Hercules

Sip on a Made in Monaco spirit at **La Distillerie de Monaco** (p94)
🚶 10mins from Gare de Monaco

Browse the book titles Grace Kelly once read at the **Princess Grace Irish Library** (p100)
🚶 25mins from Gare de Monaco

Marvel at Monaco's commitment to ocean preservation at the **Musée Océanographique de Monaco** (p96)
🚶 30mins from Gare de Monaco

Tuck into homegrown oysters at **Les Perles de Monte-Carlo** (p94)
🚶 25mins from Port Hercules

FRANCE

Pl des Moulins

Larvotto

Bd d'Italie

Monte Carlo

Casino de Monte Carlo

Bd des Moulins

Bd du Larvotto

Av Princesse Grace

Av de la Costa

Av d'Ostende

Bd Louis-II

Pl Ste-Dévote

Av Hector Otto

Bd de Belgique

Bd Rainier III

R.Grimaldi

Bd Albert 1er

La Condamine

Pl d'Armes

Av du Port

Port de Monaco

Av de la Quarantaine

Monaco Ville

Av des Pins

Bd Charles III

Palais Princier de Monaco

Av St-Martin

Av Albert II

Av des Papalins

Port de Fontvieille

Fontvieille Parc Fontvieille

MEDITERRANEAN SEA

0 ——— 500 m
0 ——— 0.25 miles

Practicalities

ARRIVING

Aéroport Nice-Côte d'Azur From the airport, millionaires hop on the helicopter (seven minutes, from €650), but everyone else heads for the Nice Airport Xpress bus (€22), taxi (€95) or train from Gare Nice St-Augustin (€5.10).

CONNECT

Buy a 1/7/30-day (€5/15/30) pass to connect to Monaco Telecom's wi-fi network.

SHOPPING

Blend in with locals at the Marché de la Condamine market. Carrefour in Fontvieille is a large supermarket.

WHERE TO STAY

Place	Pro/Con
Monte Carlo	A trio of Monaco's most prestigious five-star hotels surround the bling of Casino Sq.
Larvotto	The beach strip with a row of waterfront resorts.
La Condamine	Relaxed neighbourhood by the harbour with place d'Armes at its hub.
Fontvieille	Leafy, village vibe overlooking a smaller marina.

EATING & DRINKING

You'd struggle to write a cookbook about purely Monégasque cuisine; although don't leave before you've tasted the vegetarian-friendly national dish, the *barbagiuan*. You'll find Michelin-star fanfare in Monte Carlo and Larvotto; if laid-back experiences are more your style, check out restaurants in Fontvieille, Monaco-Ville (pictured top left) or La Condamine.

Must-try local craft brewery
Brasserie de Monaco (p95; pictured bottom left)

Best weekend brunch
Cafe Foufou (p103)

GETTING AROUND

Bus Six routes serve all corners of the principality.

Walking Monaco is small enough to cover by foot but can be very hilly. To catch your breath on steep ascents, look out for one of 79 public lifts.

Bicycle MonaBike, an electric bike-sharing scheme, has stations across Monaco (*mona bike.mc*).

MONACO FIND YOUR FEET

JAN–MAR
Bitter orange trees bearing fruit bring colour to the winter streetscape.

APR–JUN
Warm, but not stifling. Grand Prix road closures and deviations in May.

JUL–SEP
Peak superyacht season in Port Hercules. High prices.

OCT–DEC
Cooler nights bring a festive mood and Christmas market.

Made in
MONACO

HARBOURSIDE FOOD | CRAFT DRINKS | WALKING

Despite its postage-stamp size, a determined group of artisan entrepreneurs are finding space in unlikely locations across Monaco to brew beer, distill liqueurs and even farm oysters, adding an array of modern Made in Monaco flavours to accompany the principality's bite-sized national dish, the *barbagiuan*. Tasting their inventive creations is a decidedly delicious way to pass your time here.

🍴 How to

When to go Le Marché de la Condamine is open until 3pm. The Brasserie de Monaco first stirs at noon.

Cost A *barbagiuan* €1.20, a bottle of Carruba liqueur €27, a dozen oysters €28, a pint of beer €9.

Cool cocktail A splash of l'Orangerie liqueur, topped up with sparkling wine with an orange zest or strawberry slice as a flourish, the Monaco Spritz is the signature cocktail of the principality.

Top nosh Monaco's national food is a moreish morsel called the *barbagiuan*, a fried ravioli stuffed with Swiss chard. The best spot to grab a handful, along with a large side of people-watching, is at the **A Roca** stand inside the lively Marché de la Condamine food hall, although you'll find casual eateries across town with their own variations. At the edge of the breakwater in Fontvieille port, join a lunch crowd hungry for oysters reared on-site at **Les Perles de Monte-Carlo**, a marine research centre-turned-seafood counter with a delightful sun-drenched terrace. Reservations a must.

That's the spirit Tucked away in a back street of La Condamine, **La Distillerie de Monaco** takes the title of the principality's first – and only – distillery. Bitter oranges grown on neighbourhood streets are the primary ingredient in a punchy L'Orangerie liqueur, as well as one of seven

🐟 Monaco's Last Fisherman

There used to be a dozen or so fishermen in Monaco but today I'm the last one. My boat *Dédé* – named after my father, who like the two generations before him also fished these waters – is moored among the superyachts in Port Hercules. Mediterranean rockfish such as red mullet are some of the smaller fish found closer to the shore. Further out, I net tuna and swordfish. La Pêcherie U Luvassu *(ma-poissonnerie.mc)* is my fishmongers turned cafe on Quai d'Hirondelle in the harbour. Come at lunch to enjoy the morning's catch served fresh on our waterfront dining terrace.

■ Insight from
Eric Rinaldi,
Monaco fisherman
@pecheurrinaldi

locally sourced citrus fruits in its sunshine-flavoured Gin aux Agrumes. A richer cocoa-flavoured liqueur Carruba, made from the carob, Monaco's national tree, completes the hand-crafted range. Book a tour and taste all three.

Local brew The harbourfront **Brasserie de Monaco** serves up a selection of organic homebrews straight from the tank alongside a hearty burger menu. A convenient location close to the train station – and generous happy hour – makes this brewpub particularly boisterous on Friday evening with an after-work crowd.

Above Les Perles de Monte-Carlo

The Green
TOUCH

GREEN SPACES | FINE DINING | SUSTAINABLE TRAVEL

Spearheaded by the Sovereign Prince Albert II, Monaco is a small country with lofty aims: carbon neutrality by 2050. But here, going green comes with a luxury slant (of course), including sustainable Michelin-starred dining, a forward-thinking aquarium and plenty of preened, leafy public spaces. As the principality's smart tagline proclaims, 'Green is the new Glam'.

🗺 **How to**

Getting around Keep to the theme and use Monaco's electric bike scheme. Mobee *(mobee.mc)* is the car equivalent; a prepaid card unlocks a fleet that includes both snappy Renault Twizys and sleek Teslas.

Cost Monaco's Michelin-star dining doesn't come cheap – prices start at €68 for the set lunch Menu du Marché at Elsa.

Sports bar Laid-back harbourside sports bar and restaurant Stars'N'Bars also boasts its own vegetable patch and a strict single-use-plastic-free policy.

Sustainable stars The first 100% organic restaurant in the world to be awarded a Michelin star, at **Elsa** at the Monte Carlo Beach you'll dine on a menu of wild fish and vegetables grown in the terraced market gardens surrounding the principality. At the two-starred **Blue Bay** inside the Monte-Carlo Bay Hotel & Resort, delight in chef Marcel Ravin's signature Caribbean meets Mediterranean flavours, fuelled by edible flowers, heirloom tomatoes, kale and other produce grown in a vast on-site garden. Across at the Hôtel Hermitage, feast on sweeping harbour views and local, plant-based foods such as *farinata* and courgette flowers at three-Michelin-star chef Yannick Alleno's newly opened **Pavyllon Monte-Carlo**.

Marine museum A grand, neo-Baroque building rising up from a sheer cliff face, the **Musée Océanographique de Monaco** has long promoted

🌿 Green Thumb

Over 20%, or 470,000 sq metres, of Monaco is given over to green spaces. But beyond the sculpted cacti and dizzying views of the Jardin Exotique botanical garden, pockets of nature can be found across the manicured principality. The three self-guided walking tours of **Parcours Arbres Patrimoniaux** (Heritage Tree Trail) showcase almost 100 trees labelled remarkable, but even without the evergreen attractions, the circuits work as stand-alone itineraries through the streets of three neighbourhoods: Fontvieille, Monaco-Ville and Monte Carlo. Download the guide online to set off on your urban tree-spotting adventure.

marine preservation and scientific exploration. Under Prince Albert II, this important mission continues. While schools of Mediterranean and tropical fish, bright corals and a shark lagoon have long drawn visitors to its dimly lit, lower-floor aquarium, the museum's newest attraction is out in the open. *The Sea Turtle Odyssey* brings rescue and rehabilitation of these cute creatures to the fore and also maps out what to do if you spot an injured animal along the coast. Don't leave without enjoying the views from the rooftop terrace, but there are better places for lunch.

Above Musée Océanographique de Monaco

Race to the
FINISH LINE

WALKING TOUR | VIEWS | FAST CARS

▬▬▬ Walk a lap of the Monaco Grand Prix street circuit at your own speed. The most famous track in Formula One racing is actually the perfect loop for day-trippers looking to cover classic sights and admire million-dollar views on foot.

✨ Don't Miss

The name of the Fairmont Hairpin bend (pictured) has changed over the years depending on who owns the hotel located on it. However, the nature of it hasn't: this is the slowest corner of any Grand Prix circuit. You could ride your bike around the turn faster than you can drive an F1 car.

🗺 Trip Notes

Getting here Although unmarked outside of race days, the official starting and finishing line outside Palais Héraclès on bd Albert 1er is a short walk from Monaco's train station.

When to go Any time of the year except for May, when scaffolding for the race day blocks both views and access to the track.

Distance One lap of the circuit is 3.4km and reflects Monaco's hilly terrain.

■ **Tip by Allan McNish,** *Monaco resident & former racing driver @allanmcnish*

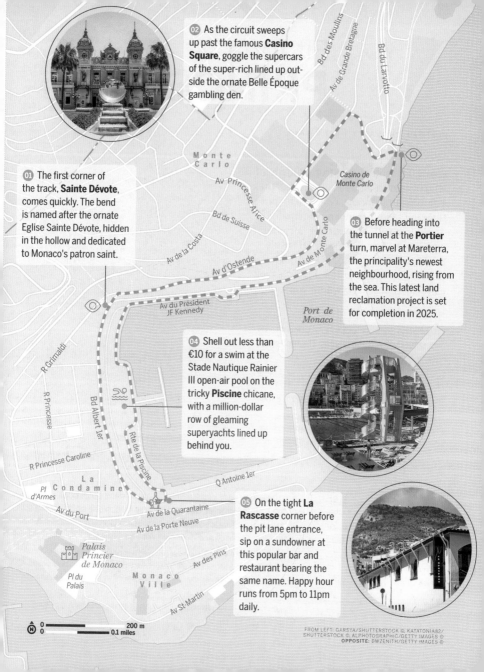

02 As the circuit sweeps up past the famous **Casino Square**, goggle the supercars of the super-rich lined up outside the ornate Belle Époque gambling den.

01 The first corner of the track, **Sainte Dévote**, comes quickly. The bend is named after the ornate Eglise Sainte Dévote, hidden in the hollow and dedicated to Monaco's patron saint.

03 Before heading into the tunnel at the **Portier** turn, marvel at Mareterra, the principality's newest neighbourhood, rising from the sea. This latest land reclamation project is set for completion in 2025.

04 Shell out less than €10 for a swim at the Stade Nautique Rainier III open-air pool on the tricky **Piscine** chicane, with a million-dollar row of gleaming superyachts lined up behind you.

05 On the tight **La Rascasse** corner before the pit lane entrance, sip on a sundowner at this popular bar and restaurant bearing the same name. Happy hour runs from 5pm to 11pm daily.

Monte Carlo

Av Princesse Alice

Bd de Suisse

Av de la Costa

Av d'Ostende

Av du Président JF Kennedy

Bd des Moulins

Av de Grande Bretagne

Bd du Larvotto

Casino de Monte Carlo

Av de Monte Carlo

Port de Monaco

R Grimaldi

R Princesse

Bd Albert 1er

Rte de la Piscine

R Princesse Caroline

La Condamine

Pl d'Armes

Av du Port

Q Antoine 1er

Av de la Quarantaine

Av de la Porte Neuve

Palais Princier de Monaco

Pl du Palais

Monaco Ville

Av des Pins

Av St-Martin

N 0 — 200 m
0 — 0.1 miles

Fit for a
PRINCESS

HISTORY | ROYALTY | CITY WALK

The golden girl from Philadelphia who became a Hollywood actress, then a European princess, Grace Kelly put this tiny Mediterranean principality on the global map with her fairy-tale wedding to Prince Rainier III inside the Cathédrale de Monaco in 1956. Four decades on from her death, her legacy can still be felt everywhere you look.

How to

When to go Summer for State Apartment tours. Spring for rose-scented blooms. Theatre season runs from September to May.

Did you know? The jersey Grace designed for the AS Monaco football club in 1960 is still its talisman. Tour their grounds, Stade Louis II, from June to October.

Further exploration Download the *Parcours Princesse Grace* map (*monte-carlo.mc/static/img/guides/parcours-princesse-grace-en.pdf*) for an outline of 25 sites of importance, each marked out by a multilingual information board.

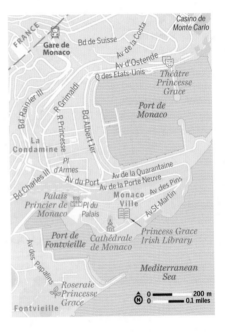

The Rock Monaco-Ville, or The Rock as Monaco's oldest neighbourhood is more commonly called, is a charming warren of narrow alleyways on a rocky promontory overlooking the sea. Apart from the daily changing of the guards at 11.55am, tours of the formal State Apartments are the only visitor experience at the **Palais Princier de Monaco**, the official sovereign residence where Grace made her Mediterranean home. You'll feel a greater sense of her passions, however, by browsing the spines of books she owned at the **Princess Grace Irish Library** (*pgil.*

mc). These quiet book rooms also house one of the world's most important collections of Irish literature, as well as a handy kids' reading corner for rainy days. Nearby, pay your respects in the **Cathédrale de Monaco**, where Prince Rainier and Princess Grace's graves lie inside the choir.

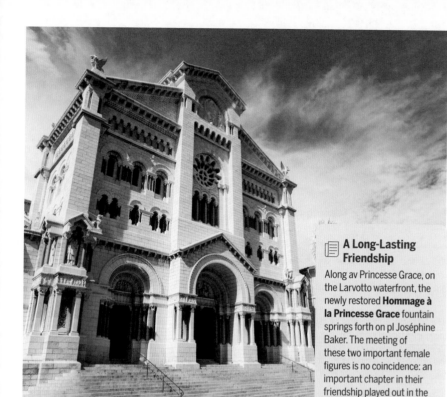

SERGEY NOVIKOV/SHUTTERSTOCK ©

A Long-Lasting Friendship

Along av Princesse Grace, on the Larvotto waterfront, the newly restored **Hommage à la Princesse Grace** fountain springs forth on pl Joséphine Baker. The meeting of these two important female figures is no coincidence: an important chapter in their friendship played out in the principality. With Grace's support, Baker, an American dancer and civil rights activist, set up home here in the 1970s. In 2021, nearly 50 years after she died, she became the first Black woman to be symbolically laid to rest in the Pantheon in Paris, France's monumental tomb of heroes. At her family's request, she remains buried in the Monaco-Louis II cemetery.

Fontvieille Those searching for a peaceful corner head to the **Roseraie Princesse Grace**, an English-style garden where a bronze statue of Grace surveys more than 6000 rose bushes.

Water views Admire Grace's artistic touch at the **Théatre Princesse Grace**; in the 1970s she was heavily involved in the redesign of its interior decor, acoustics and dressing rooms. Check out the planning to see what's on during your stay; keeping true to her vision, the venue is a platform for both established names and new talent in the dramatic arts.

Above Cathédrale de Monaco

Listings

BEST OF THE REST

Cheap Eats

Maison des Pâtes €

The wide variety of fresh, cook-to-order pasta makes this popular stand inside La Marché de la Condamine worth the queuing time.

Sexy Tacos €

Friendly Mexican joint run by an ex-Fairmont Monte Carlo chef that lives up to its name off the tourist trail near the Tour Odéon.

ICI Salad Bar €

Quick and easy compose-your-own salad bar with three outlets across Monaco: Fontvieille, La Condamine and St Roman.

Eola €

Pastel pinks and greens, all-day breakfasts, colourful poke bowls, raw desserts and cold-pressed organic juices; this photogenic cafe has carved out a hipster niche on pl d'Armes.

Chez Roger €

Little has changed on the recipe front since Chez Roger first opened nearly 50 years ago. The spot for *socca* and *pissaladière*.

Planet Sushi €

Fresh sushi on the harbourfront. The Midi menu at lunchtime (€12.90) is a cracker of a deal.

Neat for Non-Drinkers

Stars'N'Bars €

This beloved sports bar and restaurant serves non-alcoholic beer and cocktails, organic fruit juices and a spritzy kombucha brewed on-site.

Azzura Kitchen €

Enjoy a beyond-the-basics mocktails or a sober spritz or G&T beside the swimming pool at the Novotel Monte Carlo hotel.

MayaBay €

This slick Thai restaurant along the Larvotto strip serves refreshing tea-based mocktails, christened T'Tails, in a serene terrace garden.

Le Pattaya €

Bright yellow awnings mark this low-key spot on Port Hercules with comfy waterfront lounges and a refreshing selection of fruit cocktails.

Weekend Brunch

Le Teashop €€

Cute neighbourhood cafe on bd des Moulins. Hosts an organic veggie brunch on the first Saturday of the month. Reservations a must.

Blue Bay Restaurant €€€

An oyster bar and a set price inclusive of bubbles – brunch at the Monte-Carlo Bay Hotel & Resort is the creation of celebrated Michelin-starred chef Marcel Ravin.

Hôtel Hermitage Monte-Carlo €€€

Champagne served under a cupola designed by Gustave Eiffel and live cooking before your eyes. A children's playroom and dedicated kids' buffet keep younger diners entertained.

Plage du Larvotto

Cafe Foufou   €

Relaxed market cafe in Beausoleil, France (right on the Monaco border), with a fresh, organic menu of brunch favourites including chia pudding and avocado toast. Doesn't take bookings.

Brunch Azzurra   €€€

Still not cheap, but at €50 a head (and €20 for under 12s), the Novotel Monte Carlo's brunch buffet is one of the best value in town. Reservations recommended.

Like a Local

Place d'Armes

Busy market square in La Condamine where locals sip coffee and shop for fresh produce in the morning, grab a quick, tasty *plat du jour* at lunch, and relax over an *apéro* early evening.

Patinoire à Ciel Ouvert

From December to March, the swimming pool at the Stade Nautique Rainier III freezes over, transforming into an open-air ice-skating rink.

Monaco Open Air Cinema

Worth a visit as much for the Hollywood-worthy setting at the foot of the Rock as for what's on the big screen. Open June to September; movies start at sunset.

Parc Princesse Antoinette

Terraced park on bd du Jardin Exotique where you can shelter under the shade of 100-year-old olive trees and let the kids roam free. Plenty to entertain, from table tennis tables to a mini-golf course and even a petting farm.

Solarium Beach

Handy spot for a picnic and swim on the Port Hercule sea wall, accessed by a staircase near Fort Antoine. Dive off the steps in calm seas, but the water is very deep and unpatrolled.

Plage du Larvotto

Back in full action after nearly two years of serious upgrades, including spaces for new restaurants, this sandy beach fills up fast on

Monaco Open Air Cinema

weekends. **La Note Bleue** has the best position of all the posh private beach clubs.

Art & Culture Afternoons

Nouveau Musée National de Monaco (NMNM)

Two grand buildings at opposite ends of the principality, NMNM's Villa Sauber and Villa Paloma mix things up with deep dives into Monaco's history and contemporary art exhibits.

Sculpture Paths

Set off in search of over 200 open-air artworks on three leafy sculpture trails (*visitmonaco. com/en/routes-and-walks/27464/sculptures-trails*) through Fontvieille, Monaco-Ville and Monte Carlo. Each walk takes under two hours.

Jardin Exotique

Sublime setting for a prickly cactus garden. Closed for major renovation works until 2023 at the earliest; check for updates before you go.

Collection Privée des Voitures de S.A.S. le Prince de Monaco

See the types of cars that got Prince Rainier III's motor running. Turns out he had a penchant for vintage F1 specimens and sporty Ferraris. New location on rte de la Piscine on the harbour.

 Scan to find more things to do in Monaco online

ST-TROPEZ & THE VAR

BEACHES | HILLTOP VILLAGES | WINE

**Experience
St-Tropez
& the Var
online**

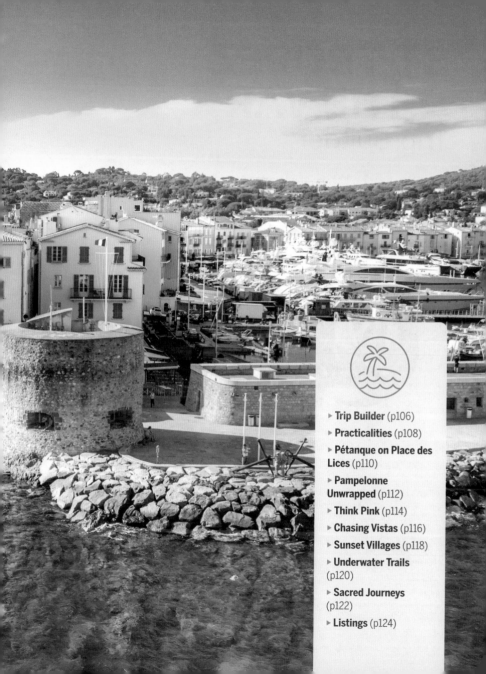

ST-TROPEZ & THE VAR
Trip Builder

Nowhere evokes the glamorous yin and grassroots yang of Provence quite like the Var: at its chic helm, jet-set favourite St-Tropez, ensnared by buttercream sands, manicured vineyards and medieval villages every wine, food and nature buff will adore.

Catch an alfresco, classical-music concert at **Château Ste-Roseline** (p114)
🚗 *1hr from St-Tropez*

Le Luc   Le Cannet des Maures

Gonfaron

Catch world music live between château ruins in hilltop **Grimaud** (p119)
🚋 *25mins from St-Tropez*

Celebrate chestnuts at an autumnal festival in **Collobrières** (p122)
🚗 *1hr from St-Tropez*

MASSIF DES MAURES

Bormes-les-Mimosas   Cavalière

Toulon

Le Pradet   **Hyères**   La Londe-les-Maures   **Le Lavandou**

Port Miramar   Cabasson

Les Oursinières

Port d'Hyères

La Capte

Giens   *Île de Porquerolles*   *Île de Port-Cros*

Learn to kitesurf on the **Presqu'île de Giens** (p121)
🚋 *25mins from Hyères*

La Tour Fondue   *Îles d'Hyères*

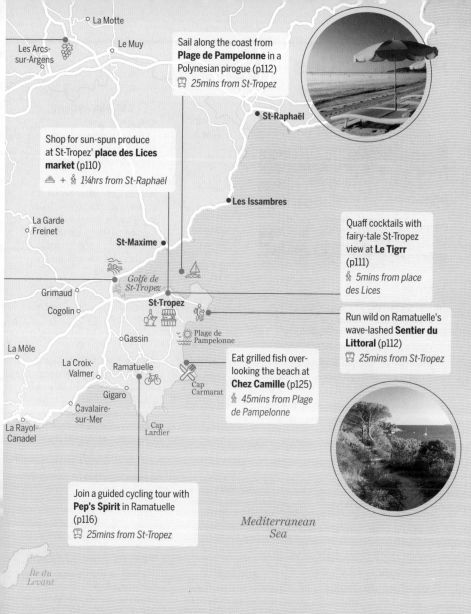

Sail along the coast from **Plage de Pampelonne** in a Polynesian pirogue (p112)
🚌 25mins from St-Tropez

Shop for sun-spun produce at St-Tropez' **place des Lices market** (p110)
⛴ + 🚶 1¼hrs from St-Raphaël

Quaff cocktails with fairy-tale St-Tropez view at **Le Tigrr** (p111)
🚶 5mins from place des Lices

Run wild on Ramatuelle's wave-lashed **Sentier du Littoral** (p112)
🚌 25mins from St-Tropez

Eat grilled fish overlooking the beach at **Chez Camille** (p125)
🚶 45mins from Plage de Pampelonne

Join a guided cycling tour with **Pep's Spirit** in Ramatuelle (p116)
🚌 25mins from St-Tropez

La Motte

Le Muy

Les Arcs-sur-Argens

St-Raphaël

Les Issambres

La Garde Freinet

St-Maxime

Golfe de St-Tropez

Grimaud

Cogolin

St-Tropez

Gassin

Plage de Pampelonne

La Môle

La Croix-Valmer

Ramatuelle

Cap Carmarat

Gigaro

Cavalaire-sur-Mer

La Rayol-Canadel

Cap Lardier

Mediterranean Sea

Île du Levant

N

0 ——— 10 km
0 ——— 5 miles

Practicalities

RUDMER ZWERVER/SHUTTERSTOCK ©

ARRIVING

Toulon-Hyères Airport VarLib *(varlib.fr)* shuttle buses link St-Tropez (1½ hours) with its closest airport, 52km southwest. Road congestion entering St-Tropez is beyond hideous in July and August.

Nouveau Port de St-Tropez Seasonal boats sail to St-Tropez' port (pictured) from St-Raphaël, Ste-Maxime, Cannes and Nice.

Gare Routière de St-Tropez Year-round to/from St-Raphaël, Ramatuelle, Toulon and others.

HOW MUCH FOR A

Sun bed on
Pampelonne
€27–30

Pastis 51 at Café
Sénéquier
€10

St-Raphaël–
Tropez boat ticket
€15

GETTING AROUND

Bus Pay €3 or €4 for a ticket covering a single ride between towns in the Var. Services out of season (October to March) can be scant. Check routes, schedules and buy tickets on zou.maregionsud.fr or via the Zou! app.

Car & Bicycle Motoring coastal areas in summer is slow-going, and parking expensive. Download the Flow app *(flowbird.fr)* to pay for parking in St-Tropez. Away from the coast, particularly in rural Massif des Maures and Haut-Var, car or e-bike is the only means of navigating hilltop villages.

Walking Use scenic coastal paths *(sentiers du littoral)* to get around the Presqu'île de St-Tropez, Îles d'Hyères and Corniche des Maures.

WHEN TO GO

APR–JUN
Few crowds, warm days and abundant sun-spun fruit and veg.

JUL–AUG
Sky-high prices, rammed beaches and congested roads.

SEP–OCT
Crowds thin; warm, mellow days usher in the grape harvest.

NOV–MAR
Beaches close; buses and boats adopt a sparser winter timetable; black-truffle season.

EATING & DRINKING

An international jet set assures a feast of world food (Indian, Thai, Japanese, Italian, you name it) in St-Tropez. Vegan and vegetarian *menus* are also abundant. The town's *tarte Tropézienne* (pictured top right) sandwiches cream between two orange blossom–flavoured sponges. Inland, village *auberges* (inns) and cult-foodie bistros with tree-shaded terraces cook Provençal classics. In September and October look for the date-like jujube fruit (pictured bottom right) at weekly markets. November to March, dogs sniff out black truffles around Aups in Haut-Var.

Best sunset terrace
Le Tigrr (p111)

Must-try rosé
Château d'Esclans (p115)

CONNECT & FIND YOUR WAY

Wi-fi Many tourist offices offer free wi-fi; high-season crowds in St-Tropez can slow connection speed.

Navigation The A8 *autoroute* slices across the Var and the A57 dips southwest to Toulon on the coast; the D98 wiggles between the Presqu'île de St-Tropez and Massif des Maures. The northern Var (Haut-Var) is a rural hinterland; download online maps.

MONEY

Accommodation and dining prices in St-Tropez and coastal hot spots in summer are sky-high – unlike inland destinations, which are good-value year-round. Parking rates in downtown St-Tropez (€3/9 for one/three hours) encourage use of public transport.

WHERE TO STAY

If you're planning on staying anywhere near St-Tropez, be prepared to pay for the privilege; even campsites are dramatically more expensive than elsewhere. Many hotels close completely in winter.

Place	Pro/Con
St-Tropez	Great shopping and dining; congested in season, expensive, and no budget accommodation.
Ramatuelle	Five-star campsites on Plage de Pampelonne. Pricey but bucolic villas and *bastides* (country houses) in wine country.
Hyères	Midsized, reasonably priced seaside town. Well placed for coastal explorations and Îles d'Hyères boats.
Haut-Var	Good-value village *auberges* (inns) and rural *gîtes* (self-catering rentals); wheels essential.
Île de Porquerolles	Seasonal, car-free island escape, only accessible by boat; luxury hotels and self-catering studios/apartments must be booked early.
Collobrières	Main base for hiking/biking/touring the Massif des Maures; village hotels and rural *gîtes* close in winter.

CENT SAVER

Shop for picnics at open-air food markets to learn what sun-spun produce is in season locally and cut dining costs. Every village has a weekly *marché* – mornings only; bring your own bag or basket.

16

PÉTANQUE
on Place des Lices

CULTURE | SPORTS | CAFE LIFE

▬▬▬ Despite its quintessential image of a bunch of old men throwing balls about on a dusty patch of gravel beneath trees, Provence's most popular pastime is a serious sport. For pros or amateurs alike, there is no more iconic spot to have a spin at *pétanque* than beneath the bucolic parasol of lime-green plane trees on St-Tropez' legendary central square.

KIRK FISHER/GETTY IMAGES ©

🎑 How to

Getting here St-Raphaël train station is 200m from the dock where seasonal boats by Les Bateaux de St-Raphaël sail to/from St-Tropez (one hour). Late October to March, take a bus or drive.

When to go Spring and early Autumn. July and August sees St-Tropez packed to bursting.

Market days Forget *pétanque* on place des Lices during its twice-weekly market (7am to 1pm Tuesday and Saturday). Shop for fruit, veg, herbs, spices and a straw bag for the beach instead.

NUTFIELD CHASE/SHUTTERSTOCK ©

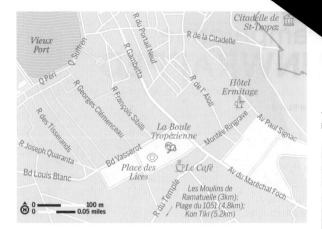

Top left *Pétanque*, pls des Lices
Bottom left Market, pl des Lices.

Ball Talk

Assuming you have rocked up in St-Tropez ball-less, whet your whistle with *un café* (espresso) or rite-of-passage pastis on the terrace of historic **Le Café**, local hangout for *pétanque* players since 1789. Drink done, head inside to borrow *une triplette* (trio) of solid metal *boules* (balls) at the traditional zinc bar.

Team up in pairs or teams of up to six players. Scratch a small circle in the gravel and stand in it to throw the *cochonnet* – not a 'piglet' but the jack players need to aim their boules at. Underarm throwing is compulsory, and players can dribble along ground *(pointer;* to point) or hurl balls high in the air to land on another player's boule *(tirer;* to shoot) and smash it away from the jack. Polishing balls with a soft cloth throughout is essential.

Watch the Pros

Place des Lices is the home ground of **La Boule Tropézienne**, the town's *pétanque* club and host to official matches and tournaments that unfold on the square. Regional championships are held on the gravel car park of **Plage du 1051** on Plage de Pampelonne. The official season runs mid-March to early November. Matches are free to watch.

Almost every **cafe terrace** on place des Lices promises a dress-circle view. Don't confuse *pétanque* HQ **Le Café** with the newer, cream-and-green-canopied Café des Arts on the square.

☆ Jet-Set Games

Embrace St-Tropez' signature cool with *une soirée pétanque* – an evening spent with friends spinning *pétanque* balls over alfresco cocktails, rosé and shared plates.

Hôtel Ermitage The city and peninsula panorama from the *pétanque* pitch at this glamorous 19th-century villa are unmatched. Invest in a drink with the jet set at **Le Tigrr** – magical terrace with St-Tropez view – to earn a complimentary game.

Les Moulins de Ramatuelle Inland towards hilltop Ramatuelle, this Mediterranean restaurant seduces with *pétanque* on tap in a flowery, fountain-clad garden.

Kon Tiki Keep your feet firmly on the ground with a *pétanque* game at this beachside campsite with Polynesian 'huts' and hot-tub-clad cottages overlooking vines and celebrity-studded Pampelonne.

pelonne
WRAPPED

...E

complete
...tive, old-
sch... Pampelonne.
One of Euro... ...nical beaches,
this shimmering s... ...of white sand
ribbons for 5km along the eastern side
of the St-Tropez Peninsula. Flaming
cocktails, entertainers on stilts, sun
butlers facilitating every last sunbathing desire: anything goes.

🗺 How to

Getting here By train to St-Raphäel, then Les Bateaux de St-Raphäel boat to St-Tropez (one hour).
Buses link St-Tropez with Toulon-Hyères airport
(1½ hours) and Ramatuelle (35 minutes).

When to go July and August for the party vibe and
celebrity spotting; May, June and September are less
high-octane.

Beach clubs Open from around 11am to 8pm daily,
March or April to September or October. Table
reservations are essential – few open after dark.

8am

Pampelonne's endless
sweep of sand is a perfect
barefoot romp in the cooler
morning air. Or don hiking or
trail-running shoes and hit the
Sentier du Littoral (coastal
path): south to France's
second-tallest lighthouse on
Cap Camarat (5km) and

offshore **Rocher des Portes**
or Bird Island, always covered
in black cormorants; or northeast around the peninsula to
St-Tropez (14.8km).

Noon

Laze over lunch with sublime
sea view at **Le 1051** on **Plage
de Tahiti**, on Pampelonne's

northern end. Maxime is at
the helm, serving wine from
his family vineyards and zero-
pesticide veg and herbs grown
on horse-ploughed farm **Jardin de la Piboule** in nearby
Cogolin. Or dine at **Bagatelle**
or **Verde**. Live music rocks the
poolside from noon to 8pm at
adult-only **Nikki Beach**.

> ### ✅ Beach Bum Essentials
>
> Pampelonne is essentially a day venue. In July and August; a handful of beach clubs stay open for dinner.
>
> **Lunch reservations** are crucial – beach clubs have two or three seatings. Reserve the first seating (noon or 12.30pm) for a more sedate experience, the second (usually 2pm or 2.30pm) and third (4pm) to party.
>
> For an upscale **siesta on the sand**, rent a sun lounger and parasol (€27 to €30 per day on private beaches). Or BYO or towel-flop for free on a section of public beach.
>
> **Family-friendly clubs** like Gigi and Jardin Tropezina provide sophisticated kids' clubs, play areas and entertainment.

3pm

Visit **Pep's Pampelonne** (*peps-spirit.fr*) for a seafaring adventure by kayak, stand-up paddleboard or Polynesian pirogue. Book a *randonnée guidée* (guided trek) in advance or rent gear and DIY. **Tiki Beach** is another water-sports hub.

5pm

Cocktail hour – most beach bars close at 8pm. Hobnob over aperitifs at original 1950s duo **Tahiti** and **Le Club 55**. Or share yellowtail fish carpaccio and truffle pizza at nomad-inspired **Indie Beach**; or enjoy dancing and DJ sets at boho-chic **Verde Beach**.

Above Plage de Pampelonne

18 Think PINK

WINE TASTING | CHÂTEAUX | LOCAL LIFE

▬▬▬ Cracking open a bottle of rosé to enjoy beneath a vine-draped pergola or sun parasol is the essence of Provençal *art de vivre* – not just for Provence-thirsty visitors dreaming of dizzying azure skies and sea, but for locals too. Discovering first-hand how the Var's celebrated AOC Côtes de Provence rosés are crafted is a privileged peek into the wine-producing region's back parlour.

🗺 How to

Getting around Drive or cycle to clandestine châteaux and *domaines* (estates) lost in a sea of vines.

When to go June for festivals (who doesn't love **Pique-nique Chez le Vigneron Indépendant** when winegrowers open their vineyards to picnic-lovers?). The grape harvest begins in mid-August. Autumn promises mellow warm days spun from beautiful colours and light.

Bring a corkscrew Screw caps are rare. Fill your own bottle with cheap *vin de table* at **wine cooperatives**.

Map labels: Aups, Châteaudouble, Barjols, Maison Mirabeau, Draguignan, Jardin Secret, Cotignac, Entrecasteaux, Château Ste-Roseline, Carcès, Les Arcs-sur-Argens, Le Muy, Le Val, Argens, Maison des Vins de Côtes de Provence, Brignoles, La Celle, Abbaye de la Celle, Le Luc, Gonfaron, St-Maxime, Carnoules, Cuers, Collobrières, Grimaud, St-Tropez, Bormes-les-Mimosas, Hyères, Le Lavandou, Château Léoube, Île du Levant, Giens, Îles d'Hyères

10 km / 5 miles

House of Wines

Discover Provence's signature rosé at **Maison des Vins de Côtes de Provence** in Les-Arcs-sur-Argens. Three-hour oenology workshops explain the appellation which sees rosé typically made from blended grenache, cinsault and syrah grapes. Taste rosés in the boutique and browse 800 different wines from 230 wineries, sold at producer prices. Road-trippers, pick up itinerary maps for **Les Routes des Vins de Provence** (*route desvinsdeprovence.com*).

Château Life

From Les-Arcs-sur-Argens drive 4.5km east to **Château Ste-Roseline**, a *cru classé* winery with top-flight tasting cellar, stunning grounds and a 13th-century Romanesque chapel decorated with a 1975 Marc Chagall mosaic. Watch for summer concerts here.

Grapes are hand-harvested at night and early morning to ensure they stay cool at pio-

ⓘ Tasting Tips

Going from winery to winery in the Var, you take in so much incredible scenery, including vineyards, lavender fields and coastal roads. Our own tasting room is a great place to stop in the charming village of **Cotignac**. A great option by the coast, with its own private beach and beach cafe, is organic **Château Léoube** (live music, film screenings and kayak-rental alert!) in Bormes-les-Mimosas.

The restaurant at **Abbaye de la Celle** in La Celle has a brilliant wine list to accompany locally sourced food. In Cotignac, catch a refreshing pink-gin cocktail at **Jardin Secret** *(loucalen. com)*, a lovely 'secret garden' address with a kitchen-garden-to-table philosophy and delicious food.

neering **Château d'Esclans**. Experience playful *The Beach* or the world's finest rosé, *Whispering Angel* – book free tastings by email or visit the château shop (daily May to September). Forget tasting *Garrus*, the world's most expensive rosé, crafted from near-centurion vines.

Going for Gin

Winemakers at Cotignac's **Maison Mirabeau** are taking Provence's pink renaissance one step further with dry rosé gin, bursting with local botanicals in a retro perfume-style bottle. Drink it with a sprig of fresh rosemary and slice of organic lemon.

■ **Recommended by Jeany Cronk,** *winemaker and co-founder at Maison Mirabeau in Cotignac,* @MaisonMirabeau

Above Rosé, the Var

Chasing
VISTAS

ROAD TRIP | VILLAGES | VIEWPOINTS

Away from St-Tropez in the Golfe de St-Tropez, an oasis of peace and tranquillity – bejewelled with Instagram-worthy panoramas of the Med and France's most mythical coastline – unravels. Bookmark this road trip around the finest viewpoints for the low or shoulder season when roads and *cols* (mountain passes) are less crowded.

🗺 Trip Notes

Getting here This circular trip begins on the coast at Plage de Gigaro, 6km south of La Croix Valmer, but you can pick it up at any point. You'll need wheels (car, motorcycle or electric-assisted mountain bike).

Sunset views Enjoy sunset from a roadside *belvédère* (viewpoint, with parking for a few cars). Pair this itinerary with **Sunset Villages** on p118 to enjoy the sundown show atop a flower-filled hamlet or hilltop fort en route.

🚲 Cycling Around

When you ride on the ridges you have breathtaking views of the Mediterranean Sea and the great Maures forest – the lung of our region. Thanks to this immensity of nature you have a feeling of living a unique experience. Planning an itinerary is important because there are so many paths and trails.

■ Tips by **Frédérique Ballarini,** *cyclist and owner of Pep's Spirit in Ramatuelle,* @pepsspirit

0   10 km
0 5 miles

03 From La Môle (D98), the **Col du Canadel** (D27) offers breathtaking views of the Massif des Maures, the coastline and its islands, before plunging down towards the coastal **Corniche des Maures**.

02 Wiggle up to Gassin along **Route des Moulins de Paillas**, named after windmills used to grind wheat for flour here from the 16th to 19th centuries. In summer, book a tour of the single windmill rebuilt (pictured opposite).

Gonfaron

La Garde Freinet

● St- Maxime

Golfe de St-Tropez

Port Grimaud

Collobrières

Grimaud

Cogolin

● St-Tropez

Col de Babaou

La Môle

Gassin

La Croix-Valmer

Ramatuelle

Col de Gratteloup

Gigaro

Cavalaire-sur-Mer

Plage de Gigaro

Col de Cagou-Ven

Bormes-les-Mimosas

La Rayol-Canadel

01 Motor west from Plage de Gigaro to pick up the inland D93. This narrow but drop-dead-gorgeous road winds up and over the **Col de Collebasse** (129m) to labyrinthine walled village Ramatuelle, 12km north.

Le Lavandou

Cabasson

Mediterranean Sea

05 The **Col de Cagou-Ven** (237m) unveils dreamy views of Bormes-les-Mimosas. Climbing north, the steep D41 staggers up to the **Col de Gratteloup** (199m) and **Col de Babaou** (415m) towards Collobrières.

04 On the Col du Canadel, watch for **Route des Crêtes** signposted on the left. This hairpin-laced road is peppered with strawberry, myrtle and eucalyptus trees and has sublime views its entire length (20km).

20 Sunset VILLAGES

ARTS & CRAFTS | FESTIVALS | FLOWERS

████ Southwest of star-studded St-Tropez unfurls a bewitching patchwork of hilltop villages, stitched from sweet Mediterranean blooms and cobbled lanes dotted with *maisons de village,* gold-stone fountains and *lavoirs* (washhouses). Scale village heights at sunset for pretty-in-pink views of vineyards, fruit orchards and exquisite flower gardens tumbling down to the Golfe de St-Tropez.

KIRK FISHER/SHUTTERSTOCK ©

🗺 **How to**

Getting here Limited bus services are run by VarLib – check schedules on zou.maregionsud. fr – but having your own transport gives you infinitely more freedom and flexibility.

When to go Avoid July and August when congested roads make road-tripping heavy work. Many hotels and restaurants close completely in winter.

Picnic supplies and apéritif fare Stock up on cheese, charcuterie and artisan breads to savour at sunset at each village's weekly open-air food market.

LENS-68/SHUTTERSTOCK ©

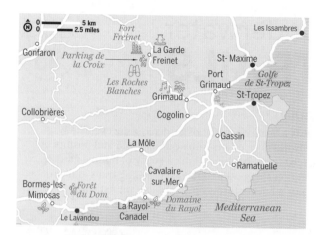

Top left Outer wall, Château de Grimaud **Bottom left** Domaine du Rayol

A Bougainvillea Balade

Not to be confused with its Venetian-style sister **Port Grimaud**, medieval **Grimaud** rises from a sea of vineyards, olive groves and oak-and-beech-clad foothills 7km inland. Late May to July, bougainvilleas cloak house facades in spectacular cascades – download the 'Balade des Bougainvilleas' self-guided walking tour on Grimaud's tourist office website. In high summer, open-air concerts fill the atmospheric château ruins with world music.

Mimosa Magic

Follow the intoxicating scent of mimosas, in bloom in January and February, to cobbled **Bormes-les-Mimosas**. The tourist office arranges guided botanical walks and hikes with a forest warden in nearby **Forêt du Dom**, and has details on the 130km-long **Route du Mimosa** (routedumimosa.com) driving itinerary: admire 30 species of mimosa in the spectacular gardens of **Domaine du Rayol** en route to Provençal perfume capital Grasse.

White Rocks

A glorious panorama of burnt-red rooftops unfolds from the 13th-century ruins of **Fort Freinet**, crowning glory of the medieval village of **La Garde Freinet**. Meet village cork harvesters, honey makers, stone masons and other artisans at heritage-driven **Conservatoire du Patrimoine du Freinet**.

Equally magnificent is the view from **Les Roches Blanches** (637m), a dramatic formation of dazzling white rocks veined with quartz. Pick up the trailhead for the 8km hike in **Parking de la Croix**, accessed via Route des Crêtes west of the village.

◎ Cogolin Pipes & Panoramas

Cogolin is renowned for its craftsmanship: pottery, carpets, reeds and pipes. At **Cogolin Courieu** savoir-faire (expertise) has been passed on from father to son for more than 150 years. This maître pipier (master piper) carves pipes from heather roots specifically farmed in the Massif des Maures. Guided tours of the workshop run year-round.

There is no finer view of the authentic old village with our beautiful Massif des Maures in the background than from **rue de la Résistance** in **Cogolin**. For a panorama of the entire Golfe de St-Tropez, continue uphill to aptly named **place Bellevue** – 'Beautiful View Square'.

■ Recommended by **Stéphanie Gualbert,** guide and interpreter, Cogolin

PHOTO: VAR MATIN ©

21

Underwater
TRAILS

WATER SPORTS | BEACHES | NATURE

The Var squirrels away a beauty pageant of gardens, some exquisitely manicured and known the world over, others intoxicatingly wild and unsung. A fascinating few are submerged in the big blue: think a string of marine gardens, open to slow-motion exploration along well-marked snorkelling trails and enticing beach lovers to strips of sands a bucket-throw off the beaten tourist track.

SAMI SARKIS/GETTY IMAGES ©

🗺 **How to**

Getting here ZOU! bus lines 7801 (St-Tropez–Toulon) and 7802 (St-Tropez–Hyères) stop in La Rayol-Canadel-sur-Mer (one hour). Bus 67 links Hyères train station with La Tour Fondue.

When to go Mid-June to mid-September (trails shut off season).

What to bring Anyone from age eight and able to swim can access *sentiers sous-marin* (snorkelling trails); bring swimmers. Some trails provide snorkel, mask, flippers and wetsuit for chillier temperatures. Check for jellyfish before diving in!

TRAVEL.FR/SHUTTERSTOCK ©

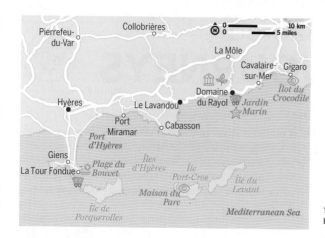

Top left Scuba diver, Île Port-Cros
Bottom left Pointe du Bouvet

Garden of Eden

Ditch the dizzying scent of Mediterranean maquis (scrub) and buzz of cicadas on dry land for a silent underwater ramble along seabeds at **Domaine du Rayol**. This lavish estate's ochre villa was built for a Parisian businessman in 1910, on a headland overlooking **Baie du Figuier**. For garden lovers, the ornamental cascade of Cretan date palms and eucalyptus, perfumed mimosa, rock roses, exotic themed gardens and terraced fruit orchards is the original Garden of Eden.

In its **Jardin Marin** don wetsuit, tuba, mask and flippers (all provided) and plunge into the shallows with a guide to learn about the kaleidoscope of starfish, sea bass, flatfish, sea cucumbers, anemones, pomfrets et al twirling around you. A conger eel cave, sea urchin beds and mother-of-pearl passage are deep-water highlights.

Shipwreck Gold

On the southern tip of **Presqu'île de Giens**, marine explorers uncover buried treasure along the **Sentier Sous-marin Archéologique de la Tour Fondue**. This free-to-access archaeology trail at Pointe du Bouvet recreates lost cargo from the *Madrague* shipwreck, discovered offshore here in the 1970s.

Admire 120 amphoras scattered on the seabed. Visual cards attached to weighted chains in the water allow to you identify flora and fauna along the 6m-deep trail. Bring your own mask, tuba, flippers (and wetsuit if necessary), or rent at **Espace Mer** (*rando-palmee.fr*), a diving and nautical-sports centre 50m from **Plage du Bouvet**.

☰ Best Island Idylls

Pair a marine-garden ramble with a boat trip or *sentier du littoral* (coastal path).

Île Port-Cros Sail from Hyères to France's smallest national park. Spot 500 algae and 180 fish types along a short snorkelling circuit, marked offshore from Plage de la Plaud. Buy the waterproof leaflet on arrival at the port-side Maison du Parc. Rent gear at Sun Plongée.

Îlot du Crocodile From La Croix Valmer's Plage du Gigaro, walk 20 minutes along Cap Lardier's coastal path to Plage de Jovat. Offshore, a snorkelling trail winds around a crocodile-shaped islet, through Posidonia seagrass beds, anemone gardens and a wrecked cargo ship.

22 Sacred **JOURNEYS**

HIKING | WELLNESS | HISTORY

▬▬▬ Rising like an island of honeyed stone in a sea of green, 12th-century Chartreuse de la Verne sits on a forested ridge in the Massif des Maures. Walking trails lead from the monastery into an ancient wilderness of *châtaigneraies* (chestnut groves) and cork oak forests. Take the slow road here – on foot – to embrace an evocative journey of stillness and sacred contemplation.

LEGNA69/GETTY IMAGES ©

🗺 **How to**

Getting here From Collobrières, follow rte de Grimaud (D14) east for 6km, turn right (south) onto the D214 and continue 6km to the monastery. La Môle is 18km from St-Tropez along the D98.

When to go Shoulder seasons are the quietest. Experience cork harvesting mid-June to mid-August; chestnut harvests and festivals (Collobrières' is the biggest) in October.

Local lunch date Reserve a table beneath trees at Collobrières' **La Petite Fontaine** for some *daube de boeuf* (beef stew), sublime fruit tarts and sweet chestnut ice cream.

JUAN CARLOS MUNOZ/SHUTTERSTOCK ©

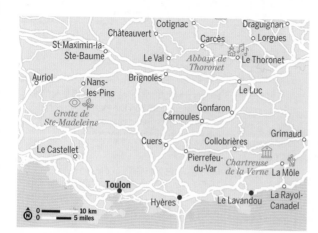

Top left Chartreuse de la Verne
Bottom left Abbaye de Thoronet

ST-TROPEZ & THE VAR EXPERIENCES

The Monks' Trail

Mystery and intrigue cloaks isolated **Chartreuse de la Verne**, founded by Carthusian monks in 1170 on the site of a temple dedicated to goddess Laverna, traditional protector of forest bandits. Park in the car park, 700m away, and enjoy a 10.4km promenade (yellow markers) to and around the monastery. Ravaged by fire, it was largely rebuilt in the 17th and 18th centuries.

Or follow in ancestral monk footsteps with a day hike (23km, 6½ hours) along the circular **Sentier des Moines** (Monks' Trail) from La Môle. Pick up the well-signed trailhead in the car park at the hamlet's western end (D98) and follow the footpath northwest, along the peaceful shores of Barrage de la Verne, and onwards through chestnut groves and perfumed maritime pines to the monastical estate.

Medieval Serenity

Prolong the moment of medieval serenity with a soul-stirring pilgrimage to other sacred sights in the Var – likewise squirrelled away in nature.

Abbaye de Thoronet Enjoy a hauntingly beautiful music concert at this masterpiece of Romanesque architecture, hidden in beech woods. One of three Provençal Cistercian abbeys, highlights include the cloisters, church, chapter house and cellars.

Grotte de Ste-Madeleine In La Ste-Baume, follow a 40-minute forest trail between centurion oaks, pines and maples to the mythical final resting place of Mary Magdalene. From the cave entrance the panorama of Montagne Ste-Victoire, Mont Ventoux and the Alps is breathtaking.

⚗ Harvesting Cork

Cork protects the tree against sun and fire; it doesn't burn. Once stripped of its bark, a cork-oak tree is unprotected for two years.

Harvesting cork is a delicate business. It's only allowed mid-June to mid-August when the tree is physiologically active. The bark must be at least 3cm thick, making the tree a minimum of 40 to 60 years old. One wrong move with the harvester's axe and *la mère* ('the mother') – the amber-coloured layer beneath the cork – is damaged.

Once the cork is removed in half-pipe sheets, the trunk is ginger, wet and wrinkly. Within a couple of months it turns brick-red; within a year, brown; and within 13 years, ready for the next harvest.

■ Insight from Fabien Tambolini, *forest technician and nature guide, Collobrières*

Listings

BEST OF THE REST

 ## Artisan Shopping

K Jacques

The strappy leather sandals handmade at this shoemaker's since 1933 are a St-Tropez icon – Picasso and Bardot both shopped here.

Sunday Saint Tropez

Flowing dresses, peasant tops and daisy-shaped straw bags stitched with 'Love' and other slogans by local brand Mana evoke boho beach vibes at this chic boutique in St-Tropez.

L'Atelier des Jeunes Createurs

'Built and made for French young creators' is the strapline of this concept store on boutique-lined bd Louis Blanc in St-Tropez. Sneakers, sunglasses, stools, swimsuits...

Poterie Provençale Augier

Brighten up your table at home with bold and colourful plates, bowls et al from this traditional pottery on place de l'Ormeau in Ramatuelle.

Meni & Fils

Drool over sausages, terrines, cured meats and ready-made *daube de sanglier* (Provençal wild-boar stew) in this tiny shop in Collobrières.

Caves des Vignerons de Grimaud

Stock up on local table wine (around €2.50 a litre) at Grimaud's wine cooperative, established by local winegrowers in 1932. Find it south of Grimaud village on the St-Tropez-bound D61.

 ## Village & Farm Feasts

Fleur de Sel   €€

Enjoy modern Provençal cuisine at this enchanting bistro, squirrelled away in a former bakery in medieval Grimaud. Alfresco dining is beneath an olive tree.

La Petite Fontaine   €–€€

Locals travel from miles around to lunch at a tree-shaded table on the leafy village square in Collobrières. Reservations are essential, as is hard cash (no credit cards).

Ferme de Peïgros   €

Marry sweeping views of the Massif des Maures with wild boar, pheasant, capon and autumnal *cèpes* (porcini mushrooms) at this rustic goat farm, 1.8km along a gravel track from Col de Babaou (8km from Collobrières).

La Rastègue   €€€

Booking is essential at this seasonal *table d'hôte*–style restaurant in Bormes-les-Mimosas. Views from its seven tables – of the Med from the sea-facing terrace and chefs at work in the open kitchen – are fabulous.

Family Fun

Île de Porquerolles

Sail to this unspoilt island, potter along un-paved trails by bicycle (rent on arrival), picnic on the beach and take a dip in crystal-clear turquoise water: old-school family heaven in a nutshell.

Village des Tortues

Observe one of France's most endangered species on a guided tour of this Massif des Maures sanctuary protecting the Hermann's tortoise. Hatching season is May and June.

Citadelle de St-Tropez

Hike up to St-Tropez' hillside citadel, built in 1602 to defend the coast against Spain. Views are fantastic and all ages love the interactive maritime-history museum in the dungeons, focusing on swashbuckling Tropezienne and Provençal sea-adventurers.

Bravade de St-Tropez

Don traditional costume and join the crowds enjoying an army of 140 musket-firing *bravadeurs* parading a bust of St Torpes, the town's patron, through the streets in mid-May.

Kitesurf on Plage de l'Almanarre

Families with teens will have a kitesurfing ball on this mythical free-rider spot, on the Presqu'île de Giens in Hyères. Beachside Kite Center 83 organises gear and lessons for all abilities, including absolute beginners.

Sweet Treats

La Tarte Tropézienne

Join the queue at this bustling cafe-bakery on place des Lices for a bite of the town's eponymous sugar-crusted, orange-perfumed cake.

La Pâtisserie Cyril Lignac

Baba au rhum topped with Bourbon vanilla whipped cream, creamy pavlova piled high with seasonal fruit, sassy lemon tarts and cherry éclairs to die for. Be prepared to don a few extra calories after a trip to St-Tropez' most gourmet cake shop.

La Maison Barbarac

Expect a rainbow of flavours at this artisan *glacier* (ice-cream shop) in St-Tropez, including some screaming Provence: candied chestnut, watermelon, cherry, even *tarte Tropézienne*.

Confiserie Azuréenne

Don't leave Collobrières without buying signature chestnuts to take home from this local producer. *Marrons glacés* (candied chestnuts), *crème de marrons* (chestnut cream) and chestnut liqueur are epicurean highlights.

Beach Dates

Les Graniers   €€

Follow the street-smart local crowd to this clandestine beach-shack restaurant in

Cycling, Île de Porquerolles

St-Tropez, with tables – quite literally – on the sand. The menu sizzles with barbecued meats and seafood, and fairy lights work their magic after dark.

Chez Camille   €€€

The wood-grilled fish at this fishing cottage, overlooking the beach 6km east of Ramatuelle since 1913, is unmatched. The fourth-generation beach restaurant turns out great bouillabaisse and steak too. Follow signs for 'Bonne Terrasse' creek.

Chez Jo   €€

The ultimate seafood-on-the-sand shack, barebones Chez Jo buzzes with barefoot beach lovers scoffing fresh seafood between sips of Côtes de Provence rosé. Find it on the southwestern end of nudist beach Plage du Layet, near Cavalière.

Couleurs Jardin   €€

Bohemian and chic, this imaginative beachside space is the place to lounge over market- (and fashion-) fuelled food and drinks on cushioned seating beneath trees or the sea-facing terrace. Find it at Plage Gigaro in La Croix-Valmer.

Scan to find more things to do in St-Tropez & the Var online

MARSEILLE

ART | SEAFOOD | NIGHTLIFE

Experience Marseille online

Embark on a snorkelling adventure from **Plage des Catalans** (p137)
🏊 15–30mins from Vieux Port

Learn about prehistoric cave art at **Cosquer Méditerranée** (p137)
Ⓜ 6mins from Gare St-Charles

Tuck into **bouillabaisse** aboard a traditional sailing boat (p134)
Ⓜ 15mins from Gare St-Charles

Mediterranean Sea

Île Ratonneau

Île Pomègues

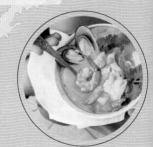

MARSEILLE
Trip Builder

▬▬▬ Bursting with cultural creativity, backdropped by history and anchored by seafaring tradition, Provence's high-octane capital rethinks traditional sightseeing. A bewitching trinity of eclectic museums and galleries, locavore gastronomy and coastal capers is the golden ticket to getting under Marseille's weathered, mistral-whipped skin.

Live the slow life afloat a **Tuba** stand-up paddleboard (p132)
🚲 45mins from Marseille's Vieux Port

Cap Croisette

Catch an exhibition at Marseille's original alternative-arts venue **La Friche La Belle de Mai** (p147)
🚶 18mins from Gare St-Charles

Dance the night away on a Marseille **rooftop** (p146)
🚶 5–20mins from La Canebière

Explore street art and open-air markets in **Notre Dame du Mont** (p138)
🚶 5mins from Cours Julien

Marseille

Blend your own pastis at **Distillerie de la Plaine** (p141)
🚶 20mins from Vieux Port

Shop for vintage fashion on bohemian **Cours Julien** (p139)
🚶 7mins from La Canebière

La Pointe-Rouge

Spend the night in a contemporary-art gallery at **Pavillon Southway** (p144)
🚎 + Ⓜ 30mins from Vieux Port

△ Mont Puget (564m)

Les Goudes

Callelongue

Sormiou

Morgiou

0
0
2 km
1 mile

Practicalities

BELLENA/SHUTTERSTOCK ©

ARRIVING

Aéroport Marseille-Provence (pictured) 25km northwest of the city. Line 91 buses go to/from Marseille's central train station in 25 minutes (single/return €10/16 or €10.90/17.40 including a public-transport ticket). Regional trains stop at Vitrolles-Aéroport Marseille-Provence train station, five minutes from the airport by LeBus +13 (€1.20).

Gare St-Charles Marseille's central train station is a junction for Marseille's two metro lines. Twenty minutes' walk to the Vieux Port.

HOW MUCH FOR A

**Glass of pastis
€4**

**Bouillabaisse
€60 per person**

**Marseille
soap cube
€3.80**

GETTING AROUND

Bicycle & Scooter Reduce your carbon footprint with shared wheels. Pay €1 for a seven-day Le Vélo bike subscription, then €1 per hour; the first 30 minutes are always free. For longer journeys, grab a free-floating e-bike or e-scooter.

Boat The loveliest way to reach Pointe Rouge, L'Estaque and Les Goudes between April and September; boats use the Vieux Port (€5). The cross-port ferry (€0.50), linking its northern and southern quays in five minutes, sails year-round.

Public Transport RTM's two-line metro, trams and buses make light work of zipping around. Services run roughly 5am to midnight and a single ticket is €1.70 (€2 from bus driver, €15 for a 10-ticket carnet).

WHEN TO GO

APR–JUN
Sun-rich days and bountiful markets.

JUL–AUG
High summer; sizzling hot with packed beaches.

SEP–OCT
Crowds dwindle; warm, mellow days usher in the grape harvest.

NOV–MAR
Coastal venues close for winter; low season can be cold, wet and windy.

EATING & DRINKING

As Provence capital and culinary heartland of the region's iconic bouilla-baisse (fish stew; pictured top right), Marseille is epicurean nirvana. Its dining scene has exploded in recent years, elevating grassroots dining and extending menus far beyond bouillabaisse and pizza. Expect a thrilling choice of traditional seafood, world food and militantly locavore, eco-French cuisine. Pedestrian streets around the Vieux Port buzz with touristy restaurant terraces – choose wisely. For world food, dine alfresco on Cours Julien (pictured bottom right) or around Marché des Capucins in multicultural Noailles.

Best plant-based cuisine
Carlotta (p151)

Must-try gastronomy
AM by Alexandre Mazzia (p150)

CONNECT & FIND YOUR WAY

Wi-fi There's free wi-fi at Marseille tourist office and 40 hotspots around town with 30 minutes' free connection. Rent a pocket wi-fi device or buy a SIM card (data-only) at the airport or in town.

Navigation The city is divided into 16 *arrondissements*. Use the Géovélo app to track dedicated cycling lanes and recommended bike routes.

MONEY

Most places accept payment by debit or credit cards alongside cash. The city centre is eminently walkable, but if you do plan to use the metro, buses and trams several times, buy a cent-saving ticket (24/72 hours €5.20/10.80).

WHERE TO STAY

Marseille has ample accommodation options for all budgets. Rates reflect comfort, service and area. Those seeking midrange accommodation will feel most comfortable in the Vieux Port area or southwest along the coast.

Neighbourhood	Pros/Cons
Vieux Port	Central. Harbour views and superb eating, drinking and sightseeing.
St-Charles	Budget hotels and hostels by train station. Excellent transit links.
Le Panier	Hillside 'hood overlooking old port; trendy cafes and bistros.
St-Victor	Ultra-hip waterfront district with great dining and drinking scene. More Airbnbs than hotels.
Corniche John F Kennedy	Upmarket and midrange coastal-road hotels. Easy access to the Prado beaches.
Les Goudes	A bus ride from downtown Marseille. Limited accommodation, with village vibe and bold sea views.

MARSEILLE CITY PASS

This good-value pass (one/two/three days €27/37/43) includes museum admissions, unlimited public transport, public-bike shares, a guided city tour and a Château d'If boat trip.

23 Village Vibe in the **EIGHTH**

NATURE | SEAFOOD | GREAT OUTDOORS

When the dizzying pace of downtown Marseille gets too much, cruise south to the serene 8e *arrondissement*. A hypnotic mirage of ochre-hued *cabanons* (fishing cottages), dusty backstreets and cactus-filled front yards by the sea, the tranquil village of Les Goudes is instant soul balm.

🗺 Trip Notes

Getting here Seasonal RTM boats from Marseille's Vieux Port or bus 19 from Rond-Point du Prado metro to La Madrague de Montredon, then bus 20 to Les Goudes. Count 12km by shared e-scooter or bike.

When to go April to October; almost everything shuts in winter.

Recommended hike A hidden beach with prickly barbary figs and remote lunch shack **Chez Le Belge** (no electricity) is the highlight of a scenic hike to Calanque de Marseilleveyre.

Les Goudes by Stand-Up Paddle

Les Goudes is a very secluded playground. I like to jump off the *calanque* in front of Tuba and paddle towards **Cap Croisette**. It's a short but sturdy ride and whatever the wind direction, you're quite safe. When the breeze is off, cruising around the **Tiboulen de Maire** is a treat!

■ Recommended by Fabrice Denizot, *Marseillais film producer and co-founder of Tuba* @tuba.club

Mediterranean Sea

04 Follow the cool crowd to eco-conscious beach club **Tuba**, with cocktail bar, restaurant and rooftop in a 1960s diving club. Tables on rocks cradle the ultimate Big Blue vista.

02 Admire traditional whitewashed *cabanons* with blue paintwork on **rue Désire Pelaprat**. Then snap **Crack Concrete** (2013), David's silhouette carved in concrete by local sculptor Boris Chouvellon.

Les Goudes

05 Stroll the coastal road to **Callelongue**, a cluster of fishing shacks in *'le bout du monde'* (the end of the world). Join **Raskas Kayak** on a sea-kayaking trek.

●Callelongue

01 Explore wild **Cap Croisette**. Ruined WWII bunkers pepper its barren slopes and a single footpath cuts through sun-scorched rocks to clandestine beach club **La Baie des Singes**. Tan on loungers and scoff seafood.

Île Maïre

03 Watch fishermen tend to their boats and nets over *un café* or the *pêche du jour* (catch of the day) on the mellow waterfront terrace of **Chez Paul – L'Auberge du Corsaire**, much-loved local gathering spot since 1948.

24 Bouillabaisse
REVOLUTION

SEAFOOD | HISTORY | GASTRONOMY

Originally cooked by fisherfolk from the scraps of their catch, bouillabaisse has been Marseille's signature dish since time immemorial. In keeping with the foodie city's experimental and creative spirit, a brigade of contemporary chefs are now shaking up the original die-hard rules to make the traditional fish stew more sustainable in the 21st century.

MICHAEL715/SHUTTERSTOCK ©

📍 **How to**

Top tip Don't trust tourist traps promising cheap bouillabaisse; the real deal is minimum €60 a head and is prepared for at least two people.

Table reservations Essential at the best addresses, a couple of weeks ahead in high season.

Etiquette Forget ordering *une entrée* (starter). Bouillabaisse is a meal in itself, served in two courses: *soupe de poisson* (fish soup) first, followed by filleted fish deboned table-side.

ARTENS/SHUTTERSTOCK ©

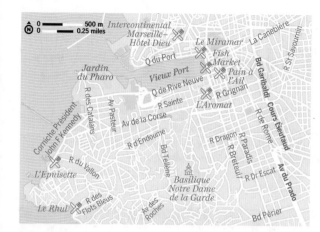

Top left Le Miramar **Bottom left** Fish market, Vieux Port

Bouillabaisse at Sea

Modern bouillabaisse is a return to its origins – to the simplicity of leftovers, scrappy fish heads... It is about lifestyle: buying fish on the quays, shopping at the market, having a drink at the bar, returning home to cook, feasting next day with friends around a *marmite* (shared pot). The best bouillabaisse is always in a family home or *chez le pêcheur* (such as the fishing hut of harpoon fisherman Sylvain Chabasse by Plage Napoléon in Port St-Louis de Rhône).

It's about conviviality. We sail on a wooden sail boat at sunset – silently, there's no motor – into a creek. From a ladder on the boat we swim and snorkel in the open sea. We share bouillabaisse, raw fish and other *petits plats* on deck.

■ **Insights from Christian Qui,** *chef and eco-creative at Bouillabaisse Turfu, Marseille www.bouillabaisse-turfu.com*

Back to Basics

Take a cookery class at **Le Miramar** to understand Marseille's emblematic dish – essential fuel for Greeks settling the sea-faring city around 600 BCE and the dish that Venus, Roman goddess of love, purportedly put husband, Vulcan, to sleep with so she could cavort with her paramour Mars.

The best bouillabaisse takes a day or two to prepare. The longer the potpourri of garlic, onions, tomatoes, fennel, olive oil and saffron simmers, the more flavoursome the resultant broth. Whip up *rouille,* a fiery garlic-chilli mayonnaise, to smear on bite-sized bread toasts and dunk in the soup.

Modern Mashups

Michelin-starred **L'Épuisette** and **Le Rhul** are elegant spots to sample the old-timer stew. Or guess which four fish are incorporated in modern mashups: sip a deconstructed Bouille-a-Baisse milkshake at **Intercontinental Marseille Hôtel Dieu**; scoff fishy bouillabaisse burgers with *panisses* fries at **L'Aromat**; or grab a **pain bouillabaisse** (fish-stew panini) from **Pain à l'Ail**.

Sustainable Marine Cuisine

Purists insist on at least four types of fish being thrown in the pot, including the obligatory *rascasse* (scorpion fish) and St Pierre (John Dory). Yet for Marseille's sustainable-marine cuisine champion Christian Qui, the most authentic bouillabaisse favours the morning's catch hauled to shore by local fishermen – whatever that might be (rarely John Dory!). Linger at the **fish market** on the Vieux Port quays to identify fish species indigenous to Marseille's Mediterranean waters today.

25 Voyage Under
THE SEA

ART | PREHISTORY | SNORKELLING

▬▬▬ The accidental discovery of Grotte Cosquer and the priceless treasure it hides, buried at sea for millennia, is the stuff of French sci-fi – the fantastical tale would sit quite comfortably in a Jules Vernes adventure story. Create your own extraordinary voyage under the sea with this deep dive into Marseille's fascinating subaquatic world and the rich biodiversity it squirrels away.

SOPA IMAGES/GETTY IMAGES ©

🗺 How to

When to go May, June and September. Risk of forest fires can close footpaths into the Parc National des Calanques in July and August.

What to bring Your tuba, mask and flippers to snorkel. Swimsuit, sun shades and skin protection too.

Avoid the crowd In July and August access to Calanque de Sugiton is limited to 500 visitors a day; reserve your spot up to three days in advance (*www.calanques-parcnational.fr*).

AVIM WU/SHUTTERSTOCK ©

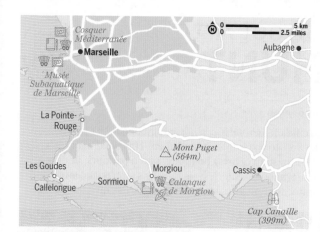

Top left Cave paintings, Cosquer Méditerranée **Bottom left** Calanque de Morgiou

ⓘ Top Tips

Marked by a white resting buoy, the Musée Subaquatique recalls the permanent link that unites man with nature – our survival depends on its state. It underlines the beauty of the sea and the need to preserve it for future generations.

Always observe the sea before going in to meet it – we are the guests in this environment. Visit in the morning when the water is calmer, clearer. Tell someone on the beach that you're going to the museum. Just like in scuba diving, visit in pairs with mask and snorkel fins, shorty or anti-UV T-shirt in summer and wetsuit in mid-season.

■ Tips by **Antony Lacanaud**, *Marseille diver, environmentalist and founder of Musée Subaquatique de Marseille @underwatermuseumfrance*

PHOTO: GUILLAUME RUOPPOLO ©

Prehistoric Booty

Fire your imagination at **Calanque de Morgiou**, one of several coves spangling the wild, cliff-carved coast south of the city. Here, in 1985, local diver Henri Cosquer discovered an underwater cave daubed with 20,000-year-old Palaeolithic rock art. Protected and off-limits today, the miraculously preserved chamber is submerged 37m deep, reached via a 116m-long tunnel.

Evoke the diver's journey with an idyllic bob around the cove's turquoise water by **kayak**, **boat** or **paddleboard**. Picture prehistoric artists approaching the cave 30,000 years ago – on dry land and 6km from shore when sea levels were 120m lower.

Cosquer Méditerranée

Plunge into the mysterious world of cave diving at **Cosquer Méditerranée** in La Joliette, Marseille's old maritime neighbourhood. 'Descend' 37m under the sea and, in semi-darkness, ride an electric exploratory vehicle through the cave – a brilliant 3D replica – plastered with a dazzling bestiary of bisons, horses, monk seals and extinct megaloceros. Come up for air in the museum's top-floor exhibition area to learn the what, why and how behind some of the world's rarest and most remarkable cave art.

The Thrill of the Underworld

Feel the thrill of the aquatic underworld at the **Musée Subaquatique de Marseille** on Plage des Catalans – deep-sea divers can shore dive with a professional diving guide. Swim 100m from the sandy shore to observe giant contemporary sculptures and accompanying flora, displayed 5m deep on the seabed.

26 Street Art
HUNT

STREET ART | CULTURE | SHOPPING

━━━━━ Load a map of Marseille's 16 *arrondissements* and infamous '111 villages' and pinch east of the Vieux Port to zoom into Cours Julien. This bohemian neighbourhood in the 16e – a mashup of artsy boutique, tattoo parlours, underground music venues and international eateries – is the city's street-art central and vintage-fashion hub. En route, hunt mosaics by iconic street-artist Invader.

JAVIER GARCIA BLANCO/GETTY IMAGES ©

🗺️ How to

Getting here Walk 1km east (15 minutes) from Vieux Port's Quai des Belges or take M2 to the Notre Dame du Mont–Cours Julien metro stop.

Opening hours Shops tend to open 2pm to 7pm Monday, and 10am or 11am to 7pm Tuesday to Saturday. After 5pm is the time to lap up the neighbourhood's electric evening vibe.

Street art Download the free smartphone app FlashInvader to track down and 'flash' the street mosaics of Invader.

OLRAT/SHUTTERSTOCK ©

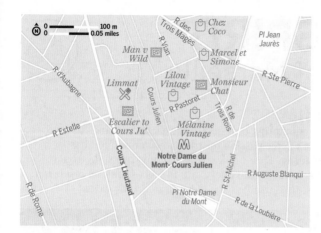

Top left Rainbow staircase, Cours Julien **Bottom left** Cours Julien

☆ Camille's Little Black Book

Fave cafe Café La Muse at 8am for a coffee and breakfast, or for *'le afterwork'* from 7pm. The chef makes an incredible crispy chicken with secret homemade sauce, and in season it has super oysters.

Boutique shopping For vintage clothes, Kosmik Palace or Le Mercato. For vinyls, Extend and Play.

Dining tips La Cantinetta for Italian and El Santo Cachon for Chilean cuisine. Brulerie Moka does a wonderful cappuccino and cinnamon roll.

And for a quick bite? Le Dernier Metro, a tobacconist-bar-bistro that has always been there! They know every client like family.

Best night out? La Bisette, a bar-club open until 2am with cool DJ line-ups Thursday to Saturday. Waaw for Saturday-night karaoke.

■ Recommended by Camille Calancha, *press officer in Marseille* @camilleclch

Rainbows & Turtles

Ascending from the Notre Dame du Mont metro station, you are hit by the 'hood's most iconic street art: the *escalier* (staircase) climbing up to Cours Ju' (as locals call the wide and elongated, partly pedestrianised square) is painted every colour of the rainbow. Snag a ringside seat at **Limmat** for a fashionable plant-based lunch with riotous art view.

On nearby rue Vian, **Mahn Kloix**' gargantuan turtle snakes grotesquely up the facade of No 5 in an artistic *Man v Wild* face-off. If you eyeball a colourfully painted portrait of a woman staring from a wall, it will be the hand of Provençal female artist **Manyoly**. Toothy-grin cats are the domain of **Monsieur Chat**.

Vintage Chic

Fashionistas scour secondhand boutiques for retro pieces on rue des Trois Mages. Garments from the 1940s to '80s fill **Marcel et Simone** (No 30); bellbottoms and hippy ponchos scream the '70s in **Chez Coco** (No 13); and the party never stops at '80s and '90s specialist **Mélanine Vintage** (No 10). On rue Pastoret you can't miss **Lilou Vintage**'s fire-engine-red facade.

To Market

Cours Julien's emblematic cultural venues and eateries moved in after the city's 19th-century central market, piled high with fruit and veg along much of its length, moved out in 1973. Small specialist markets still set Cours Julien abuzz: flowers (Wednesday and Saturday), antique books (alternate Saturdays) and stamps and/or antiquarian books (Sunday).

SPIRIT
of Marseille

ISLAND VIBES | COCKTAILS | DRINKING

▬▬▬ Marry the nation's unfaltering devotion to the sacrosanct apéritif (pre-meal drink) with Marseille's fierce passion for traditional anise-fired pastis, and you get a foolproof pairing. Throw a desert island, invasive spiky-green agave succulents and an eco-warrior distillery into the mix – and the result is a brilliant new creative twist to Marseille's age-old artisan drinks scene.

YANN GUICHAOUA-PHOTOS/GETTY IMAGES ©

🞖 How to

Getting there *Frioul If Express* boats sail between the Vieux Port and the dyke-linked Îles du Frioul.

At the bar Order pastis by brand (Ricard, Pastis 51 etc).

Drinking instructions Pastis is always served deconstructed: a 20mL shot in a glass, a jug of water and ice cubes. Dilute the amber-coloured spirit (roughly five parts water to one part pastis), watching it turn milky as you pour. Add ice afterwards.

REDAKCO/GETTY IMAGES ©

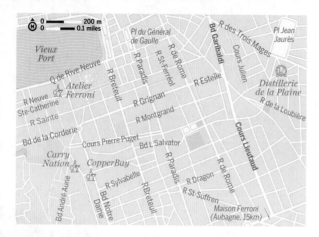

Top left Îles du Frioul **Bottom left** Pastis

Island Invasion

Several thousand kilometres away it's called tequila or mezcal. In Marseille the crystal-clear spirit is bottled as Josiane. Its hand-engraved label reads 'Product of uprooting invasive, exotic plants in the Calanques National Park and Frioul Archipelago'.

Brought from Mexico to southern France's sun-blazed gardens as an ornamental plant in the 16th century, *agave Americana* now menaces native ecosystems along Marseille's coast. From the Vieux Port sail to the **Îles du Frioul** and hike around the barren outcrops to see the giant octopus-esque plants in situ.

Artisan Alchemy

Fleshy agave hearts are crushed, pressed, fermented and double-distilled to become highly desirable Josiane. Other distillers in Marseille are practicing similar artisan alchemy to upcycle green waste: dabble in distilling gin or pastis at blending workshops run by **Distillerie de la Plaine** near Cours Julien; learn about Provence's indigenous botanicals and visit the gardens, maceration rooms and cellars at the **Maison Ferroni** distillery in Aubagne; or sign up for a gin or rum cocktail masterclass at **Atelier Ferroni** on rue Neuve Sainte Catherine, 7e.

Down the Hatch

Toast your newfound knowledge with a 'Made in Marseille' cocktail. Cocktail bar **CopperBay** (of Paris renown) partners with Distillerie de la Plaine to distill its own house pastis. Or celebrate French boutique spirits at 1920s speakeasy **Carry Nation** (reserve a table to receive address and code to enter).

⊙ Meet the Maker

Inspiration behind Josiane? Instinctive travels (my own and others) and Frioul island footpaths.

Cocktail suggestion? My friends and I prefer to drink Josiane pure. But we have mixed our own kind of Paloma-style cocktail using homemade Kombucha – it was summery and splendid!

Fave bar to drink Josiane? On the terrace of Tuba in Les Goudes, fresh out of the fridge, straight, as the opening shot of an *apéro* with good friends.

Hot tip Watch for our oak-barrel-aged Josiane, a mezcal aged by Guillaume Ferroni at Maison Ferroni in Aubagne. Try it in its bar Dans Les Arbres at Château des Creissauds.

■ Recommended by Axel Schindlbeck, *Marseille-based designer, design professor and Josiane co-founder @josianelespritdagave*

PHOTO: LORRAINE HELLWIG ©

28 The New
GALLERISTS

ART | MUSEUMS | URBAN LIFE

▬▬▬ Marseille has embraced contemporary art ever since homegrown sculptor César stuck out his thumb – all 6m of it – with such aplomb in the 1980s. Today a young generation of artist-gallerists are curating powerful exhibitions to tell new stories about their city.

How to

Getting here Use public transport or bike-share Le Vélo. For César's thumb, ride the metro to Prado then bus 23 or 45 to the Haïfa-Marie-Louise stop. For La Cité Radieuse: metro to Castellane, then bus 1 to the 'Le Corbusier' stop; continue to the Michelet Blanc stop for Southway Studio.

When to go Any time of year; early summer ushers in the season's new exhibitions.

What's on Check current exhibitions with Marseille tourist office *(marseille-tourisme. com).*

Open House

Debunking myths, breaking with traditional scenography, and immersing visitors in a story that is accessible to everyone are the fundamental goals of Marseille's new gallerists. This is a generation of young artists, designers and talent-spotters who curate provocative exhibitions – occasionally in the unlikeliest of places.

In the residential 8e *arrondissement*, buried on the 4th floor of La Cité Radieuse, it's open house at **Maison Mirbel**. This is the hybrid showroom-boutique-office of interior designer Ginie Bel where furnishings – 1950s to pieces by emerging designers – change every few months. Smaller, cabinet-of-curiosity purchases like embroidered postcards and candles celebrate 'Made in Marseille' slow design.

A few blocks south, aficionados of the mid-19th-century Arts and Craft movement

Top left Rooftop, MAMO (p145) **Bottom left** MAMO (p145)

overnight at **Pavillon Southway**, the *maison d'art* of Marseillais artist, designer and curator Emmanuelle Luciani. This unique B&B allows art lovers to spend a night in an art gallery and artist residency dedicated to 'decorative, domestic and handmade art'.

Gallery can likewise morph into inhabited interior with **Pièce à Part**, the itinerant art and design studio of Emmanuelle Oddo. The talented Marseillais curator also collaborates with **Sessùn Alma**, a riveting artisan concept store, bookshop and cafe-kitchen, at home in an old soap factory on rue Sainte, 7e. To watch local artists at work, sign up for a workshop (€30) embracing everything from floral art to vegetal silk-dyes, ceramics and plant cuisine.

Among the Clouds

When the decaying rooftop of Le Corbusier's brutalist apartment block **La Cité Radieuse** (1947–52) popped up for sale in 2010, it was snapped up by **Ora ïto** *(ora-ito.com)*. The world-famous Marseillais designer restored

🖾 Southway Studio

I make works that pay tribute to medieval culture and antiquity, as well as bas-reliefs sculpted with the symbol of Olympique de Marseille (OM). For me, everything is linked. Growing up in Marseille is to grow up on limestone rocks, a necromass of fish bones. Walls have a history spanning 2600 years. I am inevitably carried by the weight and vertigo of this vast past.

Southway Studio is installed in a pavilion from the end of the 19th century, so you can discover walls from this great period as well as works inspired by a fantasised ancient past or by its soccer club perhaps.

■ Recom-
mended by
**Emmanuelle
Luciani,** *curator,
art historian, gallerist at
Pavillon Southway Studio,
Marseille*
@pavillon_southwaystudio

PHOTO: FLORIAN TOUZET ©

☆ Best Independent Galleries

Galerie Alexis Pentcheff Magnificent paintings by southern landscape artists like Albert Marquet.

Voiture 14 Project space for emerging artistic practices, directed by Myriam Mokdes, presents a completely different vision of art.

Jogging Not a gallery, more a lifestyle store showing a fresh way to understand Marseille.

it to share with his city as a free and extraordinary 'place among the clouds devoted to art and design'.

It's hard not to fall hard for **MaMo** (an acronym of 'Marseille' and 'Modulor'). The rooftop art space stages large-scale artworks to dramatic effect and occasionally favours talented Marseille gallerists like Emmanuelle Luciani when it comes to curating its top-drawer seasonal exhibitions. More modest-sized, winter exhibitions take place in Le Corbusier's former gym, a covered space on the roof.

Back at the Museum

Return to the mainstream with Marseille's well-established contemporary-art museums. Before entering the **Musée d'Art Contemporain (MAC)**, admire César's iconic **bronze pouce** (thumb) installed in the middle of the Rond Point de Bonne-veine roundabout in front. Inside MAC, the crushed cars that the Marseille sculptor César Baldaccini (1921–98) is best known for jostle for the limelight with works by Christo, Andy Warhol, Jean-Michel Basquiat and Nice New Realists Yves Klein and Ben.

The glass-and-steel architecture of **Fonds Régional d'Art Contemporain (FRAC)** in former docks La Joliette is as arresting as the exhibitions held inside. It's the space to tune into thought-provoking installations, decorative arts and other grassroots works by artists from all over the region.

Left & above Pavillon Southway Studio **Top** *The Port of Marseille* by Albert Marquet (1916).

29 Rooftop Bar **CRAWL**

COCKTAILS | DANCING | LIVE MUSIC

Some of the best summer nights in Provence's sultry capital unfold up high on hidden rooftops. Start at sundown with 360-degree sunset views and party until dawn with drinks, dancing and expertly mixed tunes. Expect a local hipster crowd, craft cocktails and cool factor *extrême*.

HEMIS/ALAMY STOCK PHOT

♪♪ **The Place to Be**

Le Baou is a great rooftop with a view on Marseille's Quartiers Nord. Bands and DJs play here all summer.

It's not a rooftop, but **Le Cabanon de Paulette** on Plage de l'Abri Côtier, 8e, is a good place to chill at sunset over mussels and fries, beer and acoustic music.

■ Recommended by Sian Criscuolo, *Marseille communications creative @siancriscuolo*

📔 **Trip Notes**

When to go April to October; rooftops are seasonal and also shut on wet or mistral-whipped summer days.

Opening hours Typically 7pm to 1am or 2am; rooftops serving lunch from 12.30pm remain open all afternoon.

Best non-rooftop Marseille's original 'bar with million-dollar views', aka the hotly contested balcony overlooking the Vieux Port at **La Caravelle**.

Top tip Some bars are cashless; grab a rechargeable card at the entrance and load it with euros online.

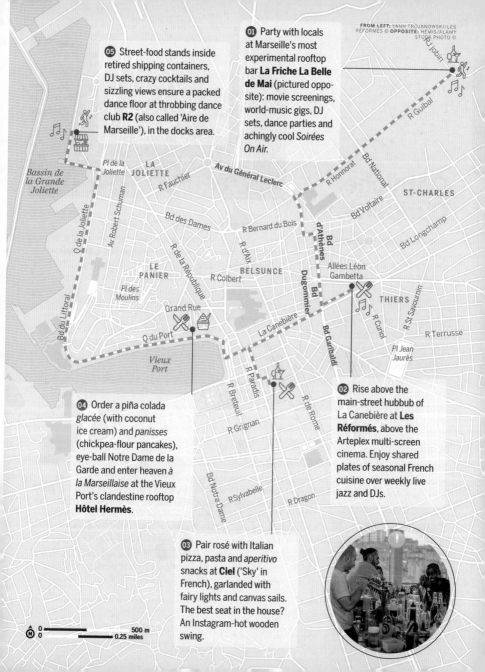

05 Street-food stands inside retired shipping containers, DJ sets, crazy cocktails and sizzling views ensure a packed dance floor at throbbing dance club **R2** (also called 'Aire de Marseille'), in the docks area.

01 Party with locals at Marseille's most experimental rooftop bar **La Friche La Belle de Mai** (pictured opposite): movie screenings, world-music gigs, DJ sets, dance parties and achingly cool *Soirées On Air.*

04 Order a piña colada *glacée* (with coconut ice cream) and *panisses* (chickpea-flour pancakes), eye-ball Notre Dame de la Garde and enter heaven *à la Marseillaise* at the Vieux Port's clandestine rooftop **Hôtel Hermès**.

02 Rise above the main-street hubbub of La Canebière at **Les Réformés**, above the Arteplex multi-screen cinema. Enjoy shared plates of seasonal French cuisine over weekly live jazz and DJs.

03 Pair rosé with Italian pizza, pasta and *aperitivo* snacks at **Ciel** ('Sky' in French), garlanded with fairy lights and canvas sails. The best seat in the house? An Instagram-hot wooden swing.

Corniche Curiosities

MYTHS AND QUIRKS ALONG MARSEILLE'S COASTAL ROAD

'La corniche' is one of those iconic strips. Sea and sunset views are gold, and the catwalk of local life that unfurls along its much-loved 5km length is intoxicating. Promenade slowly on foot, hop on a bus for bolder views from up high, or grab shared electric wheels (bike or scooter) to glide along in bewitching e-powered silence.

Two Aqueducts & an Assassination

Until the 1850s the corniche ribboning south along the coast from the historic cove of **Plage des Catalans** to **Plages du Prado** (a 1970s reclamation job, all tiny pebbles, created from backfill from excavations for Marseille's metro) was nothing more than a rocky coastal path fringed with the occasional weathered fishing hut or elegant villa with priceless sea view. In 1848 building work began on two viaducts to navigate the ancient fishing coves of **Vallon des Auffes** and **Anse de la Fausse Monnaie** (Counterfeit Money Cove). A century later, in the mid-1950s, the road was modernised and in 1963, just months after US president John Kennedy was assassinated, the new seaside road was ready to be named: Corniche John F Kennedy.

Point Zero

The exact 'point zero' from which Provence's stone-capped peak Mont Ventoux (1909m) and every other altitude in France are measured slumbers – largely unnoticed – at No 174 on the corniche. Installed in 1883, **Le Marégraphe de Marseille** is a tide gauge that mechanically measures mean sea levels each week, assisted by a digital wave-radar device since 1998. Look for an attractive, cream-stone cottage with terracotta-tiled roof and walled courtyard, perched on rocks across the cove from 19th-century villa and gastronomic icon **Le Petit Nice**.

Left Vallon des Auffes, 1905 **Middle** Le Marégraphe de Marseille **Right** Plage des Catalans

A Desert Island

Across the water from the tide gauge slumbers pinprick **Île Degaby** – an uninhabited islet pierced with an ancient fort and used as the private, paparazzi-free beach of a luxury hotel in downtown Marseille. The fort was built under Louis XIV in 1703, later used to isolate plague victims, and was gifted to music-hall star Liane Degaby by her wealthy industrialist husband in 1914. Should you be a guest at **Hôtel C2**, lounge on parasol-shaded sun beds, swim from the deck, eyeball fish with a snorkel and enjoy the thrill of decadent desert-island life.

> Love-struck teens smooch, street-smart skateboarders cruise to Prado's world-famous 'bowl' and carefree tomb-stoners leap into the sea.

Bench Mark

Throw yourself into the melting pot of local life. The silky-smooth pavement of *la corniche* buzzes with runners, cyclists and dog walkers. Love-struck teens smooch, street-smart skateboarders cruise to Prado's world-famous 'bowl' and carefree tomb-stoners leap into the sea from 14m-high rocks around **Anse de Malmousque**.

Come sunset, romantics grab a craft beer and pizza from a food truck to devour on the beach or **the world's longest concrete bench**, running much of the length of the long, wide, silky smooth prom. If you happen to be in town in summer 2024, this will be the perfect pew to watch the nautical events of the **Paris Summer Olympics**.

🛆 Say it in Bronze

Storied sculptures bookend the corniche. Join Gaston Castel's bronze female figure walking to victory beneath a sea-facing arch at the **Monument aux Morts de l'Armée d'Orient et des Terres Lointaines** (1927) – a WWI memorial opposite No 60.

Further down the prom, a 9m-high **boat propeller blade** in bronze evokes French repatriates' homecoming voyage across the Med from Algeria to Marseille in 1962. Marseille-born César Baldaccini (1921–98), after whom the French César film awards are named, sculpted the emotive tribute.

In front of the Prado sands, nod and blush at **David** – a 1903 marble replica by Marseille sculptor Jules Cantini (1826–1916) of Michelangelo's Herculean, world-famous nude.

Listings

BEST OF THE REST

Parks & Picnic Spots

Jardin du Pharo

The closest green escape to downtown Marseille, these peaceful palace gardens with pea-green lawns bejewel Napoleon III's 19th-century Palais du Pharo. With its unparalleled views, this is an ideal spot for a sunset aperitif.

Jardin des Migrations

Planted on sea-facing slopes within Fort St-Jean, this aromatic dry garden evokes cultural diversity and plant migration in the Mediterranean region. Don't miss the *potager* packed with vegetables typical to Provençal ratatouille.

Jardin de la Colline Puget

Waterfalls, sculptures, ivy-stitched grottoes and vintage stone staircases create storybook enchantment in Marseille's oldest public garden, landscaped in 1801 on the slopes of Colline Puget above the Vieux Port. Summer cocktail bar too!

Parc Borély

Follow the serenity-seeking locals and go to Marseille's prettiest park, a 17th-century love child with an ornamental lake, a château, floral botanical gardens and a giant insect hotel.

Sacred Highs

Basilique Notre Dame de la Garde

Unmatched views – the sunset show is breathtaking – unfold from Marseille's Romano-Byzantine church, teetering on the city's highest point. Its 9.7m-tall statue of La Bonne Mère (The Good Mother) has protected sailors since the 19th century.

Cathédrale Ste-Marie-Majeure de Marseille

Marseille's totemic cathedral, built in green Florentine marble and slate-grey stone from Cassis further along the coast, is well worth exploring. Finish in the 19th-century vaulted warehouses beneath the church, which have been upcycled into restaurants and boutiques.

Abbaye St-Victor

Watch for free organ and classical-music concerts at this fortress-like abbey, built on a 3rd-century-BCE necropolis and the birthplace of Christianity in Marseille. Stunning acoustics.

Modern Flavours

AM   €€€

Reserve well in advance to score a spot at Alexandre Mazzia's tiny Michelin triple-starred restaurant where flavours from around the world – including the Republic of

Parc Borély

Basilique Notre Dame de la Garde

the Congo, where the chef was born – marry beautifully with those of the homegrown Mediterranean.

La Bonne Mère €

Scoffing wood-fired pizza is as sacred in Marseille as its OM football team. Try this pizzeria near Basilique Notre Dame de la Garde for its great selection of classic pies.

Chez Étienne €

This family-friendly local favourite has long prided itself on its menu of hand-thrown pizza and other authentic Neapolitan mains. Cash only.

L'Eau a la Bouche €

Unusual ingredients like mussels, banana and Roquefort are spread across crisp pizza crusts at one of the city's best Italian spots. Booking ahead is advised.

Carlotta €

Sample the delicious new urban trend for deli dining at this gourmet *épicerie* (delicatessen) in the foodie-oriented 6e *arrondissement* – 100% plant-based to boot. Pair falafel, shakshouka, imaginatively roasted vegetables and creative salads with natural wines.

Maison des Nines €€

A trio of women working in finance ditched their Parisian day jobs to open this funky *table d'hôte* (shared table dining) and pop-up brunch venue in epicurean Noailles near Cours Julien.

Ancient to African Art

Mucem

Dip into the history and culture of the Mediterranean through events, anthropological exhibits and rotating art exhibitions at this sea-facing Marseille icon. The thrilling contemporary building by Algerian-born, Marseille-educated architect Rudy Ricciotti is James Bond–esque.

La Vieille Charité

Tribal masks, pottery and other arts and crafts from the Americas, Africa and the Pacific fill one of two museums nestled inside this grand almshouse, built by Marseille architect Pierre Puget (1620–94), in the rambling heart of old-world Le Panier.

Musée Cantini

Superb pieces of 17th- and 18th-century Provençal art, coupled with Marseille-themed works by Max Ernst, Joan Miró et al, make this 17th-century mansion turned museum a must. Sculptor Jules Cantini lived here until his death in 1916.

Coffee, Cocktails & Craft Beer

Deep   €

'Legal high for people with good taste' is the strapline of this coffee shop and roastery, the discerning address near the Vieux Port for a serious espresso or flat white over magazine-browsing or alfresco. Fantastic cakes and barista-led cuppings.

Gaspard   €€

Mixologists work with surprising ingredients, spices and flavours from the Far East (matcha green tea, citrusy yuzu) to shake truly fabulous cocktails. Decor blends retro Tiki with industrial chic.

Mucem

Livingston €€

Hipsters hobnob over *vin orange* (in a nutshell: white wine vinified like red) and other hard-to-find vintages by small independent winegrowers at this super-chill wine bar, bistro and Cours Julien hang-out. It's only open in the summer.

Zoumaï €

Organic, gourmet beers are different every season at this highly inventive artisan brewery near place Castellane. Check its Facebook page for dance parties, eco-lectures, zero-waste apéritif soirées and what's hot at its weekly farmers market.

 Wine, Biscuits & Balls

Microcosmos

Purchase small-production, organic wine from Provence's only urban winemakers Fabienne and Lukas, with a *chai* (cellar) on rue de l'Eveché and teeny vineyards dotted around Provence; advance appointments essential.

Jogging

On-trend concept store bursting with fashion, homewares, design objects and vintage by local and Mediterranean artists, designers and brands. Jogging's seaside *cabanon* (cabin) to

Jardin du Pharo (p150)

rent in Calanque de Samena is the ultimate sleep getaway.

Maison de la Boule

Buy handmade boules to take back home and play *pétanque* with. Indoor court too and a museum exploring the history of Provence's iconic sport, including the curious figure of Fanny: if you lose a game 13–0, kiss her bare bum cheeks.

Four des Navettes

Marseille's oldest bakery has been baking the city's signature *navettes de Marseille* (boat-shaped biscuits perfumed with orange blossom) and Provençal *calissons* (almond and melon sweet bites) since 1871.

30 Escape to Woolf's **PARADISE**

LITERATURE | WINE | GREAT OUTDOORS

Glamour-kissed Cassis, 30km southwest of Marseille, has been immortalised in art and literature since the 19th century when Provençal poet Frédéric Mistral sought inspiration in the then-sleepy fishing village. In the 1920s London's Bloomsbury set wrote in this bijou wine-producing haven by the sea – '*un petit paradis!*' in the words of Virginia Woolf. The seduction remains timeless.

CHRIS HELLIER/GETTY IMAGES ©

🗺 **How to**

Getting here Twenty minutes by train from Marseille (€7) to Cassis train station, then bus M1 to the waterfront village 3.5km away.

When to go Low or shoulder seasons; July and August are uncomfortably crowded.

Belle Époque bolthole
Perched on a cliff with big bold sea views and pool suspended between rocks, art deco villa-hotel Les Roches Blanches (The White Rocks) is as irresistible as it was in its 1920s heyday.

JEAN-LUC ICHARD/GETTY IMAGES ©

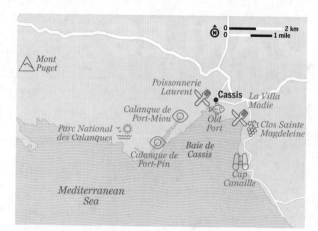

Top left Cap Canaille **Bottom left** Old port, Cassis

Catch of the day Fishing has fuelled seafaring Cassis since Ligurians settled here around 500 BCE. Mooch at the boat-filled **old port** where Winston Churchill set up his easel in the 1920s to paint the market stalls and colourful cottages *en plein air*. Take in views over local white and the day's catch at 1850s fishmonger-bistro **Poissonnerie Laurent**. Or join gastronomes feasting on sea urchins and blue lobster with a spectacular twist at triple-Michelin-starred **La Villa Madie**, overlooking pebbly cove **Anse de Corton**.

Santé! AOC Cassis is one of France's oldest wine appellations – explore on foot, by bicycle or e-bike. Pick up trail maps and lists of estates offering *dégustation* (tasting) at **Cassis tourist office**. By the port, sea-facing **Clos Sainte Magdeleine** has a viticultural pedigree stretching back to the 1800s. Post-tasting, indulge in a siesta on the pebbly beach at **Anse de l'Arène**.

Cruise the crests Experience the heart-pounding raw beauty of Cassis' majestic setting along the clifftop **Route des Crêtes**. Head south along the D141 and ribbon up to **Cap Canaille**, a sandstone cape crowned by Europe's highest sea cliff (363m). Pull over to swoon over dizzying views of Lego-like Cassis down below and **Mont Puget** (564m), the highest peak in the **Massif des Calanques**.

Turquoise creeks Pocket-sized pebble beaches slipping into gin-clear emerald waters reward those who venture into the wild **Parc National des Calanques**. From Cassis' old port, hike 1.5km to **Calanque de Port-Miou** and another 1.5km to **Calanque de Port-Pin**.

Best Outdoor Adventures

Cassis' enviable geographic location ushers in myriad ways to explore by land and sea.

Kayak a trio of calanques Hook up with Cassis-based Calanc'O to kayak from Cassis to Calanque de Port-Miou, Calanque d'En-Vau and Calanque de Port-Pin; half- or full day.

Stand-up paddle beneath sky-high cliffs Cap Canaille views are gargantuan and awe-inspiring throughout this cove-to-cove paddle with Calanc'O from Plage du Corton (Anse du Corton) to Plage de l'Arène (Anse de l'Arène).

Cruise the coast by boat Les Bateliers Cassidains runs boat trips year-round from quai St-Pierre at Cassis port along the Parc National des Calanques' crenellated coastline.

AIX TO ARLES

ART | CULTURE | FOOD

**Experience
Aix & Arles
online**

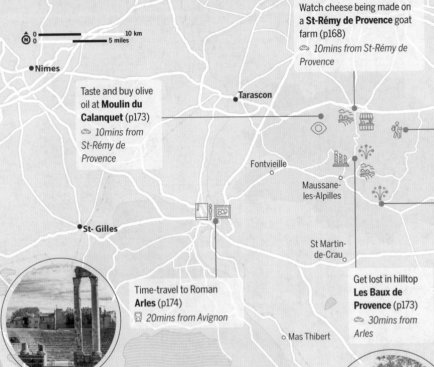

Watch cheese being made on a **St-Rémy de Provence** goat farm (p168)
10mins from St-Rémy de Provence

Taste and buy olive oil at **Moulin du Calanquet** (p173)
10mins from St-Rémy de Provence

Tarascon

Fontvieille

Maussane-les-Alpilles

St Martin-de-Crau

St- Gilles

Nîmes

0 ——— 10 km
0 ——— 5 miles

Time-travel to Roman **Arles** (p174)
20mins from Avignon

Get lost in hilltop **Les Baux de Provence** (p173)
30mins from Arles

Mas Thibert

AIX TO ARLES
Trip Builder

Be it playing the graceful *flâneur* in elegant Aix-en-Provence, touring bucolic vineyard and mountain scapes painted by Cézanne or trailing Roman gladiators in Arles, this part of Provence has it all: history, art and nature in spades.

Explore the **Côte Bleue** in a traditional wooden fishing boat (p167)
/ 1hr from Marseille

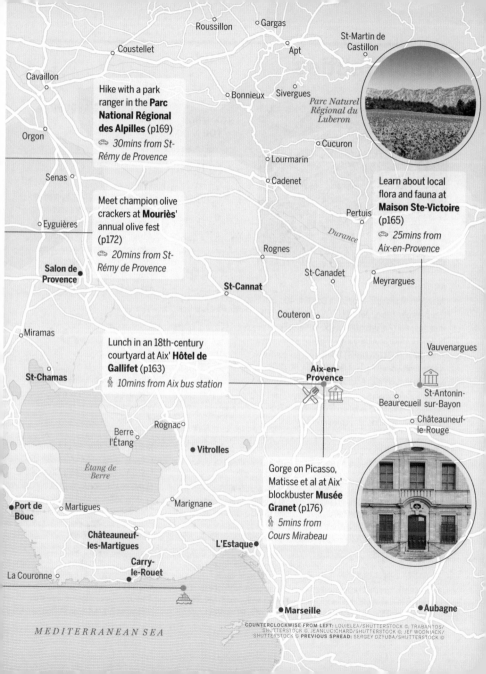

Roussillon Gargas
St-Martin de
Castillon

Coustellet

Cavaillon

Apt

Bonnieux Sivergues

Parc Naturel Régional du Luberon

Orgon

Hike with a park ranger in the **Parc National Régional des Alpilles** (p169)

🚗 *30mins from St-Rémy de Provence*

Cucuron

Senas

Lourmarin

Cadenet

Learn about local flora and fauna at **Maison Ste-Victoire** (p165)

🚗 *25mins from Aix-en-Provence*

Eyguières

Meet champion olive crackers at **Mouriès'** annual olive fest (p172)

🚗 *20mins from St-Rémy de Provence*

Pertuis

Durance

Salon de Provence

Rognes

St-Canadet

Meyrargues

St-Cannat

Couteron

Miramas

Lunch in an 18th-century courtyard at Aix' **Hôtel de Gallifet** (p163)

🚶 *10mins from Aix bus station*

Vauvenargues

Aix-en-Provence

St-Chamas

St-Antonin-sur-Bayon

Beaurecueil

Châteauneuf-le-Rouge

Berre l'Étang Rognac

Vitrolles

Étang de Berre

Gorge on Picasso, Matisse et al at Aix' blockbuster **Musée Granet** (p176)

🚶 *5mins from Cours Mirabeau*

Port de Bouc Martigues

Marignane

Châteauneuf-les-Martigues

L'Estaque

Carry-le-Rouet

La Couronne

Marseille Aubagne

MEDITERRANEAN SEA

Practicalities

SEAN NEL/SHUTTERSTOCK ©

ARRIVING

Aéroport Marseille-Provence Bus line 40 shuttles between the airport, Aix TGV train station (10 minutes) and Aix bus station (35 minutes) every half-hour from around 5am to 11pm.

Aix TGV station (pictured) 15km from Aix centre; on the high-speed Paris–Marseille line. Bus 40 links the station with Aix bus station (15 minutes).

Arles train station Regular trains to/from Marseille (one hour) and Avignon (20 minutes). The nearest TGV stations are Nîmes and Avignon.

**HOW MUCH
FOR A**

1L of olive oil
€30

Aix Festival ticket
€50–300

E-bike rental
€35–45 per day

GETTING AROUND

Train & Bus Travelling by rail between Aix-en-Provence and Arles (two hours) requires a change of train in Marseille. A handful of daily buses on line 54 link Arles and St-Rémy de Provence (50 minutes); check schedules on zou.maregionsud.fr.

Car & Motorcycle Despite the high-season headache of parking in towns, driving is the most practical way of navigating this rural area. Car-sharing service BlaBlaCar (*blablacar.fr*) works well between towns. For scenic sidecar tours and motorcycle taxis, Aix-based La Belle Chappée (*labelleechappee.fr*) is gold.

Bicycle Away from towns, quiet country lanes are bliss to cycle. Rent regular or electric-assisted wheels in Aix, Arles or St-Rémy.

WHEN TO GO

APR–JUN
Sun-blessed days, few crowds and produce-laden food markets.

JUL–AUG
Sizzling hot days; prestigious arts and music festivals.

SEP–OCT
Pleasantly warm temperatures, ideal for hiking and biking; grape-harvest season.

NOV–MAR
Low season, with occasional mistral-whipped days; olives are harvested.

EATING & DRINKING

Must-tries include Brousse du Rove goat's cheese and Alpilles lamb, salads with Saragna chicory (pictured top right), and melon- and almond-laced *calissons* from Aix-en-Provence. Arlesian dining plays with red Camargue rice (pictured bottom right), *taureau* (bull), locally farmed *fleur de sel* (salt) and *tellines* (wedge clams) pan-fried with parsley and garlic. Pays d'Aix produces top-quality olives and rosés (AOC Côteaux d'Aix-en-Provence and Côtes de Provence Ste-Victoire). For reds and whites, seek out AOC Les Baux de Provence and AOC Palette.

Best hilltop-village lunch
Dan B (p176)

Must-try wine
AOC Palette at
Château Simone (p176)

CONNECT & FIND YOUR WAY

Wi-fi Tourist offices in Aix-en-Provence and other small towns offer free wi-fi. Set yourself up with a pocket wi-fi device before leaving home or buy a SIM card (data-only) at Marseille airport or in any town.

Navigation The A54 and A7 cross the region from Arles to Aix-en-Provence; download road maps to use offline before leaving home.

CITY PASS

The **Aix-en-Provence City Pass** (aixenprovencetourism.com; 24/48/72 hours €25/34/43) covers admission to key sights, guided tours and unlimited public transport. In Arles, buy a **Pass Liberté** (arlestourisme.com; €12) valid for one month and covering six sights.

WHERE TO STAY

Choose between staying in a small town, where parking can be challenging (and expensive) in high season, or in the surrounding countryside with pool-clad hotels and *chambres d'hôte* (B&Bs) overlooking vines.

Place	Pro/Con
Aix-en-Provence	Wide range of accommodation, plentiful dining and sightseeing.
Montagne Ste-Victoire	Rural *auberges* (inns) and basic *refuges* (mountain huts) lost in nature.
St-Rémy de Provence	Chic and pricey boutique accommodation, gourmet dining and stylish shopping.
Fontvieille	Idyllic village vibe; excellent Huttopia campground and midrange châteaux and farmhouse hotels.
Arles	Great range of hotels for all budgets; cheap compared to other towns. Excellent dining, cafe and street-music scene.
Carry-le-Rouet	The seaside address. Highly affordable, with seafood restaurants in spades.

MONEY

Save money by shopping for picnics of local cheese, saucisson and artisan baguettes or bread loaves at local markets.

31 FLÂNERIE
in 17th-Century Aix

WALKING | ARCHITECTURE | ART DE VIVRE

A Provençal proverb says *'La flânerie est la gastronomie de l'œil'* ('Leisurely strolling is gastronomy of the eye'). Grab hat and cane, a dandyish demeanour and step into the honey-coloured Mazarin quarter to soak up the sights, sounds and devilishly handsome architecture of old-world Aix-en-Provence.

☕ On a Cafe Terrace

My favourite street in Quartier Mazarin is rue de l'Italie (pictured). There are lovely tea and cheese shops, and at the point where it meets Cours Mirabeau, you can sit at a little wooden table on a terrace and take in the light walls, coloured shutters and climbing plants accompanied by the occasional accordion player.

🗺 Trip Notes

Getting here Bus 40 (15 minutes) from Aix-en-Provence TGV train station, 15km away. Trains to/from Marseille (45 minutes) use Aix' city-centre station.

When to go Spring and autumn are gloriously mellow, as is live jazz in Hôtel de Caumont's gardens (mid-June to mid-September).

People-watching hotpot Fine-tune *flâneur*-essential observation skills at Aix' place Richelme **food market**.

■ Recommended by Mégane Duborgel,
Masters student at Aix-Marseille University

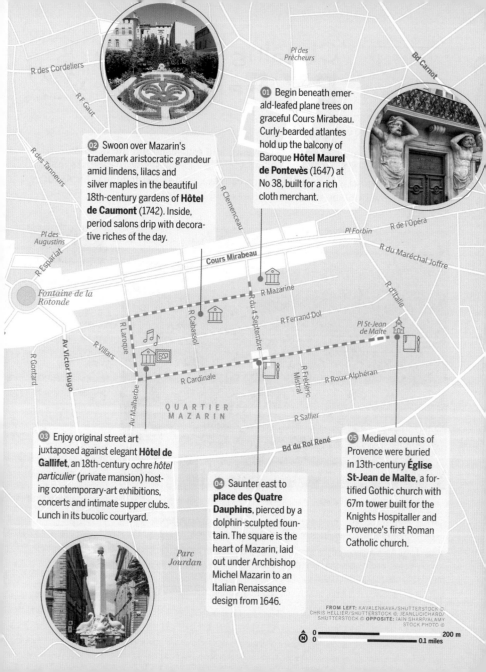

02 Swoon over Mazarin's trademark aristocratic grandeur amid lindens, lilacs and silver maples in the beautiful 18th-century gardens of **Hôtel de Caumont** (1742). Inside, period salons drip with decorative riches of the day.

01 Begin beneath emerald-leafed plane trees on graceful Cours Mirabeau. Curly-bearded atlantes hold up the balcony of Baroque **Hôtel Maurel de Pontevès** (1647) at No 38, built for a rich cloth merchant.

03 Enjoy original street art juxtaposed against elegant **Hôtel de Gallifet**, an 18th-century ochre *hôtel particulier* (private mansion) hosting contemporary-art exhibitions, concerts and intimate supper clubs. Lunch in its bucolic courtyard.

04 Saunter east to **place des Quatre Dauphins**, pierced by a dolphin-sculpted fountain. The square is the heart of Mazarin, laid out under Archbishop Michel Mazarin to an Italian Renaissance design from 1646.

05 Medieval counts of Provence were buried in 13th-century **Église St-Jean de Malte**, a fortified Gothic church with 67m tower built for the Knights Hospitaller and Provence's first Roman Catholic church.

R des Cordeliers
Pl des Prêcheurs
Bd Carnot
R F Gaut
R des Tanneurs
Pl des Augustins
R Esparlat
Fontaine de la Rotonde
Av Victor Hugo
R Gontard
R Villars
R Laroque
Av Malherbe
R Clemenceau
Cours Mirabeau
Pl Forbin
R de l'Opéra
R du Maréchal Joffre
R Mazarine
R Cabassol
R du 4 Septembre
R Ferrand Dol
R Cardinale
R Frédéric Mistral
R Roux Alphéran
R Sallier
QUARTIER MAZARIN
Bd du Roi René
Pl St-Jean de Malte
R d'Italie
Parc Jourdan

0 ... 200 m
0 ... 0.1 miles
N

32
Chasing Cézanne
BY E-BIKE

CYCLING | ART | MOUNTAINS

Pick up an e-bike in Aix-en-Provence and cruise, hot on the heels of Cézanne, into the hills of Montagne Ste-Victoire – the post-impressionist's muse which he painted extensively. Watch his canvases spring to life along this 55km loop, fringed with plane trees, olive groves and vineyards.

🐾 Nature Watch

Ophrys de Provence is a reddish, yellow and purple orchid, endemic to Provence. Admire it from March to May.

Fossils reveal the astonishing geological history of a landscape forged over a period of 150 million years. Collecting them is forbidden.

Deer are back after centuries of disappearance. Observe at nightfall.

📍 Trip Notes

Getting here Rent e-bikes, child carriers and luggage racks at **Aixprit Vélo** (3 bd Aristide Briand, Aix-en-Provence). Guided cycling tours too.

When to go April to June, September and October have fewer crowds, mellow temperatures, wildflowers and the autumnal grape harvest. The risk of summer forest fires can make hiking trails inaccessible in July and August.

Make a weekend of it Overnight at rustic-and-rural **Refuge Baudino** or **Gîte d'étape Puyloubier** (grandsitesaintevictoire.com).

■ Recommended by Jerôme Segaud, *naturalist and tour guide at Secrets d'Ici, Aix-en-Provence @secrets_dici*

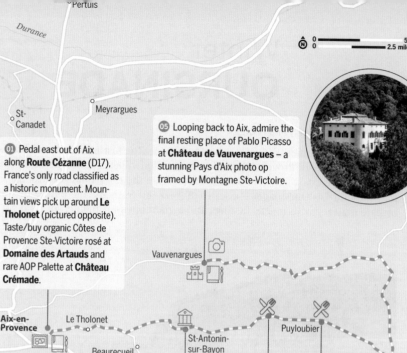

01 Pedal east out of Aix along **Route Cézanne** (D17), France's only road classified as a historic monument. Mountain views pick up around **Le Tholonet** (pictured opposite). Taste/buy organic Côtes de Provence Ste-Victoire rosé at **Domaine des Artauds** and rare AOP Palette at **Château Crémade**.

05 Looping back to Aix, admire the final resting place of Pablo Picasso at **Château de Vauvenargues** – a stunning Pays d'Aix photo op framed by Montagne Ste-Victoire.

02 Gen up on swallowtail butterflies, golden eagles and other flora and fauna at **Maison Ste-Victoire**, 6.5km east in **St-Antonin-sur-Bayon**.

04 Continue another couple of kilometres to **Puyloubier**, a foodie village that seduces with locavore cuisine and irresistible Maison Casalini lime-and-ginger sorbet from Aix at village *auberge* **La Place**.

03 After 5km pull into **Parking Saint Ser** and take a side hike (3.5km) up to 5th-century **Ermitage Saint Ser**, chiselled into rocks. Lunch at field-to-table **Le Relais de Saint Ser**, in a 19th-century Provençal *mas* (farmhouse).

33 Winter
OURSINADE

SEAFOOD | CULTURE | FESTIVALS

Forget summer. For serious seafood lovers, the tastiest time to visit this epicurean wedge of Provence is in February, when villages along the Côte Bleue (literally 'Blue Coast') west of Marseille celebrate their seasonal sea-urchin harvest with Les Oursinades – a series of weekend festivals celebrating the love-or-hate delicacy with music, tastings and a giant open-air picnic. Join the party!

EBASCOL/SHUTTERSTOCK ©

🗺 **How to**

Getting here Buses and trains link main town Carry-le-Rouet with Marseille, 35km east, and other Blue Coast villages. Journey time is about one hour.

When to go November to 15 April; Sundays in February to catch Les Oursinades.

Deep-dive into nature The entire Côte Bleue, from Anse des Laurons to Pointe des Corbières and extending 3km offshore, is a protected *parc marin* (marine park). The park office in Carry-le-Rouet organises **guided snorkelling tours** in summer.

FONDACCI MARKEZANA, JEAN ET HUNE/GETTY IMAGES ©

Far left Beach, Carry-le-Rouet
Bottom left Pan-fried *tellines* **Near left** Sea urchins

Mediterranean Caviar

Spiny *oursins* (sea urchins) can be deep purple, aubergine, chocolate brown or jet black in colour, and are served like oysters – raw and by the dozen or half. To eat, cut open the ball. Scrape off the guts and brown grit to uncover the startling rusty-orange gonads (reproduction organs) of the sea urchin, arranged in five sweet-salty strips. This is what gourmets wax lyrical about. Côte Bleue locals know them as *châtaignes de mer* (sea chestnuts).

Bob along the Blue Coast

Mooch on the quays at Carry-le-Rouet's quaint **port** to admire traditional *pointus* (painted wooden fishing boats) from which fisherfolk scooped urchins from the seabed with a claw-like *grappe* (a wooden rod with a hook at the end). Only fishing by free-diving or on foot is allowed today. Visit heritage association **Boud'mer** (boudmer.org) to bob along in your own *pointu*.

Festive Feasting

On Sundays in February follow the festive crowd to open-air food stalls lining the length of **quai Maleville**. Buy a half-dozen urchins, oysters or prawns to scoff around a shared table on the quayside. In the company of fresh lemon, crusty bread and chilled Cassis white wine is best. Giant pans of paella ensure the gonad-squeamish don't starve. Live music and an artisan market entertains between tastings.

Post-feast, stretch your legs along the **Sentier du Lézard**, a walking trail exploring rare flora and remarkable fauna (urchins included) in Carry's coastal ecosystem.

⇨ At the Fishmonger's

The best shellfish is seasonal: sea-urchin season is December to mid-April and fishing is limited to four dozen a day – free-diving or on foot. *Violets* (sea squirts), gathered in rocky shallows December to March, are an acquired taste: their chewy, iodine-infused flesh couldn't taste more like the ocean.

To cook your own *fruits de mer* feast, buy the day's catch at **Poissonnerie du Golfe** in neighbouring Sausset-les-Pins. September to May, indulge in a kilo of baby-pink, nail-sized *tellines* (wedge clams). Soak in salted water until purged of sand, drain, and pan-fry with finely chopped garlic and parsley or shallots with butter, cream and a splash of white wine.

34 Count Sheep in
ST-RÉMY

ENVIRONMENT | CULTURE | FESTIVALS

Immerse yourself in pastoral life and its grounding riches at St-Rémy de Provence's seasonal Fête de la Transhumance. Celebrating the ritual transhumance at the end of spring, it sees thousands of sheep shepherded through the handsome market town en route to cooler mountain pastures. The sights, sounds and smells – not to mention the peripheral shopping and feasting – are breathtaking.

POOL LAFARGUE/GETTY IMAGES ©

🗺 **How to**

Getting here and around Buses link St-Rémy de Provence with Arles and Avignon. Motorists, don't park in the Vieille Ville (old town) or boulevards encircling it: Parking Géneral de Gaulle (north) and Parking du Cimitière (south) are 10 minutes' walk from the flock-filled action.

When to go Pentecost Monday, in late May or early June.

Top tip Arrange a visit to **La Fromagerie des Alpilles** to learn how cheese is made on a local goat farm.

GRAHAM RIDING/SHUTTERSTOCK ©

Far left Fête de la Transhumance, St-Rémy de Provence **Bottom left** Cheeses, St-Rémy de Provence **Near left** Flea market, St-Rémy de Provence

Ancient Tracks

Join the crowds awaiting *le troupeau* on **bd Gambetta**, **bd Mirabeau**, **bd Victor Hugo** and **bd Marceau**. A chaotic symphony of clanging bells and bleats, dog barks and the rattle of carts rings in the herd's arrival from Plateau de la Crau around 11am. The sea of 4000 sheep, Rove goats and donkeys driven by cane-wielding shepherds in wide-brimmed hats, black waistcoats and colourful Provençal-print shirts is spellbinding.

After encircling the old town twice, the herd returns to Plateau de la Crau to be sorted and loaded into lorries for the modern-day transhumance. Few shepherds today make the 10-day ancestral journey from winter lowlands to higher-altitude, lush green summer pastures on foot.

On the Steppe

Follow the crowds out of town to watch shepherds demonstrate the razor-sharp herding skills of their quick-witted sheepdogs on windswept **Plateau de la Crau**, north of St-Rémy. Shepherds have wintered their flocks of woolly Arles Merino sheep on this vast desolate plain – once the delta of the Durance River, now a patchwork of hay fields and dry stone-strewn steppe – since the 16th century.

Threatened lesser kestrels, little bustards and pin-tailed sandgrouse speck the skies. Dig deeper into La Crau's rich biodiversity on a guided hike (on foot, horseback or mountain bike) with a ranger from the **Parc National Régional des Alpilles**; reserve in advance at the **Maison du Parc** on bd Marceau in St-Rémy.

🏪 To Market, To Market

Indulge in all the fun of the fair at **open-air markets** on place de la République (flea market) and bd Marceau (cheese).

If you don't find the right *chèvre* (goat's cheese) at the Transhumance's traditional Foire aux Fromages (Cheese Market), nip into **La Cave aux Fromages** where cheese is ripened in a 12th-century cellar.

Stock up on biscuits made from local Roman and Renaissance recipes at **Le Petit Duc**.

Homewares crafted from wooden pallets, paper art, candles, traditional *fuseaux de lavande* (lavender wands woven from satin ribbons and sweet-smelling lavender stems) and olive-wood chopping boards are among artisanal *objets d'art* sold at artist-collective **Le Savoir-Faire des Alpilles**.

35 Celebrating
GREEN GOLD

FOOD | FESTIVALS | SHOPPING

▬▬▬ A vital ingredient in almost every dish cooked under the Provençal sun, silken olive oil is the lifeblood of Provence's superlative cuisine. Return to the source – olive groves planted by ancient Greeks amid desolate scrubland and wild almond trees in Les Alpilles – to celebrate with locals.

🗺 How to

Getting here and around Your own wheels, two or four, is the only satisfactory way to explore the 11 rural villages scattered around provincial town St-Rémy de Provence.

When to go June to September for oil-mill tours; mid-September for the Fête des Olives Vertes; October to December for the olive harvest.

Bring your own bottle Fill it en route with local olive oil at cooperatives and mills.

AIX TO ARLES **EXPERIENCES**

Green Gold

Strung between the Durance and Rhône rivers, south of Avignon, the silvery Massif des Alpilles is a chain of limestone rocks glinting with sun-baked herbal *garrigue* (scrubland) and olive groves. It is here, in isolated villages in the Vallée des Baux, that some of France's finest *or vert* ('green gold') olive oil is pressed, bottled and celebrated in serious style. For centuries kings of France were baptised and coronated in Reims with olive oil from here.

The bulk of Les Alpilles' succulent olives, born from clusters of white flowers that blossom on the knotty old trees in May and June, are harvested between early October and late December. Table olives are the first to be picked and those destined for the olive press, the last. Mooch at **St-Rémy de Provence**'s

ⓘ Tasting Oil

Drink water first. Pour olive oil onto a plastic teaspoon and taste. It can have varying degrees of sweetness or acidity, be peppery or 'green', and clear or murky (meaning the oil is unfiltered). Aromas can be of fresh hay, cut grass, artichoke, cocoa, hazelnut, truffle, tomato leaf...

Top left Olive groves, Les Baux de Provence **Bottom left** Fête des Olives Vertes, Mouriès (p172) **Above** Olives on sale, Aix-en-Provence

Wednesday-morning **open-air market** to admire the complete range: black, round and fleshy *(grossane)*; pear-shaped with yellow tints *(salonenque)*; green and pointed *(picholine)* or pungent *(aglandau)*.

Champion Olive-Crackers

Summer's end and the upcoming olive harvest in the Massif des Alpilles is celebrated at the **Fête des Olives Vertes** (Green Olive Festival) – two days of unabashed merriment the third weekend of September in **Mouriès**, 16km south of St-Rémy de Provence.

The costumed parades, traditional Provençal dances, open-air concerts and street stands offering olive and olive-oil tastings evoke the rich cultural heritage behind the village's olive-growing tradition. But nothing matches the wild excitement – not to mention good-humoured rivalry – induced by the annual quest to find the season's new champion olive-cracker.

À Table

Mono-varietal olive oils are unique in that they have completely different flavours. Some will be soft and buttery; others, fiery with aromas of artichoke, cut herbs or pepper. *Huiles d'olives douce* ('sweet' or mild olive oils) are the perfect accompaniment to strawberry salad or fine-fleshed fish. Stronger oils are used with raw vegetables or on a hot goat's cheese, or meats.

Anchoïade remains a must on Provençal tables. Filled with a variety of vegetables accompanied by olive oil and anchovies, it takes you to the very heart of Provençal traditions. Chefs in the Alpilles have varying cuisines, but they all advocate quality of produce and *produits de terroir* (local produce).

■ Recommended by Anne & Gilles Brun, *olive farmers at Moulin du Calanquet, St-Rémy de Provence* @moulinducalanquet

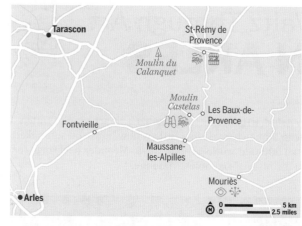

Left Anchoïade **Below** Olives on sale, St-Rémy de Provence market

Just-harvested green olives – usually Provence's popular *aglandau* variety, still firm and not too fleshy – are split open by hand with a stone from the nearby plain of **La Crau**, Europe's last protected steppe. These *olives casées* (cracked or broken olives) are simmered in salted water with fennel, pepper and bay leaves, then marinated for several days before drained and served as an end-of-summer apéritif snack called **les olives cassées**.

Mill Tours

Nothing beats poking around backstage and tasting – just like wine or cheese – on the very spot where the said olive oil was made. August is generally the last month to buy the mill's *huile d'olive* (olive oil) before it sells out.

Small-holding olive farmers around **Mouriès** and **Maussane** take their harvest to local cooperative **Moulin Coopératif des Mouriès** to be milled. Free guided tours and tastings in July and August.

Dramatic views of **Les Baux de Provence**'s clifftop ruined château are thrown in for free at **Moulin Castelas**, a mill on the fringe of the iconic, tourist-packed hilltop village.

The 20,000 olive trees at **Moulin du Calanquet** yield some 300,000 tonnes of olives and 40,000L of oil a year – five different mono-varietals alongside a traditional blend of different olive varieties.

36 Waltz Through Art
IN ARLES

ART | HISTORY | FAMILY TRAVEL

▬▬▬▬ There is far more to Arles' artistic timeline than post-impressionist Dutch artist Vincent Van Gogh, who famously lived in a little yellow house on sun-baked place Lamartine and painted 200-odd works around town. Meander backstage for an evocative waltz through art history's complete timeline.

🗺 Trip Notes

Getting here Trains link Arles' downtown train station with Marseille (one hour), Avignon (20 minutes) and beyond.

Getting around Walk, rent a bicycle, tricycle or e-bike from Taco & Co, or ride a free electric shuttle-bus (linking Luma Arles and Musée d'Arles Antique via av Victor Hugo, bd des Lices and bd Clémenceau).

When to go To pair your visit with the world-famous photography festival **Les Rencontres**, make it July to September.

🖾 Wearable Art

The inspiration for our jewellery comes from ancient Roman fashion. One of our favourite monuments is the ancient Roman theatre (pictured), simply because even today it is used for what it was built for. The crypto-porticoes are often overlooked, yet they evoke the mystery of a Roman city and are the most representative of our town's history.

■ Recommended by **Ariela & Philippe**, *jewellery designers at Taberna Anticae Arelatensis, Arles @arles_anticae_atelier*

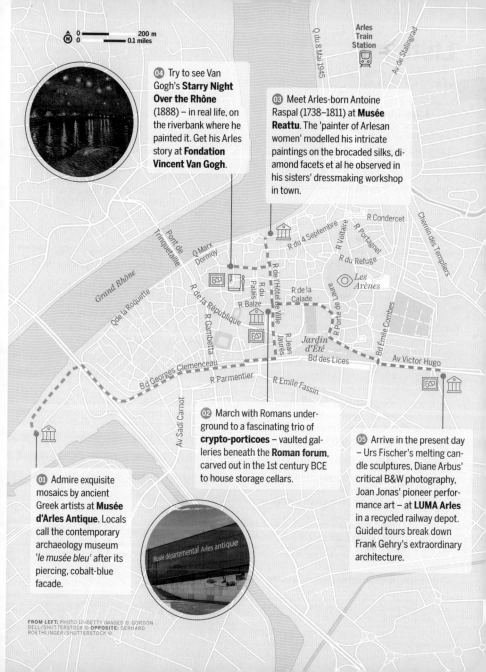

04 Try to see Van Gogh's **Starry Night Over the Rhône** (1888) – in real life, on the riverbank where he painted it. Get his Arles story at **Fondation Vincent Van Gogh**.

03 Meet Arles-born Antoine Raspal (1738–1811) at **Musée Reattu**. The 'painter of Arlesan women' modelled his intricate paintings on the brocaded silks, diamond facets et al he observed in his sisters' dressmaking workshop in town.

02 March with Romans underground to a fascinating trio of **crypto-porticoes** – vaulted galleries beneath the **Roman forum**, carved out in the 1st century BCE to house storage cellars.

05 Arrive in the present day – Urs Fischer's melting candle sculptures, Diane Arbus' critical B&W photography, Joan Jonas' pioneer performance art – at **LUMA Arles** in a recycled railway depot. Guided tours break down Frank Gehry's extraordinary architecture.

01 Admire exquisite mosaics by ancient Greek artists at **Musée d'Arles Antique**. Locals call the contemporary archaeology museum '*le musée bleu*' after its piercing, cobalt-blue facade.

Musée départemental Arles antique

Map labels:
Arles Train Station
Q du 8 Mai 1945
Av de Stalingrad
R Condorcet
Chemin des Templiers
R du 4 Septembre
R Voltaire
R Portagnel
R du Refuge
Pont de Trinquetaille
Q Marx Dormoy
R de l'Hôtel de Ville
Les Arènes
Grand Rhône
Qde la Roquette
R de la République
R Balze
R du Palais
R de la Calade
R Porte de Laure
Bd Émile Combes
R Gambetta
R Jean Jaurès
Jardin d'Été
Bd des Lices
Av Victor Hugo
Bd Georges Clemenceau
R Parmentier
R Émile Fassin
Av Sadi Carnot

0 200 m
0 0.1 miles
N

Listings

BEST OF THE REST

 ## Lazy Lunches

Les Vieilles Canailles   €€

Tuck into locavore bistro fare and curated boutique wines by independent winegrowers at this old-town bistro, footsteps from centrepiece Fontaine de la Rotonde in Aix-en-Provence.

Dan B   €€€

Exceptional dining awaits in the hilltop village of Ventabren, 15km west of Aix. Both setting (a canopied terrace with celestial view) and cuisine (inventive modern French by Michelin-starred Dan Bessoudo) are pure magic.

L'Oustau de Baumanière   €€€

Choose between dining under mulberry trees at La Cabro d'Or or the triple-Michelin-starred Full Monty at this 1940s hotel-restaurant in touristy hilltop village Les Baux-de-Provence.

Le Greeniotage   €€

Linger over sweet-onion *pissaladière,* confit lamb shank and other Provençal classics at the enchanting downtown Arles bistro of celebrity chef Jean-Luc Rabanel. End with sweet Cavaillon melon and basil sorbet.

La Chassagnette   €€€

Armand Amal's Michelin-starred farmstead restaurant near Arles celebrates local gastronomy with plant-based and 'fauna-and-fauna' menus served beneath vine-draped pergola.

 ## On the Wine Trail

Domaine de la Brillane

Organic grapes, harvested by hand and the passion of bon vivant winegrower Walter Butler, go into the esteemed reds, whites and rosés produced at this estate, 10km north of Aix.

Château Simone

Taste wines fermented in 16th-century cellars dug by monks at this honey-coloured château near Aix. Its vineyards produce 80% of wine in the boutique AOC Palette appellation.

Domaine Pey Blanc

Buy some of Aix' most beloved rosés and excellent whites at this serene eco-estate, dating to 1930 and committed to sustainibility.

Château de la Gaude

Savour rosé in the Michelin-starred restaurant or formal gardens of this majestic 18th-century château. The hotel-spa is five-star too.

Château La Coste

Art gallery, dining destination, winery and luxurious villa. Buy wine, enjoy an art-and-architecture tour or indulge in a weekend here.

Toujours Cézanne

Musée Granet

Admire nine Cézanne pieces and masterpieces by Picasso, Léger, Matisse, Monet and Van Gogh at Aix' art museum, one of France's best.

Atélier Cézanne

Poke around the Aix studio where Cézanne painted the last four years of his life; not all the tools and still-life models were his.

Bastide du Jas de Bouffan

Cézanne painted furiously in this 18th-century manor, purchased by his father in 1859. He produced 36 oils and 17 watercolours of the house, farm, chestnut alley and countryside park.

Carrières de Bibemus

Tour the dramatic rocks of this ochre quarry, east of Aix, that Cézanne captured so vividly on canvas – he knocked out 27 works while renting a *cabanon* (cabin) here in 1895.

Terrain des Peintres

Hike uphill to this bucolic terraced garden – a perfect picnic spot – from where Cézanne, among others, painted the jagged silhouette of Montagne Ste-Victoire in the distance.

Circuit de Cézanne

See where Cézanne lived, ate, drank, studied and painted in Aix-en-Provence on this self-guided walking tour through his home town. Follow plaques embedded in the pavement.

Terrain des Peintres

Festive Fun

Festival d'Aix-en-Provence

Buy tickets well in advance for a star-topped night of opera, orchestral works and chamber music to remember in the alfresco courtyard of Aix-en-Provence's former Archbishop's Palace.

Château des Baux

Make a beeline for Les Baux de Provence's clifftop castle in July and August when medieval-themed entertainment and hands-on action – shows, duels, catapult demonstrations – are staged in the maze-like ruins.

Féria de St-Rémy

Join in the fiesta with fireworks and alfresco street festivities galore at St-Rémy de Provence's party of the year in mid-August.

Fêtes d'Arles

Join the cultured pack pouring into Arles, mid-June to mid-July, to enjoy horse races, parades, costumes, theatre and music. Don't miss after-dark Pegoulado – a torchlight procession with dances in traditional Provençal costume.

Boutique Shopping

La Pastisserie

Shop for artisan pastis, lavender liqueur and other inventive spirits crafted in Provence at

this ingeniously named *cave à pastis* (pastis cellar) and gourmet *épicerie* (grocery) in Aix.

Book in Bar

Book readings, jazz evenings and an English-language book club enliven the conventional book-buying experience at Aix-en-Provence's top-dollar Anglophile bookshop.

Lait de Jument de Camargue

Shop for eco-responsible soap (the chocolate, cinnamon and milk bars are irresistible), candles, beauty and body care products made from Camargue horse milk at this horse farm on Arles' eastern outskirts.

Moustique

Handmade lamps, ceramics, clothing and clove-and-lemon-scented candles to ward off mosquitoes are among the funky homewares in this independent concept store in Arles.

Joël Durand

There is nothing sweeter to take home than a box of luxury chocolates, laced with lavender, rosemary, violet, thyme and other Provençal herbs and plants by St-Rémy de Provence's top *chocolatier*.

 Scan to find more things to do in Aix & Arles online

37

Weekend in Wild
WETLANDS

OUTDOORS | FOOD | GREAT ESCAPE

Lose all sense of time in this hauntingly beautiful part of Provence, roamed by black bulls, white horses and pink flamingos. This is go-slow, 'great escape' country – remote, wild wetlands chequered with salt pans, rice paddies, cowboy ranches and untouched wildlife in spades.

Above Flamingos, Stes-Maries de la Mer (p180) **Bottom right** Phare de la Gacholle (p180) **Far right** Camargue rice

📖 How to

Getting here and around Envia buses (*tout-envia.com*) link Arles train station with Stes-Maries-de-la-Mer (50 minutes). In situ, touring the tiny roads criss-crossing the pancake-flat region is best by car, bicycle or horseback.

When to go April to October; most camp-grounds and hotels shut in winter.

Bring Binoculars, sun hat, sun protection and mosquito repellent (or invest in some of the eco-killer stuff made from Camargue horse milk by Lait de Jument de Camargue in Arles).

Hiding with Twitchers

For birdwatchers, there are few more spectacular environments where age-old farming practices coexist with one of Europe's most precious ornithological havens. Enclosed by the Petit Rhône and Grand Rhône rivers, and protected by the 850-sq-km **Parc Naturel Régional de Camargue** and neighbouring 132-sq-km **Réserve Nationale de Camargue**, these wetlands are a vital waypoint on migratory routes between Europe and Africa.

Twitchers can potentially spot two-thirds of Europe's bird species. Walking trails beaded with foliage-camouflaged wooden hides are abundant. Observe over 300 bird species at the **Marais du Vigueirat nature reserve**, including all of Europe's heron species and – if you're very patient and lucky – the rare Bonelli's eagle, greater spotted eagle and osprey.

🏛 Fruits of the Land

Nutty red, white and brown rice Paddy fields are planted and flooded in April, harvested in September.

Salt Harvested August to mid-October from pans in Salin de Giraud.

Marsh samphire Foraging salty-tasting *salicornes* on marshland rambles is limited to 500g per person per day.

Tellines On the seashore, baby-pink fingernail-sized wedge clams hide in the sand.

The **Étang du Fangassier** notably assures nesting pink and greater flamingos – up to 15,000 couples a year – protection from predators. Visit late August and you'll find almost half of them have taken flight to winter in Spain, Tunisia and Senegal; they only return to the region in February. To admire these gracious rose-pink birds up close, walk 7km of trails and hides at the **Parc Ornithologique du Pont de Gau**.

Edge of the World

Let your soul soar with postcard views of pink flamingos strutting across desolate marshy plains from **La Digue à la Mer**. Built in the 19th century to cut the delta off from the sea and make southern Camargue arable, the 20km-long dyke can be crossed on foot or by bike: a walking and cycling track runs its length, linking seaside town **Stes-Maries de la Mer** with the 1882 lighthouse **Phare de la**

✕ Marsh-to-Menu Gastronomy

The Camargue is not truly 'wild'. Man works with nature to preserve nature, irrigates lands that would otherwise be killed by the salt. This spirit inspires La Chassagnette's 'Fauna & Flora' *menu* – a reflection in five courses of the harmony between what we grow and what we forage. 'Fauna' includes eels, shrimps, sea squirts and Mediterranean fish caught in the wild along with bull and lamb bred in the Camargue. 'Flora' marries what we grow in our vegetable garden with native foraged herbs and leaves, such as wild Swiss chard and *salicornes* (marsh samphire).

■ **Insights from Armand Arnal**, *Michelin-starred chef at La Chassagnette in Arles* @chassagnette

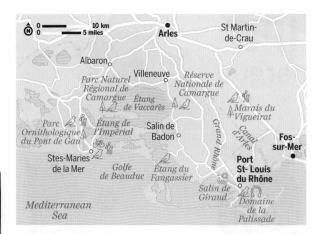

Left La Chassagnette **Below** Camargue horses, Parc Naturel Régional de Camargue

Gacholle, 12km away. Follow the trail for another 17km to **Salin de Giraud** – when the desire to dip in the Med kicks in, cut down footpaths to swathes of empty sand beach and the sea.

Gallop Like the Wind

Trek on horseback and gallop like the wind through 702 hectares of protected marshland, scrubby glasswort, flowering sea lavender (in August) and bird-specked lagoons at **Domaine de la Palissade**. Exploring the remote nature centre can easily fill the best part of a day. Non-equestrians: before hitting the scrub, rent binoculars and grab a free map of the estate's three marked walking trails (1km to 8km) from the office.

Cowboy Dreams

Immerse yourself in rural Camargue living at **Cacharel Hôtel**, an isolated 1950s *manade* (bull farmstead) at the end of an unpaved track near Stes-Maries de la Mer. Guests arriving on horseback can stable their mounts overnight with the farm's own handsome white Camargue horses and can explore the lie of the land with a traditional Camargue *gardian* (cowboy): bulls and horses were bred here for 30 years. To ensure sweet cowboys dreams post-dinner, dine on feisty *terrine de taureau* (bull-meat pâté) and traditional *gardiane de taureau* (bull stew) served with locally grown rice.

WILDLIFE
of the Camargue

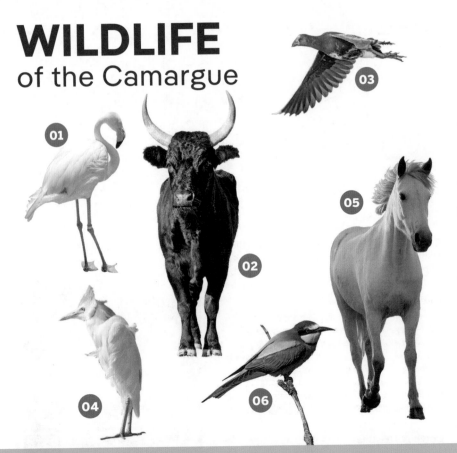

01 Flamingos
Each spring up to 15,000 pink or greater flamingo couples nest on Étang du Fangassier.

02 Black Bulls
Manades (herds) of native black Camargue bulls peppering marshlands are quintessential to the local landscape.

03 Western Swamphen
This elegant creature, also called sultana bird, adds a flourish of purple to silver-hued wetlands.

04 Cattle Egrets
If you see a small bird standing on a Camargue horse's back, it's probably a cattle egret.

05 White Horses
These wild, water-loving white horses – actually silvery grey – are brown at birth and don't need shoes.

06 European Bee-Eaters
April to August, observe colourful European bee-eaters swooping over rice fields and *salicornia* marshes.

07 Greater Spotted Eagles
The best chance of spotting a greater spotted eagle is from December to February when the predator swoops skies for wintering waterfowl.

08 Herons
Grey, purple, squacco and black-crowned night herons are among nine species of herons nesting in lagoons and reed beds.

09 Coypus
This semi-aquatic rodent was introduced to France from South America in the 19th century for its fur.

10 Red-Crested Pochards
Thousands of red-crested pochards, with distinctive golden-red heads and bright red beaks, winter here.

11 Black-Winged Stilts
Be wary of the black-winged stilt – this long-legged wader will chase you to protect its young.

12 European Pont Turtles
Wetlands provide a safe refuge for one of Europe's last remaining freshwater turtles (once eaten by monks).

13 Montpellier Snakes
At 2m long, the Montpellier snake is the most eye-catching of the Camargue's six-species snake population.

AVIGNON & AROUND

THEATRE | MEDIEVAL ARCHITECTURE | PAPAL CITY

Experience
Avignon
& around
online

Cycle up the Tour de France favourite, **Mont Ventoux** (p194)

🚗 40mins from Avignon Centre

🚲 3hrs from Bédoin

Bollène

Suze-la-Rousse

Mornas

Uchaux

Camaret-sur-Aigues

Malaucène

Beaumont-du-Ventoux

Paddle and sunbathe by the Roman aqueduct **Pont du Gard** (p190)

🚗 30mins from Avignon Centre

Orange

Violes

Gigondas

Beaumes-de-Venise

Le Barroux

Pouzilhac

Châteauneuf du Pape

Sarrians

Carpentras

Taste and buy wine like a local in a wine cooperative like **Rhonéa Cooperative** (p193)

🚗 35mins from Avignon

Roquemaure

Monteux

Pujaut

Sorgues

Pernes-les-Fontaines

Remoulins

Avignon

St-Gens

Watch theatre troupes from Festival d'Avignon on **rue des Teinturiers** (p189)

🚶 11mins from Hôtel de Ville

Fontaine-de-Vaucluse

Théziers

Visit **Pont St-Bénézet** and feel transported to the 17th century (p199)

🚶 10mins from Hôtel de Ville

L'Isle-sur-la-Sorgue

Aramon

Caumont-sur-Durance

Coustellet

Cavaillon

AVIGNON & AROUND
Trip Builder

Once home to the Popes, modern Avignon stands out for its theatre, arts and architecture. Outside the city, whether by paddling under a Roman aqueduct or cycling the giant Mont Ventoux, the region offers endless opportunities for outdoor adventure.

0 — 10 km
0 — 5 miles

Practicalities

ARRIVING

TGV Arrives from Paris, Lyon and Marseille frequently to Avignon TGV station; 7km away is Avignon Centre station, accessible by local trains.

Car Avignon is about one to 1½ hours from Marseille.

MONEY

Card and phone-pay is accepted most places, but keep cash on hand for village markets or small cafes.

FIND YOUR WAY

The Office de Tourisme provides paper city maps. The app Maps.me is good for offline navigation.

WHERE TO STAY

Place	Pro/Con
Avignon Centre	The centre is pedestrian only, so noise pollution is low.
Villeneuve-lès-Avignon	Medieval architecture; calmer than Avignon but just a 10-minute drive away.
Bédoin	Deep in the countryside, Bédoin makes you want to move to Provence.

EATING & DRINKING

In the centre of Avignon you'll find many bistros serving modern Provençal dishes. Les Halles d'Avignon is a historic food market where you'll find fishmongers (pictured top left) and small hole-in-the-wall restaurants with excellent daily specials.

Wine cooperatives across the region produce and sell wine of local appellations like Ventoux or Luberon.

Best bistrot
L'Épicerie (p202)

Must-try ice cream
La Princière d'Avignon (p203)

GETTING AROUND

Car Avignon is accessible on foot, but outside the city a car will give you the liberty to visit villages on a whim.

Bicycle Inside Avignon is flat and easily cyclable. Outside the city, pack light and rent a bike (or e-bike) with saddlebags; there are well-marked cycling paths and cars share the road relatively well.

(vertical text) AVIGNON & AROUND FIND YOUR FEET

JAN–MAR
Can be sunny. Unpleasantly cold if the mistral wind blows.

APR–JUN
Short spring brings hot weather, lush flowers and sunny days.

JUL–SEP
Hot. Do outside activities early/late or plan to go swimming.

OCT–DEC
Lovely weather in town or countryside. Beware the mistral wind.

38 Avignon sur **SCÈNE**

THEATRE FESTIVAL | CONVIVIAL | APÉRO

For nearly three weeks each July, the city of Avignon transforms into a stage – more than 1000 shows are performed all over the city in France's oldest performing arts and theatre festival. But...what if you don't speak French? There's still plenty to enjoy.

PHOTOPROFI30/SHUTTERSTOCK ©

📍 How to

When to go The festival spans 2½ weeks starting in mid-July.

Need to know The festival draws big crowds from France and all over the world; book your accommodation well in advance. Park on Île Piot and take the free shuttle into town.

Tickets Depending on the show, tickets sell out in advance. Prices range from €10 to €45. Last-minute ticket resales can be found at the Cloître St-Louis.

YK01/GETTY IMAGES ©

Far left Street performer, Festival d'Avignon **Bottom left** Street performers, Avignon OFF **Near left** Performance, Festival d'Avignon

Immerse yourself in the ambience The festival is actually two festivals going on at once: **Avignon ON**, the official program released by the Festival d'Avignon, and **Avignon OFF**. You're more likely to find international shows with English performances at the ON. Tickets are released online on a rolling basis, or you can try to buy seats the day of at the ticket office in Cloître St-Louis.

Apéro on rue des Teinturiers A narrow street that feels like the artery of the city, rue des Teinturiers holds a long and industrious past: over the centuries it has been home to ateliers for silk-makers and tapestry-makers. Today those workshops are largely transformed into bistros and bars, and the street is one of the liveliest places during the festival. Grab a table well before 6pm, as this is one of the best *apéro* spots in the city.

See a show without going anywhere One of the most original characteristics of the Festival d'Avignon is the tradition of theatre troupes and performers taking to the streets to advertise their show – in full costume! While you're sipping rosé on rue des Teinturiers, you'll be treated to miniature scenes from a slew of acts. The performers are not pushy – they'll offer you a flyer for their show, which you can accept or refuse, in order to invite you to their performance.

🎭 The Whole City's a Stage

What's wonderful about the Avignon festival is that it creates a space for a cultural bridge, where anyone can discover culture in different ways: there are theatre performances but also dance, music and art expos. My must-do during the festival is to attend performances in sublime locations: the Cloître des Carmes, the Cloître des Célestins, la Cour d'Honneur or the Jardin de la Vierge du Lycée St-Joseph. These are places where the performances take place under the stars.

■ **Recommended by Ghislaine Beaudout,** *stage producer for troupe Le Regard du Loup and children's book author from Paris who attends the Festival d'Avignon each year*

39 PONT DU GARD
by Land or by Water

ROMAN AQUEDUCT | ARCHITECTURE | ACTIVE VISIT

Built in 60 CE, the Pont du Gard gives weight to Roman engineering ingenuity. Today 52 arches remain standing on this aqueduct found between Avignon and Nîmes. Rather than just stopping by on your way between cities, stay for a night and explore the Gardon river and the villages around Pont du Gard.

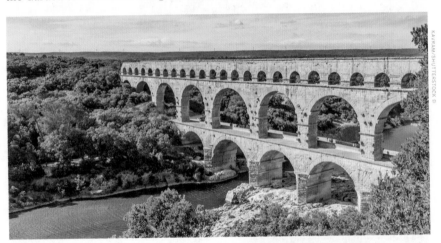

KAVRAM/SHUTTERSTOCK ©

📲 How to

Getting here By car it's the halfway point between Avignon and Nîmes. Stay the night in villages like Collias or Uzès.

Top tip Join one of the first canoe launches of the day to have the river to yourself.

Costs Day parking in the 'Rive Droite' is €9 per day. Tickets to the museum, expos, or for guided visits are €6.50 to €15. Children's tickets are free or reduced.

NURPHOTO/GETTY IMAGES ©

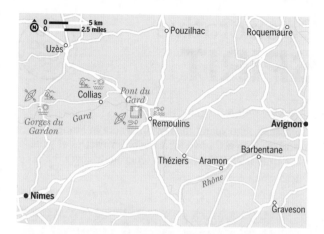

Architectural and natural heritage The Pont du Gard and the Gorges du Gardon are both Unesco-ranked sites, and it's no surprise they're heavily visited. The municipality has gone to great lengths to streamline visitors while still offering an interesting experience. There is a walking trail on the *rive gauche* (left bank) side of the aqueduct, and if you're a fan of Roman architecture, it might be worth going on a guided tour to get a real sense of the building of the aqueduct, and the human stories behind it. In July and August, when the bridge is very hot to visit during the day, consider a night visit. You'll find an enchanting surprise: light and audio shows that project artworks across the bridge.

Grab a paddle And pack a picnic lunch: a day spent canoeing the Gardon river and passing under the Pont du Gard is a day well spent. The Gardon river flows down from the nearby Cévennes massif. The waters are clear and cool all summer long. The sparkling white beaches of the Gorges du Gardon are the ideal spot for a picnic. Several companies offer semi-autonomous canoeing departures from the village of Collias. Once you've reached the end of the route there are shuttles to take you back to your car in Collias (the last shuttles leave at 6pm, don't be late!).

Top left Pont du Gard **Bottom left** Swimming, Gorges du Gardon

≈ Take a Dip

Not feeling up to a canoeing trip but want to get into the water? Here are three sites for sunbathing and swimming:

Pont du Gard Crowded, but beautiful and picturesque, it's possible to relax on the beaches right below the Pont du Gard.

Collias Clear water, good beaches for picnics, and if you're staying the night you can walk from your lodgings.

Remoulins Five kilometres from Pont du Gard, near the centre of Remoulins, and easily accessible, less crowded.

40 Cooperative SPIRIT

UNIQUE WINES | COMMUNITY | EXPLORING

▬▬▬ A vineyard tour is a classic way to spend the day anywhere in France. But if you're short on time and want to get a feel for a region's varieties of wine, visiting wine cooperatives is a time-friendly option that lets you discover the wine of the Vaucluse region.

DANIELE SCHNEIDER/GETTY IMAGES ©

🗺 How to

Getting here and around Each cooperative is less than an hour's drive from Avignon. Or, make use of the region's extensive cycling paths.

Tip Cooperatives usually have the region in the name: Cave de Luberon or Cave de Gigondas.

Weird fact In the 14th century, the Pope so appreciated north Vauclusian wines that the area was annexed into his domains. Today this 'Enclave des Papes' produces a variety of wines.

BARMALINI/SHUTTERSTOCK ©

HILKE MAUNDER/ALAMY STOCK PHOTO ©

Far left Vineyards, Vaucluse **Bottom left** Grapes, AOC Luberon, Vaucluse **Near left** Rhonéa Cooperative wines

Wine for the People!

In France, wine cooperatives have a historic status and heritage, and must adhere to strict standards. Tasting and shopping for wine in a cooperative does not mean sacrificing quality! Grape farmers pool their harvest and share the costs and facilities for making, stocking and selling the wine. Some of the cooperatives in the Vaucluse are approaching their 100th anniversary, and hold celebrations throughout the year – check online to see if you can catch one.

Like in most of France, in the Vaucluse, organic and sulphate-free wines are growing in popularity. Côtes-du-Rhône, Gigondas and Châteauneuf-du-Pape appellations have earned international recognition. While in the region, try instead the lesser-known appellations like Beaumes-de-Venise, Ventoux or Luberon.

By the bottle or by the litre? Of course, you can buy wine by the bottle in cooperatives, and even by the case. But since locals tend to frequent these shops, many cooperatives also offer the option to buy by the litre. Bring your own bottle or get an empty one from the cooperative and fill it up.

Team Ventoux or Luberon? Two AOCs that you can't miss while in the region are Ventoux and Luberon. Both wines come in red, white and rosé. Where the Alps meet the Mediterranean, wines with the Ventoux appellation are vinified. And from the plains below the Luberon comes the sun-drenched Luberon appellation.

Four Cooperative Cellars to Visit

Demazet Vignobles is close to Avignon and carries the classics: AOP Côtes-du-Rhône and AOP Côtes-du-Rhône Villages.

Rhonéa Cooperative is northeast of Avignon in Beaumes-de-Venise, a microregion where you can find the AOC Beaumes-de-Venise, a sweet muscat dessert wine.

Gigondas La Cave is located in the heart of the Dentelles de Montmirail, and you'll find richly aromatic Gigondas and Vacqueyras wines.

Cave du Luberon in Coustellet has a large selection of Luberon and Ventoux wines, only 30 minutes from Avignon. Its whites seem made for drinking on a hot day under a plane tree.

41

Cycle Mont
VENTOUX

BRAGGING RIGHTS | CYCLING | ICONIC

The giant of Provence, the rocky sides of Mont Ventoux tower over the region. Famous for its wind-whipped flanks and recurring presence in the Tour de France, Mont Ventoux attracts cyclists all year round.

How to

When to go Spring, autumn, or very early on summer mornings. Winter temps can reach -30°C at the summit, and ice or snow can result in road closures.

Need to know It's very windy on Mont Ventoux

240 days of the year: bring a windbreaker or risk being very cold.

Fun tip Have a drink at the top, or at the restaurant at Chalet Reynard on the way down.

A Cyclist's Bucket List

The challenge? Reach the summit of 1909m without putting a foot down! Cyclists can depart from Sault, Malaucène or Bédoin depending on their fitness. It's possible to rent a road bike or e-bike. You may decide to go with a guide who will manage all the logistics and help keep you motivated on your ride to the top. There are freelance photographers on the edge of the route during the last few kilometres – they'll hand you their card to check the photos online later, so be sure to give them a smile!

Cycling from Sault? Here's what to know: This is the 'easiest' route up Mont Ventoux: 25.7km/1152m+. The route will take you through a few lavender fields before the hard part of the climb kicks in. Since 1515, the market square in Sault bustles each

A Tragic Tour

Tragedy occurred on Mont Ventoux during the 1967 Tour de France. British cyclist Tom Simpson was racing up the mountain when he collapsed. He later died of heart failure from exhaustion, aggravated by doping and alcohol abuse. A memorial stands at the section of road where he collapsed.

Top left Cycling, Mt Ventoux **Bottom left** Final stretch, Mt Ventoux **Top right** Tom Simpson Memorial

Wednesday morning. During the summer season, up to 50 stands sell local, seasonal or organic fruit and veg, as well as Ventoux or Vacqueyras AOC wines, and speciality cheeses like AOP Banon goat's cheese, which comes wrapped in a chestnut leaf. At Chalet Reynard, the route meets the route coming from Bédoin, and cyclists ride together for the final kilometres.

Leaving from Malaucène? This is tied for most challenging route up to the summit.

It's technically the shortest in distance (21.2km/1535m+) by a few hundred metres, but it has several painfully steep segments, with occasional flat stretches. Climbing Mont Ventoux from the north side reveals a totally different vegetation: conifer forests, and a view over the Drôme stretching all the way to the Alps. Sometimes there is less car and motorcycle traffic on this side. Staying in Malaucène village but not really a cyclist? There's a nice hike to be had along the sharp

🚲 After the Climb, the Descent!

A lot of people focus on reaching the summit: they come prepared with sunscreen and water bottles. But you need a bit more for a great ride! Climbing the Ventoux you have to hold back a bit to not burn out. It's a very psychological ride.

Once at the top, though, there are some things you should have ready:

- A windbreaker – even if it's 30°C out.
- Sunglasses – once I rode down without sunglasses and caught bugs in my eyes the whole way!
- Focus – you'll pick up a lot of speed racing down the mountain; you need to watch for cars and motor-cycles on their way up.

■ **Tips by Phil Welch,** *cycling coach and guide with eight Ventoux tours under his belt* philwelchmtb.com

Far left Pro cyclist, Mt Ventoux **Near left** Sault market (p195) **Below** Cycling, Mt Ventoux

ridge of the Dentelles de Montmirail, followed by an AOC Beaumes-de-Venise wine tasting.

Starting point Bédoin? Bédoin is considered the classic route up Mont Ventoux. Be ready to pedal 21.3km/1589m+ before you reach the summit. In the village streets are filled with shops selling Ventoux jerseys. Many of the designs you won't find elsewhere, and given the physical effort you're about to embark on, you might as well treat yourself! Another strategic treat: *pâte de coing* (quince paste) is a thick block of what might be compared to a fruit leather. Try it for a natural energy boost rather than sports bars or goos. The ascent from Bédoin is more difficult than from Sault, but the gradient is more consistent than Malaucène. The route first winds through the lively village before leaving town. As your altitude increases, you'll pass through fields, forests and rocky surroundings before finally entering the long stretch to the top.

42 Seen in a Different **LIGHT**

PAPAL CITY | WALKING | HISTORY

Avoid the crowds and the heat by visiting Avignon by night. Let your imagination sweep you away as you explore the squares that popes, artists, and even Napoléon Bonaparte wandered. From the Porte de l'Oulle to the Pont d'Avignon and the Palais des Papes, connect with the influence of the past on the present in this bewitching city.

Connect with History

There is a feeling of intimacy when visiting Avignon at night. Standing nearly alone on the place des Palais (pictured), you experience a direct connection with the heritage; you take time to notice the centuries-old details in the architecture during the day you might pass without a second glance.

🗺 Trip Notes

Getting here Avignon has a TGV station 7km outside of town, with frequent trains from Paris, Marseille and Lyon.

When to go Spring, early summer, autumn. Late July to September is hot. Winter can be nice, or very cold with harsh wind.

Tip Ambience is key on a night stroll. Download an audio tour or book with a trusted guide to get the full story of the city.

■ Recommended by **Vincent Pasquinelli,** *Avignon native with a passion for history, who leads English- and French-language tours* @lesnoctammbules davignon

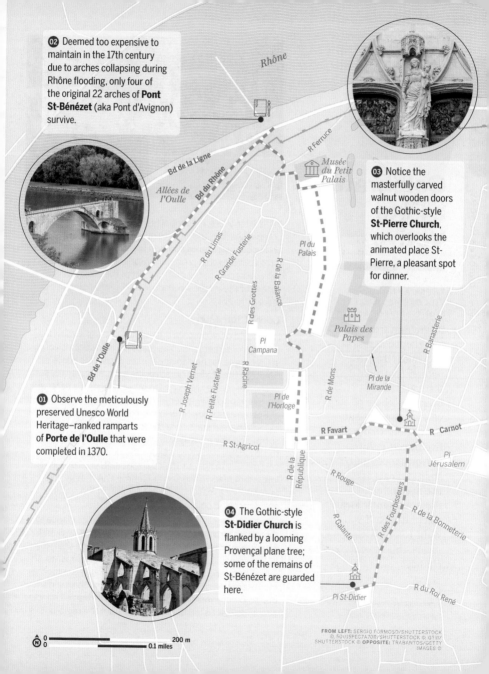

02 Deemed too expensive to maintain in the 17th century due to arches collapsing during Rhône flooding, only four of the original 22 arches of **Pont St-Bénézet** (aka Pont d'Avignon) survive.

03 Notice the masterfully carved walnut wooden doors of the Gothic-style **St-Pierre Church**, which overlooks the animated place St-Pierre, a pleasant spot for dinner.

01 Observe the meticulously preserved Unesco World Heritage–ranked ramparts of **Porte de l'Oulle** that were completed in 1370.

04 The Gothic-style **St-Didier Church** is flanked by a looming Provençal plane tree; some of the remains of St-Bénézet are guarded here.

Rhône

Bd de la Ligne

Allées de l'Oulle

Bd du Rhône

R du Limas

R Ferruce

Musée du Petit Palais

R Grande Fusterie

Pl du Palais

R des Grottes

R de la Balance

Pl Campana

Palais des Papes

R Banasterie

R Joseph Vernet

R Petite Fusterie

R Racine

Pl de l'Horloge

R de Mons

Pl de la Mirande

R Favart

R Carnot

R St-Agricol

Pl Jérusalem

R de la République

R Rouge

R des Fourbisseurs

R de la Bonneterie

R Galante

Pl St-Didier

R du Roi René

Bd de l'Oulle

N 0 — 200 m
0 — 0.1 miles

CHRIS HELLIER/GETTY IMAGES ©

AVIGNON & AROUND ESSAY

Celebrate a Fête Votive

THESE ANNUAL VILLAGE FESTIVALS LIGHT UP PROVENCE

Stretching from the Languedoc across Provence, the *fêtes votives* (patronal festivals) take over the centre of villages throughout the region. Dances, live music, cultural performances and shared meals are the highlights of these authentic local celebrations. If you want to mix with locals, this is your chance!

Left *Farandole* dancers **Middle** *Soupe au pistou* **Right** *Pétanque* players

In his later years, influential Provençal writer Jean Giono complained that the villages in Provence were dying out and becoming homogenous in identity. A visit to any two *fêtes votives* would prove him wrong! Each of these festivals, dedicated to the patron saint of the village, reveals details of the village's collective history that couldn't be more different.

Local Character

How could one compare the herding of bulls through the narrow streets that take place during the *fêtes votive* in Camargue to the dancing horses of the *fête votive* of Goult? In the Alpilles, horse racing and games on horseback take centre stage, and in other villages it's *pétanque* tournaments that garner most of the attention. The village of Robion hosts concerts in the Théâtre de Verdure, an exceptional natural site at the foot of the Petit Luberon, surrounded by rosemary and cedar trees. The origins of these celebrations are religious. Some villages still hold ceremonies to honour their patron saint, or even reenact important feats in the saint's lifetime. But mostly, the festivals are a reason to come together in the summer to eat, dance and celebrate.

Each village organises their festival in accordance to their traditions, which usually lasts the whole weekend. These events are open to all. Activities include open-air movie screenings, live music, *pétanque* tournaments, art expositions and theatre performances. *Pétanque* tournaments are taken very seriously, so practice throwing a few boules before you sign up. You might find yourself dancing a *farandole*, a distinctive line dance from the region.

Share a Table

Bigger festivals may have food trucks catering the festivities, but in smaller villages, like Lacoste, there is the possibility of joining the communal meal. Imagine the cuisine as a way to soak up the real history of a place: you may find yourself eating a *soupe au pistou*, the fragrant vegetable, pasta and *pistou* (pesto) soup that signifies summer in many parts of the Luberon. Or it may be a *joue du porc confite*, simmered for hours in a vegetable stew seasoned with *herbes de Provence* and red wine. Some villages host picnics, and serve a Provençal classic: homemade aïoli dip, a garlicy type of mayonnaise, served with steamed white fish and vegetables.

> Some villages still hold ceremonies to honour their patron saint, but mostly, the festivals are a reason to come together in the summer to eat, dance and celebrate.

Children are welcomed and celebrated during these festivals. Most villages set up an area with games and activities for kids. At some point over the weekend, the town hall tends to treat all attendees to an *aperitif* on the house, to kick off the evening's ball. Whether partygoers are dancing to traditional music with Provençal singers, or the town has decided to go modern and book a DJ, there is no better way to feel like a local than attending a *fête votive*.

⁂ Must-Visit Fêtes Votives

Visiting Avignon or the Luberon in summertime? It seems like there is a *fête votive* every weekend! There are no 'living museum' vibes when you visit a *fête votive* – you'll be welcomed and encouraged to join the fun. Here is a non-comprehensive list of festivals you might visit for a real immersion in Provençal culture:

May Monteux and Grambois

June Morières-lès-Avignon and Mévouillon

July Rustrel, Lagnes, Apt, Beaumes-de-Venise, Collias and Lacoste

August Carpentras, Oppède, Pertuis, Uzès and Lourmarin

September Gigondas, Robion, Goult, Lambesc and St-Rémy de Provence

Listings

BEST OF THE REST

Catch a Show During the Festival d'Avignon

Cour d'Honneur

In the heart of the Papal Palace, surrounded by imposingly regal walls, get swept away by the drama of the stage. Check Avignon ON festival for tickets.

Cloître des Célestins

Dimly lit arches and towering plane trees in the square add a mysterious natural touch to any play or piece of art that takes place here.

Carrière de Boulbon

Fifteen kilometres from Avignon Centre, this former quarry in the middle of nature is a surreal location to see a play or contemporary dance performance. Parking nearby.

A Drink Before (or After) Dinner

La Cave des Pas Sages €€

On Avignon's lively rue des Teinturiers, this wine bar has a curated selection of local wines as well as beer on tap and plates to share. Grab a table early during summer!

Au Fut et à Mesure €

Good choice of beer with a shaded terrace in the centre of Avignon. Don't be put off by the fact this is a small chain in France – the quality of product and ambience make it feel one of a kind.

Sham's Bar Théâtre €

Known as 'Le Shams' among locals, this cocktail bar often hosts themed nights with theatre and music performances all year long. Check its Facebook page for events.

People-Watching Cafes

Le Grand Café Berretta €

Underneath a large tree on place St-Didier in Avignon, this is a perfect people-watching cafe with good coffee, an airy atmosphere and professional service.

Maison Violette Place des Corps €

Technically a bakery (and a wonderful one at that), the small terrace of Maison Violette is a great spot to watch the residents and visitors of Avignon traverse the place des Corps.

Dinner in Avignon

L'Épicerie €€

On place St-Pierre in the centre of Avignon is a charmingly simple restaurant serving dishes like lamb shank with apricot, and Ventoux wine glazed beef filet.

Pollen €€€

Word on the street is this one-star Michelin restaurant in Avignon will soon have two stars. Chef Mathieu Desmarset's six- or eight-course meals are local ingredients prepared to present a refined and creative ensemble.

Café Roma €

Next to Avignon's Utopia Cinema, the bright and airy Café Roma serves seasonal Provençal and Mediterranean dishes, with many vegetarian, gluten-free and lactose-free options.

Au Jardin Des Carmes €€

A shaded garden off place des Carmes in Avignon houses Au Jardin Des Carmes. Carefully prepared seasonal dishes might include a fish of the day with hazelnut butter and a grapefruit and chives sauce.

Ice-Cream Fix

Regusto

A humble ice-cream stand near Les Halles, Regusto serves creamy Italian ice cream. Though French people rarely eat and walk, ice cream is the exception! Get your fill here.

La Princière d'Avignon

In summer the line can stretch around the block for the award-winning artisanal ice cream from La Princiere d'Avignon. Alongside classic favourites are flavours like fig, green tea and bergamot, and lime and basil.

 ## Museum Day

Musée Angladon Collection Jacques Doucet

One of Avignon's best museums, with a wide collection of art from the 18th, 19th and 20th centuries including works by Cézanne, Van Gogh and Picasso.

Musée Louis Vouland

Near Avignon's ramparts is the Louis Vouland museum in a former mansion displaying a collection of 17th- and 18th-century furniture, porcelain, tapestries and paintings.

Le Grenier à Sel

In a former salt warehouse in Avignon, Le Grenier à Sel brings together audiovisual artwork and living art. This is a space on the edge of avant-garde. Free entry.

Musée Calvet

Avignon's beaux arts museum: visitors will find paintings, decorative objects, sculptures and more from the 16th to the 20th centuries. The sculpture collection is especially well cultivated with works by Camille Claudel, Francesco Laurana and Giambologna. Free entry.

DANIELE SCHNEIDER/GETTY IMAGES ©

Chapelle Notre-Dame d'Aubune

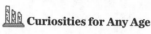 ## Curiosities for Any Age

Sarcophagi of Mazan

A little more than a half-hour's drive from Avignon is the village of Mazan, and its 64 sarcophagi dating from the 5th and 6th centuries, exhumed from an early Christian necropolis.

Chapelle Notre-Dame d'Aubune

A gem of Romanesque architecture and wonderfully preserved, the Notre-Dame d'Aubune Chapel and its medieval gardens offers free entry and free guided visits the first Saturday of every month. About 30 minutes from Avignon.

The Fires of Mont Ventoux

On 24 June, the flanks of Mont Ventoux are alight with flames, to celebrate the day of St-Jean. About 40 minutes from Avignon.

Le Mur de la Peste

Three hundred years ago, a wall to separate communities during the plague was built in the region. It's easiest to visit and learn the history in Cabrières d'Avignon, Lagnes or Venasque. Forty minutes to one hour from Avignon.

 Scan to find more things to do in Avignon and around online

THE LUBERON

HILL VILLAGES | BIODIVERSITY | OUTDOOR ADVENTURE

Experience
the Luberon
online

0
0
10 km
5 miles

Enjoy clear skies and go stargazing in **Murs** (p212)
🚗 1½hrs from Avignon

Carpentras

Mazan

○ Monteux

○ Pernes-les-
Fontaines

Scale **Le Mourre Nègre**, the highest point of the Luberon (p209)
🚗 2hrs from Avignon

Cruise on a wobbly *négo chin* boat in **Isle-sur-la-Sorgue** (p211)
🚗 45mins from Avignon

L'Isle-
sur-la-
Sorgue

● Murs

Joucas ○

Gordes ○

Roussillon ○

○ Goult

Apt

Take your time exploring the uncrowded village of **Robion** (p209)
🚗 1hr from Avignon

Coustellet
○

● Robion

Cavaillon

Bonnieux ○

*Parc Naturel
Régional du Luberon*

Vaugines

Taste farm-to-table food at the **Lauris producers market** (p217)
🚗 1hr from Avignon

Orgon ○

La Tuillie

Lauris

Lourmarin

Cucuron

○ Cadenet

Durance

Pay homage to writer Albert Camus' grave outside **Lourmarin** (p219)
🚗 1½hrs from Avignon

THE LUBERON
Trip Builder

A final huff of the Alps before the plains stretch out towards the Mediterranean Sea: the Luberon massif is home to bucolic agricultural traditions as well as rich biodiversity and beautifully preserved hill villages. What more is there to ask for?

Practicalities

ARRIVING

TGV Begin your travels through the Luberon from Marseille, Avignon or Aix-en-Provence. All three have TGV train stations.

Air By air you'll land in Marseille-Provence, outside Marseille.

FIND YOUR WAY

Apps like Maps.me and Komoot offer driving navigation but also download-able hiking and biking paths.

MONEY

Card and phone-pay is accepted most places, though for small purchases in food or antique markets, it can be cash only.

WHERE TO STAY

Place	Pro/Con
Apt	A medium-sized village home to a busy market but calm atmosphere.
Bonnieux	Narrow streets, bustling restaurants and a sun-drenched sunset over vineyards.
Isle-sur-la-Sorgue	Dividing the Luberon and the Monts de Vaucluse, Isle-sur-la-Sorgue is an oasis.

EATING & DRINKING

Local fruits and vegetables are abundant: try a Cavaillon melon (pictured top right), local cherries, or the Lagnes pepper. If you're visiting mid to late summer, try *soupe au pistou* (pictured bottom left), a hearty soup. Candied fruits from the town of Apt make their way to holiday tables all over France.

Best desserts
Chez Jarry (p221)

Must-try snack
Anchoïade – stuffed tomatoes, olive tapenade and goat's cheese (p216).

GETTING AROUND

Car Driving is the fastest way to visit multiple villages around the region. Be careful though, some village roads can be twisty and narrow.

Bicycle The region has a large network of bike paths and many backroads not frequented by cars.

JAN–MAR
Can be sunny, or very cold. Beware the mistral wind.

APR–JUN
A quick spring; May is excellent. By June it's hot.

JUL–SEP
Morning: Outdoor activities. Afternoon: Listen to cicadas from the shade.

OCT–DEC
Lovely time to visit, autumn is colourful and mild.

43 Hidden in
THE HILLS

HISTORIC VILLAGES | FEWER CROWDS | LIMESTONE

Gordes, Roussillon, Lourmarin, Fontaine-de-Vaucluse; we're not saying skip these villages. But we are saying leave some time in your itinerary for other villages, a little more laid-back, a little less crowded, and just as picturesque as the big names of the Luberon.

QUENTIN BOEHM ©

🗺 How to

Getting here The Luberon is easily visited by car, but there are well-mapped cycling routes. It's possible to rent regular or e-bikes with saddlebags. This is an ecofriendly way to see the region, and you'll notice details and meet people you'd otherwise miss.

When to go Spring, early summer, autumn. July and August are very hot.

How long Three to four days minimum to explore the Luberon without rushing.

QUENTIN BOEHM ©

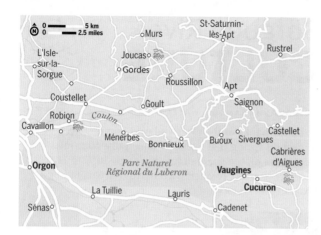

If you like... you'll love... If the neatly restored stonewalls and *bories*, ancient structures commonly seen around Gordes, come to mind when you think of the Luberon, you should try **Joucas**. Perched on a hill just a few kilometres from Gordes, Joucas has similar architecture but is smaller and less crowded. After shopping for artisanal crafts in Gordes, you'll marvel at the art of Heybroek-Plaud that decorates the village centre in Joucas.

At the foot of the Petit Luberon Maubec and Ménerbes are frequently visited hill villages bordering the Petit Luberon at the western edge of the massif. In the summer, avoid the crowds and visit the village of **Robion** instead. The historic centre is small but with charming shops and stellar bakery La Croûte Céleste. Take the kids to slide down a rock known as the *glissette* (ask locals to point it out to you) and watch the evening approach while drinking a pastis under the large plane tree at the Café de la Poste.

Luberon Sud: into the maquis Lourmarin and Cucuron are the typical choices to visit on the south side of the Luberon. But just a few kilometres past Cucuron is **Cabrières-d'Aigues**. Known as the '*village papillon*' because of its butterfly shape when viewed from above, Cabrières-d'Aigues is the best spot to stay if you plan to hike up to Le Mourre Nègre, the highest point of the Luberon.

Top left Joucas **Bottom left** Café de la Poste, Robion

Le Mourre Nègre

In the local Provençal dialect, Le Mourre Nègre means the black muzzle. From Cabrières-d'Aigues it's a two- to three-hour hike to the summit one way. Bring water and a picnic lunch and follow the trails that wind up small valleys covered by maquis (short, shrubby trees). Check restrictions in town before leaving – during the dry season it may be forbidden to climb due to the risk of fire. From the top, spot the Durance river and dozens of hill villages that make up the south Luberon, and in the distance, the Montagne Ste-Victoire, the muse of Cézanne.

Sorgues River
CULTURE

ANTIQUE MARKETS | GALLO-ROMAN | TRANQUIL WATERS

Cool off in summer on the banks of the clear and cold Sorgues river. Fed by a mysterious underground spring that even the famed diver Jacques Cousteau couldn't find the bottom of, the waters remain a chilly 10°C to 14°C year-round. In the village centre, canals are lined with narrow streets hiding artisanal shops, art studios and fine restaurants.

QUENTIN BOEHM ©

🗺 **How to**

Getting here Isle-sur-la-Sorgue is accessible by train and it's easy to rent a bicycle to get around, but many folks come by car. Isle-sur-la-Sorgue is about 40 minutes from Avignon.

When to go March to November. July and August are the hottest and busiest months.

Fun tip There are many famous artists who live or retire in Isle-sur-la-Sorgue. If you happen to dine in a certain riverside restaurant on Fridays, you may just cross paths with the singer of the French classic song 'Le Mistral Gagnant'.

QUENTIN BOEHM ©

Far left Riverside home, Sorgues
Bottom left *Négo chin*, Sorgues **Near left** Antique shops, Isle-sur-la-Sorgue

Between Cobblestone & Canals

No, this isn't Venice! Pre–Roman Empire, local fishermen slowly tamed the rivulets of the Sorgues, building an intricate network of canals. *Flâneurs*, who love wandering with no destination in particular, will love the variety of shops with local goods like soap, herbs and handicrafts. But the real shopping delight in Isle-sur-la-Sorgue is for antiques lovers.

The brocanteurs of Isle-sur-la-Sorgue This Provençal town is home to a renowned upscale flea market, which is second in size only to Paris'. Sundays year-round, av des Quatre Otages fills up with antique and secondhand dealers selling their wares. If you're not there over a weekend, there are dozens of brick-and-mortar shops across the village. The *brocanteurs* managing the stands are well-versed in shipping decorative items and furniture all over the world. If you've got the cash, there's no reason not to leave with that Louis XV Provençal buffet that caught your eye.

Go upriver to the source At the base of the cliffs of Fontaine-de-Vaucluse is a special kind of spring that draws water from an underground basin called a karst: it's the source of the Sorgues. Conflicting fairy tales recount its origins, and the whole village feels pulled from a storybook. Join locals in taking a dip across from the old paper mill near the source, or further downstream, at Chemin Noir (between Fontaine-de-Vaucluse and Isle-sur-la-Sorgue), or Partage des Eaux (Isle-sur-la-Sorgue).

⚓ Drown the Dog Boats?

In Provençal the name of these *négo chin* boats means 'drown the dog', due to their inherent wobbliness. Adapted to the shallow, clear waters of the Sorgues, their handlers manoeuvre them using a long oar. Today, traditional net fishing is forbidden and the boats are used for pleasure.

Each year in mid-July, the Confrérie di Pescaïre Li-len, the local fishing guild that dates back to 1593, hosts **La Pêche d'Antan** festival featuring these boats, with traditional fishing method demonstrations, races through the canals, boat rides and a floating market. It's a total culmination of our river culture.

■ **Insight from Alain Pretôt,** *artisanal 'water-carpenter' of négo chin boats, Isle-sur-la-Sorgue*

45

A Sky Full of
STARS

ASTRONOMY | BESPOKE | NIGHT ACTIVITY

━━━ The calm inspired by a getaway to the countryside comes with a surprising fringe benefit: small villages usually have little light pollution. Around the villages of Murs, Buoux, or even the larger village of Manosque, amateur astrologists can fill their eyes with stars. As a romantic date or with family, this is an experience that gives perspective.

🗺 How to

Before you go Book a discovery session at an observatory (€15 per adult, groups up to 60 people), a private evening with an astrologer (€80 per person up to 8 people) in the village of your choice, or observe the stars with your naked eye.

When to go Any time of year as long as the sky is clear.

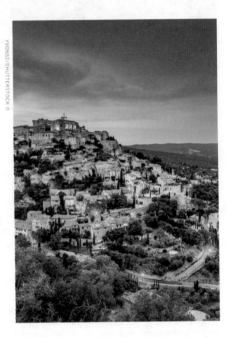

YVON52/SHUTTERSTOCK ©

Stargazing in the Luberon
The Luberon region of Provence has some of the lowest light pollution in all of France. Multiple observatory stations are set up in the hillsides for research and public education. Every Monday night in summer near the village of Manosque, the

Centre d'Astronomie St-Michel l'Observatoire hosts an English-speaking astronomy initiation. There are also independent astronomy guides like **Astrobivouac** who bring their telescope to you.

An uninterrupted view This is the key to observing stars. Along with having little light

pollution, the Luberon and the Monts de Vaucluse have a few climatic advantages, making the region an attractive locale for astronomers. The mistral wind, which holds a large place in local lore, can be a friend to those who look to the heavens; the violent gusts of this wind which usually

🔭 Accessible to All

Don't fret if you haven't got a telescope. All you need is a clear night and you can observe the heavens. Applications like Stellarium can show the configuration of the stars on a certain night using GPS. Many constellations are possible to see with the naked eye, or with low-light binoculars.

The easiest planets and stars to see with the naked eye are Jupiter, Venus and the Big Dipper. But with a telescope, I love to gaze at the rings of Saturn – I could look at them every day and not get tired of it.

■ Recommended by **Stephen Rater,** *a French astronomer who helps people discover the stars* @astrobivouac

blow for days at a time are quite adept at keeping the skies clear. Also, thanks to the mistral and the general dryness of the terrain, the vegetation – namely white oaks – does not usually grow very high. Almost any hilltop in Provence is therefore a ready-made astral obser-

vatory if you're determined enough.

If you plan to observe the stars close to your lodgings, stay in a quiet hill village with a view but little light pollution. Villages like Murs, Joucas or Buoux are good choices to reflect on our place in the universe.

Top left Nighttime, Gordes **Top right** Centre d'Astronomie St-Michel l'Observatoire

46

Producers or
PROVENÇAL?

**FARM TO TABLE | LOCAL
SPECIALITIES | MARKETS**

▬▬▬▬ Connect with the culinary traditions of Provence as you wander the stalls of the outdoor markets. Meet farmers at traditional *marchés paysans*, or be dazzled by produce from all over the region at the *marchés Provençaux*.

TRABANTOS/SHUTTERSTOCK ©

🗺 How to

When to go Market days are available online, or stop in at the town hall where you're staying.

Money Bring your own basket and cash; some merchants accept card payments but most prefer cash in small bills.

Fun tip In summer, keep an eye out for a third type of regional market: the *marchés du soir* are outdoor markets that take place during the cooler hours of the early evening.

FRANZ MARC FREI/GETTY IMAGES ©

Forget the Supermarket

The Vaucluse is one of the most fertile regions for fruits and vegetables in France. During the summer, there is a market every day of the week if you just know which village to visit. But the type of market you choose to visit is important too.

Staying for a few days? Before you visit one of the bustling Provençal markets, try a **marché paysan**. This is the French equivalent of farm to table; the stalls are reserved for the producers of the food. These markets skew heavily on seasonal and small-batch homemade goods. Locals tend to love these markets for their weekly shopping. Often the products are certified organic or in transition towards organic. A convivial ambience hangs in the air as you peruse the stands showcasing the region's best crop.

QUENTIN BOEHM ©

🌿 Aroma of Provence

Sachets of *herbes de Provence* – a mix of dried thyme, rosemary, oregano, *sarriette* and basil – are all over Provençal markets. Some of these herbs you can pick on your own. Let your nose lead you while hiking in the Luberon and you'll easily stumble upon swathes of wild thyme and rosemary!

Top left Marché d'Apt **Bottom left** Marché agricole de Petit-Palais **Above** Cheeses, Marché Provençal de Pernes les Fontaines

Need to see it all in one shot? If you're not one to dilly-dally at the market, or you want to taste local specialities while having the option of buying all the souvenirs you promised you'd bring home, better to go to a **marché Provençal**. Not limited to producers only, these markets have pretty much everything you'd like, usually local, and always keeping the traditions of Provence close to heart. You'll find more selection of artisanal home goods, like tablecloths, napkins, olive-wood cutting boards and tableware in these markets too. These larger markets can be busy and it might be worth booking a guide to show you the best stands and keep things animated.

Where to Go

Marchés paysans On the Luberon valley floor is the **marché paysan de Coustellet** (Sunday mornings) and the **marché agricole de Petit-Palais** (Saturday mornings). The south side of the Luberon is home to two more: the **marché paysan de Cadenet** takes

☀ **The Perfect Provençal Morning...**

...looks like tasting the artisanal specialities in the Provençal markets! The nougat, stuffed tomatoes, *brandade*, *poischichade*, as well as local cheeses and olive oils, all taste like the sunny days of Provence.

On summer mornings I like to take photos of the lavender fields before sunrise, visit the market early before the crowds arrive, and then go for a picnic to enjoy the contents of my shopping bag.

■ **Recommended by Ashley Tinker,** *a painter, photographer and market tour guide in Provence @curiousprovence*

Left Floating market, Isle-sur-la-Sorgue **Below** *Herbes de Provence* (p215)

LEFT: JOSE NICOLAS/GETTY IMAGES © RIGHT: JAYNE DUNCAN/SHUTTERSTOCK ©

place behind the church of one of the area's most inviting hillsides. And the **marché paysan de Lauris** takes place on Thursday evenings. It's a made-to-order place to find everything you need for a Provençal-inspired *apéro*. On the flanks of the Luberon massif there is also the Sunday morning **marché paysan de Saint Martin de la Brasque**.

Marchés Provençaux Overflowing the pedestrian streets of the canal-riddled village of **Isle-sur-la-Sorgue**, the Provençal market on Sunday mornings is the painting of a Provençal market. Saturday morning the action takes place at the **marché d'Apt**, a town at the base of the Luberon massif with narrow streets that fill the cities ramparts. Also on Saturdays on the northwest end of the massif, in the heart of Monts de Vaucluse, is the **marché Provençal de Pernes les Fontaines**, where up to 50 stands line up underneath the shady plane trees.

Splendid
SAUNTER

TROGLODYTE HOMES | CHÂTEAU | EASY HIKE

▬▬▬ Let your feet follow the trail, made from rocks bleached white by the sun, as you hike a loop from the south Luberon villages of Lourmarin and Cadenet. This hike is good for those who want a nice ramble without risking getting lost in the maquis or stuck on the steep limestone cliffs – common features of many hikes in the region.

KEVIN OKE PHOTO/SHUTTERSTOCK ©

🗺 Trip Notes

When to go Try to go very early in the morning if you go in summer.

What to bring A windbreaker is essential if the weather forecast includes wind. Pack water – there are fountains in the village but not on the trail.

Level up The departure for hiking Régalon Gorges is not far from Lourmarin. There are a few passages involving ladders bolted to the rocks, making it less family-friendly.

🗺 Extend Your Path

It's up to you if you choose to start in Lourmarin (pictured) or Cadenet.

Add a little distance without difficulty by continuing from Cadenet down to the banks of the Durance. You'll be rewarded by a view of the village with a backdrop of the Luberon to the north. Or add an activity by booking a truffle-hunting tour with Les Pastras.

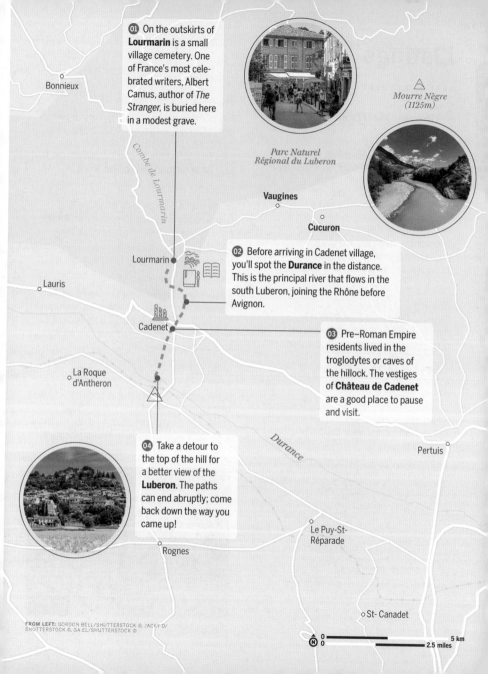

01 On the outskirts of **Lourmarin** is a small village cemetery. One of France's most celebrated writers, Albert Camus, author of *The Stranger*, is buried here in a modest grave.

Bonnieux

Mourre Nègre
(1125m)

*Parc Naturel
Régional du Luberon*

Vaugines

Cucuron

Lourmarin

Lauris

02 Before arriving in Cadenet village, you'll spot the **Durance** in the distance. This is the principal river that flows in the south Luberon, joining the Rhône before Avignon.

Cadenet

03 Pre–Roman Empire residents lived in the troglodytes or caves of the hillock. The vestiges of **Château de Cadenet** are a good place to pause and visit.

La Roque
d'Antheron

04 Take a detour to the top of the hill for a better view of the **Luberon**. The paths can end abruptly; come back down the way you came up!

Durance

Pertuis

Le Puy-St-
Réparade

Rognes

St- Canadet

Combe de Lourmarin

N
0   0   5 km
0   0   2.5 miles

Listings

BEST OF THE REST

 Sunset Meal from the Luberon

Bistrot le 5 €€

Atop the village of Ménerbes, try sardines, truffle-infused charcuterie, or a selection of spreads: olive tapenade, hummus and more. The dinner menu changes by the season but is Mediterranean-inspired bistro fare.

Le Cercle Républicain €

Though it looks unassuming from the outside, the door to a small, intimate terrace is hidden at the end of the cafe. Located in Gordes.

Un Jardin sur le Toit €€

Above the city of Apt lies the village of Saignon. On the table you'll find regional aromas and dishes like veal filet mignon served with grilled vegetables andaubergine caviar.

 Provençal Abbeys

Abbaye de Silvacane

Outside of Pertuis this charming abbey has a long and storied history – built in the 12th century, the abbey once was used as a quarry, and as a farm.

Abbaye Notre-Dame de Sénanque

Surrounded by lavender fields in a shallow valley hidden in the limestone hills between Gordes and Cabrières d'Avignon is the Abbaye Notre-Dame de Sénanque.

 Traces of Great Writers

The Home of Jean Giono

Muse and reflect in the gardens and chambers of celebrated Provençal writer Jean Giono outside the city of Manosque. Le Paraïs can be visited only with reservations.

The Grave of Albert Camus

Pay homage to the great writer and philosopher Camus, author of *The Stranger*, in a quaint cemetery outside Lourmarin.

 Museums Worth the Visit

Fondation Villa Datris

In Isle-sur-la-Sorgue, the Fondation Villa Datris has rotating contemporary sculpture exhibits in a transformed bourgeois townhouse. Dozens of artists' work is on display in the house and gardens. Free entry.

Musée de la Vannerie

Basket-weaving flourished in the village of Cadenet during the 19th and 20th centuries. The museum houses a large collection of woven objects and also audiovisual exhibits elaborating on the craft.

Musée d'Histoire Jean Garcin 39–45

A WWII museum that exhibits daily life in occupied France. A special section is dedicated to 'La Resistance' effort in the Vaucluse department. An intimate look at how artists, writers and poets were engaged in the resistance.

Village des Bories

Musée de la Lavande

Near Coustellet, learn how lavender is grown and distilled into oils, fragrances and more. Includes historic tools linked to lavender cultivation and a real understanding of the plant.

Satisfy Your Sweet Tooth

Chez Jarry €

A truly outstanding pastry and chocolate shop: stop here if Cavaillon is on your route. An eclectic decor with candies hidden everywhere gives this shop a fantasy feel. Recently started doing lunch (also excellent).

Pâtisserie Volpert €

Award-winning pastry chef Théodore Volpert's shop in Ansouis is home to a signature pastry, the 'Ansousien', mixing rosemary and apricot flavours in a way you won't soon forget.

Outdoor Marvels

Village des Bories

Spectacularly well preserved, the Village des Bories allows you to visit the dry-stone houses used from the Bronze Age to the 18th century.

Colorado Provençal

A former industrial site to collect ochre to use as dye, the Colorado Provençal is a popular hiking spot near Rustrel. A less crowded option than visiting the red walls in Roussillon.

Claparèdes Plateau

This hiking or picnic spot near Buoux is the spot to see all the colours of Provence: green olive trees, grey oaks, purple lavender and lush wildflowers in spring, under the bluest of skies.

Pont Julien

A Roman bridge dating back to 3 CE, the Pont Julien stretches wide over the Calavon river. Between Apt and Bonnieux, this well-preserved bridge has withstood sudden rises and floodings of the Calavon for centuries.

Pont Julien

Hungry for Adventure

Climbing the Limestone Cliffs

The Luberon region has hundreds of practicable rock-climbing routes. Those not to miss include the cliffs of Buoux and the Rocher des Abeilles à St-Martin-de-Castillon. Contact the tourism office for a list of guides.

The South on Horseback

In French, 'Le Sud à Cheval' lets you tour the Luberon from a saddle. Seasonally themed rides on a herd of Camargue horses last two to five days with nights spent in B&Bs or camping.

Mountain Biking the Luberon

Bonnieux or Coustellet are good starting points for a mountain-biking adventure through the Luberon. There are e-bike shops such as Sun E-Bike with mountain bikes (VVT in French) for rent in both villages.

Trail Luberon

Trail runners will love the region's steep climbs and rocky paths. The Trail du Luberon race takes place each May leaving from Cabrières d'Aigues and has 15km and 30km options.

 Scan to find more things to do in the Luberon online

THE LUBERON REVIEWS

MARKETA1982/SHUTTERSTOCK ©

ALPES-DE-HAUTE-PROVENCE

OUTDOORS | NATURE | LAVENDER

**Experience
Alpes-de-
Haute-
Provence
online**

ALPES-DE-HAUTE-PROVENCE
Trip Builder

Take the road less travelled as you drive the mystical **Route du Temps** from Sisteron (p234)

🚗 *2hr round trip, without stops*

Where wide, sun-drenched plateaus teeming with fragrant lavender meet remote mountain slopes speckled with mirror lakes and rural *refuges*, the Alpes-de-Haute-Provence is the Côte d'Azur's wild sibling. Fasten your seatbelt for an adventure of epic proportions: you're about to see Provence in a whole new light.

St-Geniez

Sisteron

○ Sault

Châteauneuf-Val-St-Donat ○

Château-Arnoux St-Auban

Banon○

Peyruis ○

Les Mées

Aiglur

Simiane-la-Rotonde ○

※ ○ Lurs

Tuck into melt-in-your-mouth lamb from Sisteron at **La Terrasse de Lurs** (p231)

🚗 *12mins from Forcalquier*

○ Mane

○ Oraison

Brunet

○ Apt

Reillanne ○

Volx ○

Puimoisson ○

Manosque ○

Valensole

Riez ○

Sample the local pink drink at the winegrower's co-op in **Pierrevert** (p231)

🚲 *30mins from Manosque*

Durance

Play a role in the sustainable future of Provence's lavender fields on the **Plateau de Valensole** (p228)

🚗 *25mins from Manosque*

Pertuis ○

St-Paul-lès-Durance ○

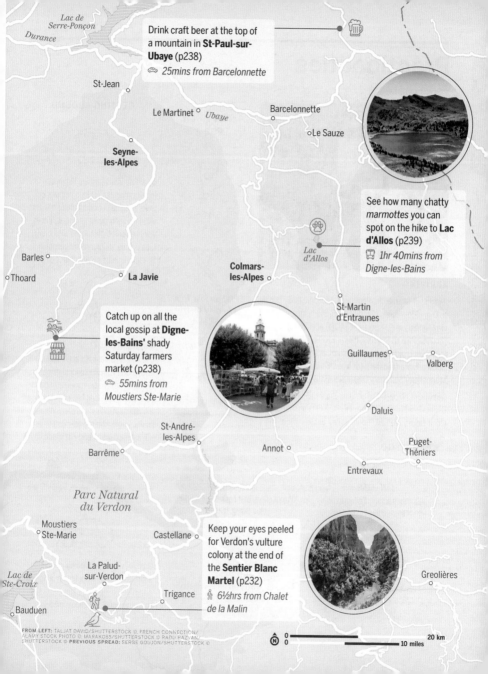

Drink craft beer at the top of a mountain in **St-Paul-sur-Ubaye** (p238)
🚗 *25mins from Barcelonnette*

See how many chatty *marmottes* you can spot on the hike to **Lac d'Allos** (p239)
🚆 *1hr 40mins from Digne-les-Bains*

Catch up on all the local gossip at **Digne-les-Bains'** shady Saturday farmers market (p238)
🚗 *55mins from Moustiers Ste-Marie*

Keep your eyes peeled for Verdon's vulture colony at the end of the **Sentier Blanc Martel** (p232)
🥾 *6½hrs from Chalet de la Malin*

Lac de Serre-Ponçon
Durance
St-Jean
Le Martinet ○ *Ubaye*
Barcelonnette
○ Le Sauze
Seyne-les-Alpes
Barles ○
○Thoard
○ **La Javie**
Colmars-les-Alpes ○
Lac d'Allos
St-Martin d'Entraunes ○
Guillaumes○
○ Valberg
○ Daluis
St-André-les-Alpes ○
Annot ○
Puget-Théniers
Entrevaux ○
Barrême ○
Parc Natural du Verdon
Moustiers Ste-Marie ○
Castellane ○
Greolières ○
La Palud-sur-Verdon
Lac de Ste-Croix
Trigance ○
○Bauduen

Ⓝ 0 — 20 km
0 — 10 miles

Practicalities

EQROY/SHUTTERSTOCK ©

ARRIVING

Aéroport Marseille-Provence Multiple daily buses to Digne-les-Bains (Zou! LER26, 2½ hours, €21.90) via Manosque (1½ hours, €14.10) and Sisteron (Zou! LER26 to Peyruis, then LER29, 2½ hours, €20.80). Buy tickets onboard or at the airport kiosk. Book private transfers (at least €145/220/280 for Manosque/Sisteron/Digne-les-Bains) in advance.

Aéroport Nice-Côte d'Azur Zou! LER31 stops at Digne-les-Bains (3½ hours, €23.60) and Sisteron (four hours, €29.70) on its way to Grenoble.

HOW MUCH FOR A

Craft beer
€4

Plat du jour in a country bistro
€14

Pedalo rental
€20 per hour

WHEN TO GO

JAN–MAR
A smorgasbord of winter sports in the ski resorts.

APR–JUN
Warm days but less foot traffic on hiking trails.

JUL–SEP
Flowers in bloom. Busy, especially around the Gorges du Verdon.

OCT–DEC
Fewer crowds on lakes. Pretty autumnal colours.

GETTING AROUND

Bus The Zou! Lignes Express Régionales (LER) bus network links the main towns and smaller villages with daily services. Fares vary: check timetables and calculate prices at zou.maregionsud.fr. Tickets can be purchased onboard (cash only).

Mountain Bike Over 4000km of trails across vast floral plateaus, above dizzying limestone gorges and over dramatic mountain passes make these heights of Provence a mountain-biker's dream. What's more, you'll find a well-oiled infrastructure already in place, from bike hire to bike repair. Keep tourism-alps-provence.com/mountainbike handy while planning. An e-bike scene is simmering.

Car As well as at the airports in Marseille and Nice, international car-hire companies have offices in Manosque, Sisteron and Digne-les-Bains.

EATING & DRINKING

Expect a heavier cuisine than you'd find on the coast, one where butter is chosen over olive oil, particularly as you make your way north. Sisteron's prized lamb (pictured top right) and Banon's goat's cheese are the products of reference, with a reputation that has spread well beyond Provence. Don't leave without trying a local liqueur made from curious-sounding mountain flora and lunching in at least one Bistrot de Pays. You'll develop a whole new appreciation for exactly how these rural tables bring together small communities.

Best produce markets
Forcalquier (p238; pictured bottom right)

Must-try mountain liqueur
Génépi (p231)

CONNECT & FIND YOUR WAY

Wi-fi Public hotspots are few and far between and network connectivity patchy on mountain tops and along riverbeds, no matter your network operator. In the bigger towns, most cafes and bars have a wi-fi network you can log into.

Navigation Download your planned routes for offline navigation before you set off. Mountain passes freeze over in winter.

WHERE TO STAY

Chic hotels and polished B&Bs are a perfect match for pretty lavender blooms. The vibe is less glossy, but equally charming, the further you head into the region's alpine heart.

Place	Pro/Con
Barcelonnette	Lively mountain community at the foot of the ski slopes. Cosy B&Bs with welcoming hosts.
Sisteron	Commanding setting at the base of the striking Rocher de la Baume. Known as the 'Pearl of Haute-Provence'.
Digne-les-Bains	Regional capital, spa town and gateway to the Unesco Géoparc de Haute-Provence.
Manosque	Biggest town. Shaded squares and photogenic pedestrian streets. Close to Valensole's lavender fields.
Moustiers Ste-Marie	Almost too pretty to be true. Smart boutique hotels with swimming pools.

CHARGING POINTS

For electric vehicle drivers, the Réseau eborn website *(eborn.fr)* maps out local charging points with real-time availability.

MONEY

You'll find your euro goes just that little bit further now you're back from the coastal resorts, but supermarket prices are fairly comparable. Cash is king at local markets.

48 LAVENDER,
Sustainably

FLOWERS | NATURE | DAY TRIP

Row after row of purple lavender flowers in full bloom are one of the most emblematic images of Provence – even more so now, thanks to social media. In late June and July, day-trippers flock to the lavender fields of the Plateau de Valensole in search of that perfect Instagram shot. Here's how to join them, but consciously.

BERT CANDAELE ©

🗺 How to

When to go Valensole's lavender fields burst into bloom in mid-June. Harvest can start as early as 1 July.

Getting around Having your own transport is recommended as you can stop and start at your leisure. Check out the Routes de La Lavande (*routes-lavande.com*) for itinerary suggestions.

Spot the difference *Lavandin* is the main variety on the Plateau de Valensole. Near Sault in the Vaucluse, *lavande* flourishes at altitude.

VEGGIE ONLY/SHUTTERSTOCK ©

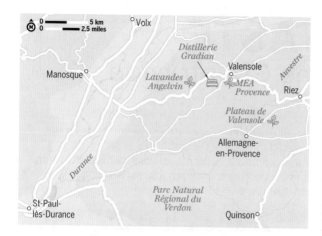

Top left Sustainable lavender field, Provence **Bottom left** Lavender ice cream

Strong roots Don't shy away from multicoloured lavender fields; these are the sustainable fields of tomorrow. The local industry has come together to form the **Fonds SPLP**, a lavender empowerment fund to preserve Provence's unique lavender culture. 'Today when we think of lavender, we imagine a blue line of flowers and a brown line of soil, but that's not natural,' says Jean-Charles Lhommet of L'Occitane Group. Supported by the foundation, the region's growers are now covering soils with plants; not just to protect from erosion but also to nourish and capture carbon. While it's natural to look for the 'perfect' lavender field for your photos, the most responsible ones are now those where the lavender blues are matched by the whites and yellows of diverse flora sprouting from the earth. Take a walk around the Plateau de Valensole and you'll soon be able to spot the difference.

Tours and more While Valensole's growers are more than happy for you to take photographs in their pretty fields, further exploration of their craft is encouraged. You'll be shown harvest and distillation techniques on a free guided tour of the family-run **Lavandes Angelvin** (lavande-valensole.fr) during July and August. **MEA Provence** (lavande-valensole.com) has a sprawling site at the foot of the village that includes a collection of historic equipment, part of an interesting exhibition space. During the season, you'll also be able to snack on no-frills cuisine in its casual, lavender-fringed outdoor restaurant. To stay a while, **Distillerie Gradian** (lafermeduriou.com) rents out self-catering accommodation.

⚘ Lavender in All Senses

See Look around the Plateau de Valensole and you'll find almond orchards, olive groves, crops of cereals such as wheat and spelt, fennel, sage and thyme all growing. This diversity is so important – if lavender was the only crop, these soils would be very poor.

Listen Close your eyes and listen to the buzz of busy bees at work, an essential aspect of a healthy field.

Smell Breathe in the signature floral, but slightly herby, fragrance of lavender bloom.

Taste Honey, ice creams and calissons: you'll taste lavender in a range of local produce.

Touch Visit the L'Occitane en Provence factory and museum in Manosque and take a tactile walk through our garden!

■ Recommended by **Jean-Charles Lhommet,** Biodiversity & Sustainable Ingredients Manager, Manosque, L'Occitane Group @loccitane

49

TASTE
the Countryside

FOOD | DRINK | VIEWS

Get to know the Alpes-de-Haute-Provence through its rural restaurants and home-grown drinks scene. The region is the cradle of the **Bistrot de Pays** association, created to champion France's under-threat country bistros. To stop for a meal is not only supporting the community, but also savouring a cuisine that promotes local products and fair prices.

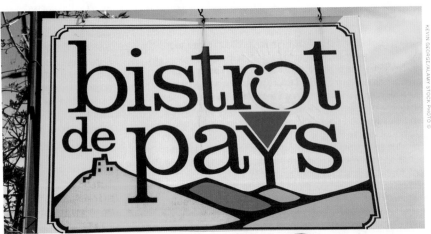

KEVIN GEORGE/ALAMY STOCK PHOTO ©

📸 How to

Cost Reasonable prices are a hallmark of the Bistrot de Pays label. Expect to pay €10 for a tour and tasting at Domaine des Bergeries de Haute-Provence, a price that's waived if you buy wine.

Sleep L'Azimut and Le Lupin Blanc are two

Bistrot de Pays that also offer accommodation.

On your bike Route Napoléon, a winding, mountainous road Napoléon took in 1815 as he marched towards Paris, is the region's great motorbike journey.

PIERRE ALLAIRE ©

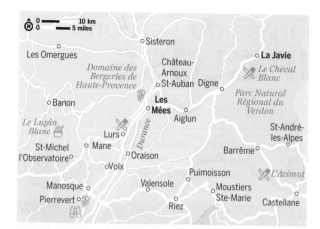

Top left Bistrot de Pays sign **Bottom left** Génépi, Distillerie Lachanenche

⚠ Best Mountain Liqueurs

Génépi Made from a plant that grows only in the alps at an altitude of 2000m, this spirit is appreciated for its medicinal properties.

Larch liqueur The wildflowers from this southern alps pine tree are harvested in spring to make a strong, slightly bitter, resin-flavoured liqueur.

Thyme liqueur Also from wildflowers picked in spring, this digestive from Haute-Provence has intense thyme flower aromas.

Hyssop liqueur This wildflower is harvested in the Vallée de l'Ubaye in summer. Herbaceous flavoured with peppery notes.

Raspberry liqueur Sweet and fruity alcohol drunk neat as a fresh digestive or with white wine in an *apéritif*.

■ Recommended by Jérôme Million

Rousseau, *co-owner, Distillerie Lachanenche, Méolans-Revel* @distillerie_lachanenche

Country bistros At the edge of the Gorges du Verdon, **L'Azimut** in Senez is a haven for bikers travelling the route Napoléon who lap up Guillaume Chevallier's traditional, yet seasonal, cuisine. In the thyme-fringed village of Pierrerue near Forcalquier, restaurateurs Céline Martignon and Jean-François Garçia met in St-Tropez and bring its breezy coastal vibe – and their beloved collection of vintage finds – to **Cocotte**. Just 30 minutes' drive from Valensole, **La Terrasse de Lurs** wows with incredible valley views and a signature lamb on the spit. You'll be charmed by the homemade desserts and bucolic setting of **Le Lupin Blanc** in the picturesque village of Revest-des-Brousses in the Luberon. On a wide grassy plain surrounded by snow-dusted mountains near Digne-les-Bains, **Le Cheval Blanc** in Marcoux is a welcoming refuge for hikers.

Local wine The vineyards around Pierrevert, just outside Manosque, have a small but growing reputation for high-quality wines grown at altitude, particularly rosé. Local grower's co-op **La Cave Coopérative Petra Viridis de Pierrevert** (petra-viridis.com) serves a dual purpose: a wine shop and the starting and finishing point of **Le Sentier des Vignerons**, a 4.5km-long winegrower's trail through swathes of vines and shady olive groves. Outside of the AOC Pierrevert, in an idyllic location south of Sisteron, the fully organic **Domaine des Bergeries de Haute-Provence** (domainedesbergeries.fr) has carved out a niche as the first winery in the region to propose cellar tours and on-site accommodation.

50

Gorges du Verdon
UP CLOSE

OUTDOORS | HIKE | DAY TRIP

The 14km Sentier Blanc Martel is the classic hike along the riverbed of the 'Grand Canyon of Europe'. Come armed with sturdy boots and plenty of water; although nothing can prepare you for the majestic beauty of the terrain you'll cover.

🗺 Trip Notes

When to go Avoid winter, rainy days and weekend crowds in July and August.

What to pack Hiking boots, plenty of water, a hat, sunscreen and a torch for tunnels. Swimming is not allowed in this section of the gorge.

One way Both Chalet de la Maline and Point Sublime serve as starting points, although the former tends to be the preferred setting-off point to avoid a steep ascent at the finish.

🚌 Transport Tip

Negate the need for two cars (one at the start and one at the end) by pre-booking your drop-off at Chalet de la Maline and pick-up from Point Sublime on the *navette* Blanc-Martel (*navette.parcdu verdon.fr*). Leaving from La Palud sur Verdun, the shuttle-bus service operates from April to September.

■ Tip from **Gilles Gravier**, *Verdon Tourisme, Castellane @dessourcesaux gorgesduverdon*

*Parc Naturel
Régional
du Verdon*

05 Look out for the famous vultures of the Verdun sweeping above you at **Point Sublime**, the finishing line at the edge of the sleepy village of Rougon.

04 Turn on your light to navigate the trio of tunnels. The longest, the **Tunnel du Baou**, is over 600m long. Even in summer, don't be surprised to find it chilly inside.

o Rougon

La Palud-
sur-Verdon

Trigance o

01 Set off from **Chalet de la Maline**, the last chance for creature comforts before you emerge on the other side. Watch out for slippery stones in loose soil at the start of the trail.

Verdon

03 Spectacular yes, but also secure. Wedged in a tight space between two cliff faces, the dizzying staircases at **Brèche Imbert** were fully restored 15 years ago.

Artuby

02 A detour to the **Passerelle de l'Estellier**, a low-lying footbridge over the Verdon, will add about 30 minutes onto the hike but is a chance to set foot on the other side of the river.

51

La Route
DU TEMPS

NATURE | MYSTERY | ROAD TRIP

▬▬▬ Embark on a sweeping adventure deep into the Unesco Géoparc de Haute-Provence on La Route du Temps, a little-known route through wild landscapes and mysterious sites with a connection to time. These are the unmissable highlights, according to local vintage car rental specialist, Julie Hoffmann (*lesbelleslurettes.fr*).

HEMIS/ALAMY STOCK PHOTO ©

🖼 Art Detour

The *Sentinelle de la Vallée du Vançon*, British nature artist Andy Goldsworthy's installation near Authon, is more than worth the detour. The stone cairn is one of a trio he has placed along an ancient 150km agricultural hiking route. You'll find one in each of the three valleys of the Unesco Géoparc de Haute-Provence, a colossal open-air geology museum.

📖 Trip Notes

When to go Any season except winter, when the Col de Font-Belle is closed.

Starting off Pay a visit to the Office de Tourisme in Sisteron to pick up a map of the Unesco Géoparc de Haute-Provence and pointers on La Route du Temps.

So chic Navigate this route in style. Les Belle Lurettes' vintage 2CVs (with matching names like Bertille and Fanny) can be hired by the half-day, day or longer.

■ **Itinerary by Julie Hoffmann,** *owner, Les Belles Lurettes, Salignac @lesbelleslurettes*

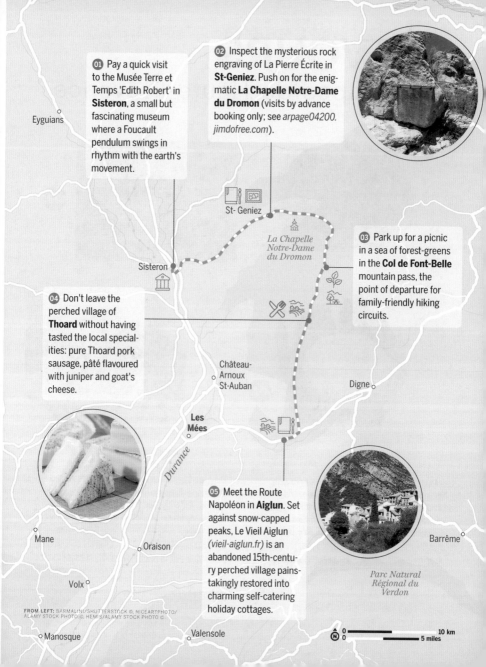

01 Pay a quick visit to the Musée Terre et Temps 'Edith Robert' in **Sisteron**, a small but fascinating museum where a Foucault pendulum swings in rhythm with the earth's movement.

02 Inspect the mysterious rock engraving of La Pierre Écrite in **St-Geniez**. Push on for the enigmatic **La Chapelle Notre-Dame du Dromon** (visits by advance booking only; see *arpage04200.jimdofree.com*).

03 Park up for a picnic in a sea of forest-greens in the **Col de Font-Belle** mountain pass, the point of departure for family-friendly hiking circuits.

04 Don't leave the perched village of **Thoard** without having tasted the local specialities: pure Thoard pork sausage, pâté flavoured with juniper and goat's cheese.

05 Meet the Route Napoléon in **Aiglun**. Set against snow-capped peaks, Le Vieil Aiglun (*vieil-aiglun.fr*) is an abandoned 15th-century perched village painstakingly restored into charming self-catering holiday cottages.

Eyguians

St-Geniez

La Chapelle Notre-Dame du Dromon

Sisteron

Château-Arnoux St-Auban

Digne

Les Mées

Durance

Mane

Oraison

Barrême

Volx

Parc Natural Régional du Verdon

Manosque

Valensole

(N) 0 / 0 — 10 km / 5 miles

FLAVOURS
of the Alpes-de-Haute-Provence

01 Annot Chestnuts
A centuries-old chestnut production is being revived in the sandstone soils of the Grès d'Annot and the result is a sweet chestnut spread.

02 Banon Cheese
Peel away the chestnut-leaf wrapping to reveal this highly prized whole raw milk goat's cheese from the lavender-scented village of Banon.

03 Haute Durance Apples
Soil and sunshine are two key factors that set these golden delicious and gala apples grown in the Vallée de la Haute Durance apart from the rest at the region's morning markets.

04 Honey
Pick your flavour: lavender, chestnut, rosemary – the variety of local honeys reflects the rich array of crops and plants cultivated in the region's soils.

05 Haute-Provence Einkorn (Spelt)
Both good for the soil and good for health, this rare small spelt cereal traditionally used in soups has long been cultivated between Vachères and Banon.

06 Valensole Almonds
The other crop of Valensole's lavender-scented plateau, particularly popular as an ingredient in nougats, macarons, marzipan and calissons (oval-shaped Provençal sweets).

07 Périgord Truffles
The treasured Périgord truffle thrives in the poor soils and nearly year-round sunshine on the plateaus of Forcalquier and Valensole. In truffle terms, that's as good as growing conditions get.

Listings

BEST OF THE REST

 ## Museums & Cultural Spaces

Musée de Préhistoire des Gorges du Verdon

On the banks of the Gorges du Verdon, vine-fringed Quinson is the unlikely location for a bold Norman Foster–designed building. Inside, treasures dug up from over 60 local archaeological sites trace millennia of human history.

Musée de Salagon

Visit this priory turned museum near Forcalquier as much to lose yourself in the delightful gardens cultivated according to themes (including perfume flowers and a medieval garden) as to delve into the heritage of the region.

Musée de la Faïence

Famed around the world for its pretty Provençal ceramics, Moustiers Ste-Marie is a fitting home for this small but fascinating museum displaying five centuries of delicate craftsmanship.

Citromuseum

Those with a thing for vintage 2CVs won't want to miss this private collection of post-war Citroëns in original condition in Castellane. The stories these cars have to tell…

Maison Alexandra David-Neel

Fully restored in 2019, Alexandra David-Neel's home in Digne-les-Bains is a colourful celebration of the life and travels of the pioneering adventurer, orientalist and feminist.

 ## Provençal Markets

Digne-les-Bains

Set under the leafy canopy of bd Gassendi, this farmers market is considered one of the most beautiful in Provence. Wednesday and Saturday mornings, year-round.

Forcalquier

Monday morning's farmers market is the social event of the week for not just the village, but the entire region. Pick up garden-fresh fruit and veg, as well as flowers and bright Provençal fabrics.

Moustiers Ste-Marie

The Marché Nocturne night markets light up Wednesday evenings in July and early August in this most picturesque of Verdon villages. Come ready to taste regional products and browse local crafts, all in a cheery vacation atmosphere.

Gréoux-les-Bains

Typical Provençal market teeming with the colours, flavours, scents – and hot gossip – of the region. Thursday mornings.

Riez

Your basket will be brimming with fragrant produce and too-tempting cheese and charcuterie after a morning at these village markets. Perfect for picnic supplies before heading to the nearby Plateau de Valensole. Wednesday and Saturday mornings.

 ## Craft Breweries, Wineries & Distilleries

La Sauvage – Brasserie des Hautes Vallées

About as far away from the breezy beaches of coastal Provence as you can get, this remote craft brewery on a sparsely populated mountain slope in St-Paul-sur-Ubaye is a special treat. Savour the view from the terrace on a summer's day. Bookings a must.

Distillerie Lachanenche

Family of fruit growers turned distillers who draw inspiration from the alpine plants and botanicals of the Ubaye Valley to craft an organic range of traditional mountain spirits. The still is located 1100m above sea level.

Brasserie Artisanale Cérévisia

Honey, almonds and *génépi* are just some of the local flavours you'll pick up in Isabelle and Christophe's artisanal beer brewed in pretty Oraison. Visits by appointment Monday, Wednesday and Thursday.

Brasserie de L'Aubrée

A friendly welcome and a well-stocked shop on the main square is drawing the region's craft-beer enthusiasts to the small mountain village of Selonnet, the gateway to the Chabanon ski resort. Takeaway only; check for up-to-date business hours before you go.

Domaine La Blaque

In the foothills of the Luberon, this impressive Provençal *bastide* is open for tastings every day of the week except Sunday. The dreamy indoor courtyard is the stuff of rustic chic design dreams.

Sports for All Seasons

Ski

Not far from Barcelonnette, Pra Loup is a sunny winter resort with something for everybody: skiing, snowboarding, snowshoeing, alpine and cross-country skiing and a cosy après-ski scene. Gets bonus point for new lifts.

Hike

Lac d'Allos, the highest natural lake in Europe (2200m), can be reached by a family-friendly 45-minute hike from the Parking du Laus. Inquisitive *marmottes* treat the grassy slopes as their personal playground. How many can you spot?

Skiing, Pra Loup

Cycle

La TransVerdon is a revered 260km mountain-bike trail across the region's ever-changing patchwork of epic landscapes, including the plunging Gorges du Verdon and the perfumed plateau of Valensole. Can also be undertaken on an electric equivalent.

Sail

Pedalo, canoe, motor boat, wakeboard; whatever your mood, there's a smorgasbord of choice to get you out on the water at Lacs du Castillon and Ste-Croix in the Gorges du Verdon. Get in early in summer.

Fly

There's something about the local thermals – and almost guaranteed blue skies – that make St-André-les-Alpes a mecca for paragliders around the world. Aérogliss is the go-to name, especially for nervous newbies.

Climb

The sheer limestone cliff faces of the Gorges du Verdon are a classic climbing destination. For the best bouldering, nothing beats the mystical sandstone formations of the Grès d'Annot.

Scan to find more things to do in Alpes-de-Haute-Provence online

ALPES-DE-HAUTE-PROVENCE REVIEWS

Practicalities

ARRIVING

242

GETTING AROUND

244

SAFE TRAVEL

246

MONEY

247

RESPONSIBLE TRAVEL

248

ACCOMMODATION

250

ESSENTIALS

252

LANGUAGE

254

Right Lignes d'Azur tram, Nice (p243)

EASY STEPS FROM THE AIRPORT TO THE CITY CENTRE

Most air passengers arrive at Nice-Côte d'Azur airport, France's largest regional airport, 7km west of downtown Nice by the sea. Free electric shuttle buses link its two terminals: check on the airport website which terminal your airline uses before departure (Delta and Ryanair usually Terminal 1, easyJet Terminal 2). Airports near Marseille, Toulon and Avignon are also popular arrival points by air.

AT THE AIRPORT

LONG.ION/SHUTTERSTOCK ©

SIM CARDS
Sold at six different red-fronted branches of Relay, including in the departures halls of both terminals. Or buy one in any *tabac* (newsagents) in town.

FOREIGN EXCHANGE
Bureaux de change operate in arrival halls at both terminals, but you won't get the best bang for your buck. The best rates come direct from ATMs in terminals and the city centre.

FREE WI-FI
Available throughout the airport – select the network NiceAirportFreeWifi, open your web browser, and follow the prompts.

ATMS
ATMs dotted around both terminals accept all types of cards (Visa, Eurocard/Mastercard and American Express).

CHARGING STATIONS
Charge phones and other devices with two-pin plugs and USB sockets on shuttle buses and in most eating and drinking areas in both terminals.

CUSTOMS & REFUNDS
Duty free For goods from outside the EU, limits include 200 cigarettes, 50 cigars, 1L of spirits, 2L of wine and 50mL of perfume.

Refunds VAT refunds for purchases made in France over €175 are available to non-EU residents. Claim refunds at self-service refund machines (if you have a tax-refund slip with barcode) or at Interchange offices in both terminals.

GETTING TO THE CITY CENTRE

TRAM

Line 2 *(lignesdazur.com)* of Nice's sleek tramway connects both terminals with Port Lympia in half an hour between 5am and midnight. Trams run every eight to 20 minutes. Get off at the Jean Médecin stop for the city centre and Nice-Ville train station, an 800m walk away.

BUS

Line 12 *(lignesdazur.com)* links the 'Aéro-port/Promenade' stop (Terminal 1) with Promenade des Anglais, place Masséna and Jardin Albert 1er (for Vieux Nice) in about 30 minutes. Buses to/from Aix-en-Provence, Cannes, Monaco, Sisteron and elsewhere use the bus station at Terminal 2.

HOW MUCH FOR A

Taxi
€32
15–45min

Tram
€1.50
30min

Bus
€1.50
30min

TAXI
Official taxis charge a fixed flat rate of €32 (no meter) for the 15- to 45-minute journey, traffic depending, into town.

RIDE-SHARE
Low-emission option Uber Green typically costs around €20 to get into town in a hybrid or fully electric car.

TRAM & BUS TICKETS

Automatic machines at tram and bus stops accept cash and card payments from €1. A single-journey ticket costs €1.50 but if you're spending the day/week in Nice, passes (€5/15 for a 24-hour/seven-day ticket) are unbeatable value. Or buy tickets via the Nice Ticket app.

OTHER POINTS OF ENTRY

Air Marseille's Aéroport Marseille-Provence, 25km northwest in Marignane, is served by year-round flights to many major French and European cities. Smaller Aéroport Toulon-Hyères, 25km east of Toulon, has seasonal flights to about 10 destinations, including Paris, London, Brussels, Luxembourg and Corsica. TUI Fly operates seasonal flights to/from Antwerp and FlyBe to/from Birmingham and Southampton out of Aéroport Avignon-Provence, 8km southeast of Avignon.

Sea Car and passenger ferries cross from Nice, Marseille and Toulon to Corsica (France), Sardinia (Italy) and North Africa. Reservations essential. Fares vary a lot depending on demand and sailing times.

Rail High-speed trains operated by SNCF *(sncf-connect.com)* whisk you from Paris to the Côte d'Azur in under four hours; trains between Paris' Gare de Lyon and Charles de Gaulle airport, Avignon TGV station and Marseille St-Charles are numerous. Low-cost, high-speed Ouigo trains *(ouigo.com)* link Paris' Gare de Lyon and Nice in six hours. For slow-travel enthusiasts nothing beats the Paris' Austerlitz–Nice night train (12 hours), with four-berth and six-berth couchettes. Eurostar *(eurostar.com)* trains from London St-Pancras to Marseille require a change of train in Paris or Lille. Nice is a major rail hub on the busy Barcelona–Rome line.

TRANSPORT TIPS TO HELP YOU GET AROUND

The region was clearly created with the whole gamut of travel styles and budgets in mind. Efficient, high-speed trains zip between major cities and towns; boats yoyo between the mainland and offshore islands; and a myriad of serene country lanes and dizzying cols (mountain passes) pander to motorists and e-bikers keen to make the journey a destination in itself.

CAR

In rural areas (Haute-Provence, Luberon, Haut-Var, Camargue, Arrière-Pays Niçois and notably Nice's iconic Grande Corniche) it is challenging to village-hop and explore remote parks without your own vehicle. In forested areas, fire roads signposted 'DFCI' are off-limits to private vehicles.

BICYCLE & SCOOTER

Provence is made for cycling with its quiet back roads and bike paths. Most towns have bike-rental outlets, with city and mountain bikes (regular and electric-assisted), plus kids' bikes and tandems. Enjoy public-shared bikes and e-scooters in Nice, Monaco, Marseille and Avignon.

CAR RENTAL PER DAY

From about €30/day

Petrol approx €1.80–2/litre

Motorway tolls €15/100km

CAR HIRE

Airports in Nice and Marseille are car-hire hubs, with all the major firms (like Avis, Budget, Enterprise Rent-a-Car, Europcar and Hertz) operating booths in arrival halls till 10pm, plus in TGV train stations and major town centres. At Nice-Côte d'Azur airport, French firm ADA offers self-service vehicles accessible 24/7. Automatic-transmission cars are rare: reserve well ahead.

ROAD CONDITIONS

Autumn to spring, driving is pleasurable. In July and August intense traffic chokes coastal roads – count hours to cover a few kilometres. For English-language traffic reports, tune into 107.7 MHz FM and autoroutes.fr. Calculate toll and fuel costs at viamichelin.com and mappy.fr.

BOAT & SEA TAXI

Ferries sail to islands and along the coast; boat or pricier sea taxi from Ste-Maxime or St-Raphaël is the loveliest way to reach St-Tropez. Key ports include Cannes (for Îles de Lérins), Marseille (Îles du Frioul), La Tour Fondue, Le Lavandou and Hyères (Îles d'Hyères).

DRIVING ESSENTIALS

 Drive on the right; the steering wheel is on the left.

 Speed limit 130km/h on motorways, 110km/h on dual carriageways, 50km/h in urban areas unless signposted otherwise.

 The blood-alcohol limit is 0.05%.

 Beware France's priorité à droite rule: give way to vehicles entering on the right.

 Snow chains are legally required in winter on some mountain roads.

TRAIN & BUS

High-speed TGVs connect cities; towns are served by slower TER trains, occasionally supplemented by SNCF buses. Remember to time-stamp paper tickets in a *composteur* (yellow machine at train-platform entrances) before boarding – avoid by purchasing e-tickets online *(sncf-connect. com)* or via the SNCF Connect app. *Autocars* (regional buses) are operated by multiple companies, but services can be limited; tourist offices have schedules or check Zou! *(zou.maregionsud.fr)*.

CAR & RIDE-SHARES

BlaBlaCar *(blablacar.fr)* is France's 'go-to' *covoiturage* (ride-sharing) hub and OuiCar *(ouicar.com)* facilitates car rental from private individuals. In Nice, reserve public-shared electric vehicles with MobilizeShare *(share.mobilize.fr)*; Mobee *(mobee-fo.vulog. center)* runs Monaco's self-service e-buggies.

WALKING

Provence is crossed by long Grande Randonnée trails and *sentiers balisés* (marked footpaths); IGN has the best walking maps. Risk of fire in close forested areas from July to mid-September.

KNOW YOUR CARBON FOOTPRINT

A domestic flight from Paris to Nice would emit about 190kg of carbon dioxide per passenger. A bus would emit 100kg for the same distance, per passenger. A train would emit about 130kg. There are a number of carbon calculators online. We use resurgence.org/resources/carbon-calculator.html

ROAD DISTANCE CHART (KMS)

	Arles	Aix-en-Provence	Avignon	Cassis	Digne-les-Bains	Forcalquier	Marseille	Menton	Monte Carlo	Nice
Aix-en-Provence	75									
Avignon	37	80								
Cassis	120	50	135							
Digne-les-Bains	183	110	197	160						
Forcalquier	154	79	94	130	48					
Marseille	94	33	104	25	138	110				
Menton	280	206	290	222	173	216	230			
Monte Carlo	270	198	282	213	164	208	221	10		
Nice	248	175	260	191	143	189	204	30	20	
St-Tropez	206	120	220	111	157	172	133	135	130	105

SAFE TRAVEL

As destinations go, Provence and the Côte d'Azur is a safe place to visit. Keep your wits about you and petty theft, pesky mosquitoes and the occasional street scam should be the worst you'll encounter.

THEFT

Theft from luggage, pockets, trains and laundrettes is widespread, particularly along the Côte d'Azur. Beware pickpockets and phone snatchers in crowded tourist areas. Motorists, leave nothing of value in parked cars and in Marseille, keep doors locked and windows up – aggressive thefts from cars occasionally happen at red lights.

STREET SCAMS

A new trick pops up each season. Keep your wits about you and don't be fooled by the thief who finds a gold ring in your path, lays a newspaper on your restaurant table, or promises you a handsome monetary win if you play a card game. Be wary of children with clipboards, especially those playing deaf.

FOREST FIRES

From early July until mid-September, sizzling summer temperatures increase the chance of forest fires tenfold. Never walk in a closed forested zone – fires spread incredibly fast. In fire emergency, dial 18. Check local noticeboards for *un arrêté municipal* forbidding campfires and barbecues between certain dates.

MOSQUITOES These are particularly rife in the Camargue. May to November, bring repellent. On the Côte d'Azur, isolated cases of chikungunya and dengue fever, carried by tiger mosquitoes, have been reported.

FRANK6.0/SHUTTERSTOCK ©

LILIGRAPHIE/SHUTTERSTOCK ©

ON THE BEACH Don't leave valuables unattended when swimming – take turns instead. On Marseille's Prado beaches put valuables in one of the free lockers. In the water, watch for pale-purple jellyfish.

STORMS

Sometimes violent and dangerous, storms are common in August and September. Check weather (*la météo*) before hiking. Carry rain gear and extra layers to prevent hypothermia. Year-round, bitter mistral winds can last for days and madden beyond belief.

COVID-19

Download France's tracking app TousAntiCovid to see statistics and up-to-date news about the virus in France, and know if you have been exposed to a positive case. Pharmacies sell face masks and antigen tests.

QUICK TIPS TO HELP YOU MANAGE YOUR MONEY

CREDIT CARDS

Credit and debit cards are widely accepted, although some restaurants and B&Bs only accept cash. Nearly everywhere requires a card with a chip and PIN. North American cards with magnetic strips don't work at some autoroutes toll booths and unattended 24-hour petrol stations – which can leave you in a sticky situation if you have no alternative method of payment.

PAYING THE BILL
While most cafes and restaurants have table service, some require you to pay *l'addition* (the bill) directly at the bar.

TIPPING
By law, restaurant and cafe bills include 15% service, so there's no need to leave a tip. Most customers nonetheless leave a few euros.

DISCOUNT CARDS

Many museums and sights sell *billets jumelés* (combination tickets). Several cities, like Aix-en-Provence, Arles, Avignon, Nice and Marseille, have museum passes. The French Riviera Pass (frenchrivierapass.com; €28/40/59 for 24/48/72 hours) covers entry to all Nice's paid attractions, plus many nearby. Those over 60 or 65 get discounts on public transit, museums and cinemas.

CURRENCY

euro

HOW MUCH FOR A

Un café (espresso)
€2–5

Glass of Côtes de Provence rosé
€5–15

Midrange meal
€20–40

BARGAINING Other than at flea markets, bargaining is not the norm in France. Avoid buying knock-off Louis Vuitton handbags – or anything – from illegal street hawkers.

ATMS
Distributeurs automatiques de billets or *points d'argent* are the easiest means of obtaining cash, although some banks charge foreign-transaction fees (usually 2% to 3%), plus a per-use ATM charge. Check with your bank.

MONEY-CHANGERS
Bureaux de change in towns and cities change currency and open reasonably long hours. Some post offices exchange travellers cheques and banknotes, but charge €5 for cash; most won't take US$100 bills.

SAVING MONEY

Prices fluctuate wildly within the region – summertime accommodation, meals and drinks in celebrity St-Tropez or chichi Cannes are at least double that of prices charged in remote Haute-Provence.

Public transport Purchase multi-ticket or day passes instead of single tickets.

Restaurants Order *une carafe d'eau* (jug of tap water) instead of bottled mineral water.

Soft drinks Replace fizzy drinks with a flavoured syrup mixed with water; mint, grenadine and peach are favourites.

RESPONSIBLE TRAVEL

Tips to leave a lighter footprint, support local and have a positive impact on local communities.

ON THE ROAD

Ride-share. Join a motorist going your way on blablacar.fr.

Select 'Uber Green' when booking with Uber to ensure a fully electric or hybrid ride.

Hire an electric or hybrid car. Find charging stations around the region, including at many top-end countryside hotels.

Book accommodation through a sustainable, community-powered platform like FairBnB *(fairbnb. coop)*, operational in Marseille and growing fast.

Verify eco-credentials of hotels, campsites and B&Bs. Green labels include Clef Verte (Green Key), the EU Ecolabel, Green Globe and EarthCheck.

Choose eco-conscious restaurants using local seasonal products; Michelin flags its green choices with a clover leaf alongside stars.

Consume fish responsibly. Check fish recommended by sustainable program Mr Goodfish *(mrgoodfish.com)* to avoid eating an overexploited species and further endangering it.

GASPAR JANOS/SHUTTERSTOCK ©

GIVE BACK

Book accommodation with FairBnB – 50% of the booking fee goes to a local community project.

Visit national parks and nature reserves, and support organisations conserving wildlife and biodiversity.

Support Europe's first solar-powered restaurant, Le Présage *(lepresage.fr)* in Marseille. A bio-gas installation transforms organic waste into gas enabling chefs to cook after dark and on cloudy days.

Help clean up beaches and massifs with a litter-picking event organised by Clean My Calanque *(cleanmycalanques.fr)* or donate to Un Déchet par Jour *(1dechetparjour.com)*.

Volunteer. Plenty of local organisations welcome keen helpers. Working-holiday platform Workaway *(workaway.info)* also lists volunteer ops, many agricultural (farm work tending to sheep, lamas and fields) or heritage-focused (building dry-stone walls and cobbled streets, restoring old barns and chapels).

DOS & DON'TS

Don't your turn nose up at *pieds paquets* (lamb trotters and offal simmered in wine) or *saucisson de taureau* (bull sausage). These and other regional dishes are hallowed, and testimony to Provence's rich cultural and gastronomic heritage.

Always say 'bonjour' when entering shops.

Greet friends with *la bise*, a light kiss on each cheek.

LEAVE A SMALL FOOTPRINT

Go wild. Make the most of national parks, multi-day hikes, spectacular mountain refuges, nature reserves and campsites and nature reserves.

Travel slowly. Ditch the hire car for e-bikes, solar-powered electric boats and the occasional public-shared vehicles.

Bring your own bottle or container to the village cooperative to fill up with olive oil or wine.

Fountains in many villages and small towns spout *eau potable* (drinking water) – bring your own water bottle!

QUENTIN BOEHM ©

SUPPORT LOCAL

Buy at the source: olive oil direct from the *moulin à l'huile* (mill) where it's made, wine from the *vigneron* (winegrower) and the catch of the day from fishers in port.

Shop at weekly food markets, urban farms and rooftop gardens for picnics and self-catered meals – bring your own straw basket or bag.

Spurn mass-produced tourist tat for handmade products crafted by local artists and artisans.

CLIMATE CHANGE & TRAVEL

It's impossible to ignore the impact we have when travelling, and the importance of making changes where we can. Lonely Planet urges all travellers to engage with their travel carbon footprint. There are many carbon calculators online that allow travellers to estimate the carbon emissions generated by their journey; try resurgence.org/resources/carbon-calculator.html. Many airlines and booking sites offer travellers the option of offsetting the impact of greenhouse gas emissions by contributing to climate-friendly initiatives around the world. We continue to offset the carbon footprint of all Lonely Planet staff travel, while recognising this is a mitigation more than a solution.

RESOURCES

fairbnb.coop
cleanmycalanques.fr
1dechetparjour.com
blablacar.fr

PROVENCE & THE CÔTE D'AZUR POSITIVE-IMPACT TRAVEL

UNIQUE & LOCAL WAYS TO STAY

Belle Époque folly on the Riviera or eco-bolthole squirrelled away in the untouched wilds of a national park, accommodation covers all bases. Chambres d'hôtes and hotels in farmhouses and châteaux unwrap life in local agricultural and winemaking communities, while active souls thirsty for soul-soaring wildernesses can bag a bunk with view in a mountain refuge or rural gîte d'étape.

HOW MUCH FOR A

chambre d'hôte
€70–300

4-person *cabanon*
€100–180

Hotel breakfast
€10–30

MAS

Originally a farmhouse, a Provençal *mas* is anything from a countryside hotel or B&B with traditional wooden shutters to a luxury self-catering villa with outdoor pool and manicured grounds. Many *mas* remain part of a working farm, with tent pitches in fields and outbuildings upcycled as *gîtes ruraux* (rural, self-catering cottages). Most are seasonal, closing in winter.

CAMPING & REFUGES

Wild camping, including on beaches, is illegal. Campsites along the Côte d'Azur tend to be more like holiday parks, with fully equipped tents and cabins, pools, playgrounds and myriad activities.

At the other extreme, *refuges* (mountain huts) in Haute-Provence and other rural areas sport little bar bunkbeds in a shared dorm and zero organised entertainment beyond chatting over beer or pastis with other walkers and mapping out tomorrow's trails. Some *refuges* and *gîtes d'étape* (rural accommodation with basic dorm rooms) will let you pitch a tent.

CHÂTEAUX

Some of the region's most charming hotels languish in centuries-old châteaux ('castles' or mansions, many on winemaking estates). Some have four or five stars; others bypass official star ranking for a healthy dose of vintage eccentricity and original architecture that doesn't allow for a lift or other star-prescribed mod-con.

CHAMBRES D'HÔTES

Chambres d'hôtes (B&Bs) are no second-rate option in Provence. All budgets are catered for and they provide a precious opportunity to meet locals at home and experience Provençal life. You might stumble upon *chambres d'hôtes* in restored orangeries and olive mills, sailing boats, treehouses, floating lake cabins, riverside lodges, or troglodytes.

Breakfast Non-optional and included in nightly rates. Served at a pre-agreed time around a shared table in the kitchen or outdoors. The traditional continental feast of breads and pastries invariably includes homemade jams, cherry clafoutis or tangy *gâteau de citron* made with lemons from the garden perhaps, creamy yoghurts and fruit sourced from local farms.

Table d'hôte Some *chambres d'hôtes* offer an optional *table d'hôte* – a fixed-price dinner with other guests around one table.

Facilities Range from nothing more than a room to the whole shebang. Many offer cookery workshops or wine tasting in situ, have an outdoor pool, *pétanque* pitch, bicycles to borrow and a garden perfumed with exotic fig, quince, kaki and jujube trees. Remember you are a guest in someone's home. Check with your host which parts of the *maison* (house) and *jardin* (garden) are accessible to you and when.

BOOKING

Find and reserve lodgings online; tourist offices also have accommodation lists and some make reservations. Book once your trip dates are set. In high season the best places to stay get snapped up fast – up to a year in advance for some farmhouses and châteaux.

Logis *(logishotels.com)* 'Logis de France' groups together small, independent hotels, with a personalised welcome and often decent restaurant.

Relais & Châteaux *(relaischateaux.com)* Hotels in (mostly top-end) historic châteaux.

Cabanes de France *(cabanes-de-france.com)* Treehouses and *cabanes* (wooden huts or modest chalets) immersed in nature.

Bienvenue à la Ferme *(bienvenue-a-la-ferme.com)* Farms with fields to pitch tents in, green camping-car spots, B&Bs and self-catering cottages.

Fleurs de Soleil *(fleursdesoleil.fr)* Search for authentic *chambres d'hôtes* by theme: romance, family-friendly, wellness, oenology, gastronomy, walking, ecology and so on.

Gîtes de France *(gites-de-france.com)* Self-catering accommodation, including eco-properties in regional parks and nature reserves.

One Off Places *(oneoffplaces.co.uk)* Quirky spots: hobbit houses, hanging pods, windmills...

CABANONS

Overlooking sandy coves in the wilds of Marseille's Les Calanques and elsewhere on the coast, vintage *cabanons* (seaside huts) – many built for fishermen – entice visitors looking to shack up in simple, self-catering solitude.

ESSENTIAL NUTS & BOLTS

ACCESSIBLE TRAVEL

Cobbled old towns and hilltop villages with steep lanes and few pavements can be impossible to navigate in a wheelchair.

Train travellers can arrange assistance through SNCF's Accès Plus and Accès TER services (accessibilite.sncf.com).

Public transport is becoming more accessible thanks to wide doors and easy-access platforms for wheelchairs on trams. Tactile strips at bus and tram stops help the visually impaired to board.

Mobil'azur (mobilazur.org) offers on-demand bus services for disabled visitors in and around Nice.

Wheeliz (wheeliz.com) is a car-sharing service offering wheelchair-adapted vehicles; rental from €45 per day.

Some public beaches, like Nice's Plage du Centenaire and Plage de Carras, have ramps into the water, amphibious wheelchairs and dedicated parking and restroom facilities for disabled visitors.

Find hotels, restaurants and more adapted for travellers with disabilities on accessible.net.

Accessibility filters on the Jaccede smartphone app (jaccede.com) allow travellers to search 100,000 accessible addresses in France.

RogerVoice (rogervoice.com) is a handy app for hearing-impaired visitors.

Useful resources include My Provence (myprovence.fr/tourisme-handicap) and Tourisme & Handicaps (tourisme-handicaps.org).

Download Lonely Planet's free 'Accessible Travel' guides from (shop.lonelyplanet.com/categories/accessible-travel).

FAST FACTS

Time Zone
Central European Time

Country Code
+33

Electricity
230V 50Hz

GOOD TO KNOW

The legal drinking age is 18. In restaurants over 16s can be served wine or beer when dining with their parents.

Campfires are forbidden. Forest-fire risk means barbecues are forbidden in many areas in July and August.

Dress modestly in churches: cover bare shoulders with a scarf.

Baring all is obligatory on plages naturistes (nudist beaches).

Visas are not generally required for stays of up to 90 days. Some nationalities require a Schengen visa.

SWIMMING
When a yellow or red flag is flying on beaches, skip the sea dip.

TABLE MANNERS
Wish fellow diners around the table 'bon appétit' before picking up your cutlery and tucking in.

SMOKING
Smoking is illegal in public interiors, including in restaurants, cafes, bars and public transport.

DRESS CODE

Going topless is routine on Côte d'Azur beaches, but a no-no anywhere else. Save bare chests and bikinis for the beach.

PUBLIC TOILETS

Major public beaches have toilets and showers. On streets in towns free *sanisettes* (self-cleaning cylindrical toilets) are open 24 hours.

OPENING HOURS

Most businesses and museums close for lunch (usually between noon and 2pm). Do as the locals do and head for the nearest restaurant.

FAMILY TRAVEL

At state-run museums and sites, admission is free for under 18s. Otherwise, children aged six to 12 are usually half-price. Some venues offer good-value family tickets covering two adults and two children.

Many outdoor activities (rafting the Gorges du Verdon, canoeing the Sorgues river, horse riding with Camargue cowboys etc) have a minimum age, often six or seven years.

Children under four get free train travel; discounted tickets are available for older kids.

STAYING CONNECTED

Public free hotspots and wi-fi-clad cafes in coastal areas mean you're always connected – unlike in Alpes-de-Haute-Provence, Massif des Maures and other rural areas. If wi-fi on tap is vital to you, rent a pocket wi-fi device (*hippocketwifi.com*) before departure.

DINING OUT

- Toast dining companions by raising your glass and saying '*Santé!*' before sipping.
- *une carte* is a menu listing what's cooking
- *un menu* is a multi-course meal at a set price
- *une formule* is a fixed, two-course lunch deal, often with coffee included

JIM JOWILL/SHUTTERSTOCK ©

LGBTIQ+ TRAVELLERS

Same-sex relationships are legal, but away from cities France is fairly conservative in its attitudes – discretion remains wise.

Notably LGBTIQ+ friendly cities, with thriving gay communities and pride festivals (*pride-marseille.com*) each summer, include Nice, Marseille, Aix-en-Provence, Avignon and Toulon. Nice's all-white Dolly Party (p49) is a highlight.

Many establishments in Nice display the city's gay-friendly Irisée Naturellement (Naturally Iridescent) label. Gay Séjour (*gay-sejour.com*) and Gay French Riviera (*gayfrenchriviera.com*) are handy for listings region-wide.

LGBT+ PACA (*lgbt-paca.org*) for regional news, events and listings of local LGBTIQ+ associations across the region.

LANGUAGE

Standard French is taught and spoken throughout France. The heavy southern accent is an important part of regional identity in Provence, but you'll have no trouble being understood anywhere if you stick to standard French, which we've also used in the phrases on this page.

The sounds used in spoken French can almost all be found in English. There are a couple of exceptions: nasal vowels (represented in our pronunciation guides by o or u followed by an almost inaudible nasal consonant sound m, n or ng), the 'funny' u (ew in our guides) and the deep-in-the-throat r. Bearing these few points in mind and reading our pronunciation guides below as if they were English, you'll be understood just fine.

TIME & NUMBERS

What time is it?	Quelle heure est-il?	kel er ay til
It's (10) o'clock.	Il est (dix) heures.	il ay (deez) er
It's half past (10).	Il est (dix) heures et demie.	il ay (deez) er ay day·mee.

morning	matin	ma·tun
afternoon	après-midi	a·pray·mee·dee
evening	soir	swar
yesterday	hier	yair
today	aujourd'hui	o·zhoor·dwee
tomorrow	demain	der·mun

1	un	un	6	six	sees
2	deux	der	7	sept	set
3	trois	trwa	8	huit	weet
4	quatre	ka·trer	9	neuf	nerf
5	cinq	sungk	10	dix	dees

BASICS

Hello.	Bonjour.	bon·zhoor
Goodbye.	Au revoir.	o·rer·vwa
Yes./No.	Oui./Non.	wee/non
Please.	S'il vous plaît.	seel voo play
Thank you.	Merci.	mair·see
Excuse me.	Excusez-moi.	ek·skew·zay·mwa
Sorry.	Pardon.	par·don

What's your name?
Comment vous appelez-vous? — ko·mon voo·za·play voo

My name is ...
Je m'appelle ... — zher ma·pel ...

Do you speak English?
Parlez-vous anglais? — par·lay·voo ong·glay

I don't understand.
Je ne comprends pas. — zher ner kom·pron pa

EMERGENCIES

Help!	Au secours!	o skoor
Leave me alone!	Fichez-moi la paix!	fee·shay·mwa la pay
Call the police!	Appelez la police.	a·play la po·lees
I'm lost.	Je suis perdu/perdue.	zher swee pair·dew (m/f)

Index

'Via Nissa's Robert Levitt taught me to look around, not through Vieux Nice's windows. We identified so many small tokens of the city's history!'

CHRISSIE MCCLATCHIE

'Years later my children still talk about Richerenches' cloak-and-dagger truffle market, the *rabaisseurs* (hunters) furtively dealing from the back of their cars. It hasn't changed one iota.'

NICOLA WILLIAMS

'I spontaneously cycled up Mont Ventoux "for research." If I can do it, so can you.'

ASHLEY PARSONS

THIS BOOK

Design development
Lauren Egan, Tina García, Fergal Condon

Content development
Anne Mason

Cartography development
Wayne Murphy, Katerina Pavkova

Production development
Mario D'Arco, Dan Moore, Sandie Kestell, Virginia Moreno, Juan Winata

Series development leadership
Liz Heynes, Darren O'Connell, Piers Pickard, Chris Zeiher

Commissioning editor
Daniel Bolger

Product editor
Clare Healy

Cartographer
Mark Griffiths

Book designer
Catalina Aragón

Assisting editors
Melanie Dankel, Andrea Dobbin, Gabrielle Stefanos

Cover researcher
Hannah Blackie

Thanks Gwen Cotter, Sandie Kestell, Alison Killilea, Amy Lynch, Darren O'Connell, John Taufa